Reviews

If you are applying to MSW programs, Reyes' guide...will quickly become a favorite resource.

Tara Kuther, Ph.D.
About.com Guide to Graduate School
Assistant Professor, Western Connecticut State University

Reader Comments

I read this book chapter by chapter, and it has tons of information and helpful tips inside. I loved the dos and don'ts at the end of each chapter

Carrietta Sepowitz

Not only did this book reassure me that I was making the right decision by entering the social work field, but it also guided me step by step through the somewhat intimidating graduate school application process.

Melissa Hawk, MSW student

I loved the book so much that I have recommended it to many people and as a result many have purchased it!

Lisa Lusczynski, MSW student

I recommend this book to anyone interested in applying to MSW programs. It's worth its weight in gold!!!

Zo'graphia Z. Scharn, MSW student

I lost this book halfway through the application process, so bought another. I guess that says how helpful it was. Reading a book written by someone experienced in recruiting students, specifically social work students, made the application process much more comfortable and much less intimidating for me. I feel it gave me an advantage over other applicants.

Craig Morris, MSW student

THANK YOU, THANK YOU!! This book was exactly what I needed and what I was looking for. It has the answers to my questions and helped alleviate some of my fears about applying to graduate school.

Janet Berch, BSW

Even though I only applied to one graduate school, my copy of GUIDE TO SELECTING AND APPLYING TO MSW PROGRAMS, 4TH EDITION (the previous title of THE SOCIAL WORK GRADUATE SCHOOL APPLICANT'S HANDBOOK) was dog-eared and well-worn by the time I received my letter of acceptance from the University of Michigan. Having this book in my possession gave me a feeling of confidence and comfort, which really helped make the application process less stressful.

Deborah Kesling, MSW student

Every applicant can find something useful in this procedural manual. Even with a very talented career counselor guiding me through the application process, I still found this guide to be an excellent focal point for my efforts.

Larry Backilman, MSW student

THE SOCIAL WORK GRADUATE SCHOOL APPLICANT'S HANDBOOK

The Complete Guide to Selecting and Applying to MSW Programs

Second Edition

THE SOCIAL WORK GRADUATE SCHOOL APPLICANT'S HANDBOOK

The Complete Guide to Selecting and Applying to MSW Programs

Second Edition

Jesús Reyes, AM, ACSW

White Hat Communications

Harrisburg, Pennsylvania

The Social Work Graduate School Applicant's Handbook
The Complete Guide to Selecting and Applying to MSW Programs
Second Edition
by Jesús Reyes

Published by:

White Hat Communications

2001 N. Front St., Bldg. 2, Suite 325
Post Office Box 5390
Harrisburg, PA 17110-0390 USA
717-238-3787 Voice
717-238-2090 Fax
http://www.socialworker.com

ISBN: 1-929109-14-8
ISSN: 1529-711X

The material in Appendix C is reprinted with the permission of the Association of Social Work Boards (ASWB) from the ASWB Web site at *http://www.aswb.org*.

Graduate Record Examinations and GRE are registered trademarks of Educational Testing Service. Miller Analogies Test and MAT are registered trademarks of Harcourt Brace and Company.

Cover photos: © 2001, 1999 PhotoDisc, Inc.

To

Our son Jesse and his wife Laura,
their first child, expected this year,

and

all our grandchildren yet to come

You hold the promise of the future

The Social Work Graduate School Applicant's Handbook (2nd Edition)

TABLE OF CONTENTS

Preface

This is the newest incarnation of an idea born almost a decade ago as I prepared to work as Assistant Dean for Enrollment and Placement at the School of Social Service Administration of the University of Chicago. One of my two main tasks was to recruit and advise applicants to the School's master's and doctoral programs. My research uncovered many works on how to prepare and apply to medical school, business school, law school, and other programs. Much to my surprise, I found that no books existed for potential applicants to social work programs. My work with hundreds of students only reinforced the thought that potential graduate students of social work were in great need of a handbook to guide their preparation and search.

The first edition of this work in 1996 (published as *The Guide to Selecting and Applying to Master of Social Work Programs*) sought to provide a starting point and perspective for potential applicants to evaluate their interests and how schools may or may not meet their needs. It attempted to provide insight into how to better prepare, both through class and field experiences, for the graduate study of social work. It also sought to provide the potential graduate student of social work with information on how to best compose the application. The present edition has the same central purposes.

This edition marks the continuation of an association of this work and White Hat Communications, its publisher. I selected the publisher of *The New Social Worker* magazine to handle this work for very specific reasons. Linda Grobman, founder of White Hat Communications, is herself a social worker and shares my commitment to serving the needs of the very special population of aspirants to a career in social work. Her unique insights have resulted in many excellent additions to this and previous editions. Readers of previous editions have also provided valuable suggestions, through surveys conducted via White Hat Communications' Web site.

The latest innovation to this work had its genesis during a lunch meeting I had with Ms. Grobman in Chicago last summer. We talked of ways to increase the usefulness of this work and agreed that expanding its focus to include social work graduate programs in Canada would be a worthy goal. I am pleased that the process has begun in this edition. The social work traditions of Canada and the United States have a great deal in common, as do our core values as expressed in our very similar approaches to educating our practitioners.

The principal sources that guided me in defining the structure and content of this *Handbook* were the hundreds of potential applicants I met across the country during my years in recruitment at the School of Social Service Administration (SSA) of the University of Chicago. In addition, over the course of the last several years, I've had the wonderful opportunity to talk, correspond by postal and e-mail, and meet many readers of previous editions. Their questions and commentaries are always insightful, intelligent, and challenging. Although no single person asked all the questions I address in this work, all originated with potential students. I am grateful to every one of them for their dedication and persistence in learning about our profession and how it trains its practitioners.

My colleagues at SSA as well as in other institutions across the country were equally invaluable sources. The many colleagues and mentors I've had the good fortune to know through my years in college, graduate school, and in many settings within the profession informed much of the content of this *Handbook*.

The types of graduate programs and the backgrounds of potential students vary a great deal. Through this *Handbook*, you will get a sense of the variety of programs available, their possible strengths and weaknesses, and the sorts of factors to explore.

This *Handbook* also presents the reader with a feel for how graduate schools approach the formidable task of sorting through the myriad of backgrounds and interests represented in each year's applicant pool. How do schools decide who is to be offered admission and who is not? How do they make an inherently subjective process work?

An understanding of how schools look at applicants will help the reader better prepare in college and through other means and to better present his (throughout this book, I refer to applicants, students, and professionals alternately as "he" or "she," since social workers come in both the male and female variety) own case for admission. Each school is genuinely invested in selecting applicants who will benefit from and contribute to the school's programs and, ultimately, to the profession and the people it serves.

Yet, schools must make decisions purely on what is contained in the applicant's file. Knowing what to highlight in a way relevant to schools can make all the difference. As a result of my experiences in this field, I am convinced that each year many applicants who would make excellent students and professionals are denied admission. Often, it is not because their credentials are lacking; rather, it is because they failed to highlight aspects of their experiences that could have made a big difference to the school.

I hope this *Handbook* proves a faithful companion in your search for the right graduate program for you.

On a personal note, I express my eternal gratitude to my wife, Bobbi, for her steadfast support and encouragement. On a professional note, I express my eternal gratitude to my publisher, White Hat Communications and, more specifically, its founder, Linda Grobman. She has the patience of Job in understanding the demands of my busy schedule. She has given me the privilege of contributing to her book, *More Days in the Lives of Social Workers,* depicting a day in my life as a criminal justice administrator. *The Social Work Graduate School Applicant's Handbook* has grown more comprehensive largely due to her ever present innovative spirit, gentle encouragement, and patience. I also wish to thank Gary M. Grobman of White Hat Communications for handling the arduous task of editing the responses from graduate programs that may be found in the *In Their Own Words* section of this book.

Jesús Reyes, AM, ACSW
March 2005

Part I

What Applicants Should Look For In Schools

What Applicants Should Look For In Schools

Most programs of social work will provide you, on request, with catalogs and brochures free of charge. All schools prepare their materials in good faith and without any attempt to misrepresent their programs or misguide the reader. Aside from their content, catalogs and brochures are useful in that they convey a sense of how the institution views itself by virtue of its choices of the aspects of its program to emphasize, general format, and photographs. Some catalogs are rich in style but lacking in substance while others, sometimes not as pleasing to the eye, are rich in content.

Some schools have more funds than others to devote to publicity materials. Usually, but not always, schools that are named after an individual have added funds from endowments provided by that individual. This sometimes results in beautifully composed and produced brochures. Look beyond the workmanship of the brochure to its content. The two do not always match, but in many cases, they do. Whichever catalogs land in your mailbox, it is important that as a consumer, you look beyond what each school chooses to present.

Part I of this book will provide you with a template for looking at social work programs. It will begin with a look at general criteria to evaluate in social work programs, including program accreditation and its implications to your ability to be licensed as a social worker, and how to interpret program rankings. Questions to ask schools about financial aid, application procedures, and factors to consider about aid will follow. The focus will then turn toward common types of academic programs (both in the classroom and in the field), dual-degree, and specialty programs and how you can assess if they meet your needs. Ways of assessing faculty background, qualifications, and interests will also be discussed, as will methods of evaluating support services such as academic and career counseling, physical facilities, libraries, computer facilities, and job placement services. Part I concludes with suggestions for assessing the achievements of alumni (by their fruits ye shall know them).

Chapter 1

The MSW Decision

The profession of social work has been said to be counter-cyclical; that is, jobs in social work appear to be more plentiful during economic downturns and slightly less so during better economic times. This is logical because, as a general rule, people are in greater need of social services during tough economic times. Application rates to graduate social work programs appear to increase and decrease accordingly. According to the Council on Social Work Education*, full-time master's enrollment increased steadily from the mid-1950s to 1978, bottoming out in 1986. Enrollment then increased once again except in 1989, 1995, and 1998. 1999 saw an increase of approximately 9% over 1998, only to see enrollment return to the same approximate levels of 1998 by the year 2000.

The Council on Social Work Education conducted a series of annual surveys from 1995 to 2002 of accredited and in candidacy master's programs, with a response rate of 81.4% in 2002. The surveys found that the number of applications to first-year status in master's programs was 43,024 in 1995, 44,968 in 1996, 40,075 in 1997, 34,533 in 1998, 34,239 in 1999, 30,262 in 2000, 25,752 in 2001, and 26,834 in 2002. In the period from 1995 to 2002, there was an overall decline of nearly 38%. During the same period, there was an increase in the number of accredited master's programs from 117 to 152. Despite the downward trend in applications, the percentage of applicants accepted and actually registered is on the rise. Of the 26,834 applicants in 2002, 70.4%

---

* *The source for statistics cited in this Handbook is* Statistics on Social Work Education in the United States: 2002, *published by the Council on Social Work Education (CSWE). These statistics refer to schools of social work in the U.S. Appendix G lists CSWE's postal address and Web site, where you can obtain that publication and others.*

were offered admission and 43% registered. The corresponding figures for the 30,262 applicants in 2000 were 68.8% and 42.4%. This means that an increased number of graduate programs of social work were competing with one another for a shrinking number of applicants—making it, in essence, a buyers' market.

Please be cautious to not allow the state of the market to make you feel over-confident. The extent of the competition varies according to the number of programs in a given geographic area. Some states have, at most, less than a handful of programs. Other states have experienced a larger growth. The majority of programs are located in the eastern half of the United States, with the Midwest having the highest concentration. Highly-ranked, more prestigious schools continue to compete at a national and even international level for the most highly qualified candidates.

If the theory of social work being a counter-cyclical profession holds up, the economic downturn prompted by events of September 2001 may, if the downturn persists, result in application rates increasing yet again. Whatever the application rates, a good undergraduate preparation coupled with exposure to the profession through voluntary or paid experiences will remain the key to successful application for admission.

A few words about the demographics of the profession are in order. The profession of social work has historically been one that attracts predominantly women. The ratio of women to men is certainly not as high as some other helping professions, such as nursing, but remains disproportionate. According to the Council on Social Work Education, as of November 2002, 83.9% of full-time and 81% of part-time master's students were female. A total of 30.3% of full-time and 31.4% of part-time master's students were students of color. African Americans were 15.9% of full-time and 17.9% of part-time students, Native Americans 1.2% and 0.9%, Asian American 2.9% and 2.0%, Mexican Americans 2.3% and 3.0%, Puerto Rican 1.8% and 0.8%, and others were 1.2% and 1.3%, respectively. The profession seeks to mirror the population it serves. Therefore, qualified male students, as well as qualified students of color, particularly bilingual and bicultural candidates, are highly recruited by most programs.

Whether you are a "first-timer" selecting your first career after college, a "career-changer" who has been in a non-social work career for a number of years, or a "career-enhancer" who has been in social service for a fair amount of time and seeking additional training in social work, the decision to seek a Master of Social Work degree merits serious thought. In a survey of current MSW students and recent graduates, *The New Social Worker* magazine found that respondents felt the best advice they could give prospective MSW applicants was to be realistic about graduate school expectations. Many emphasized the need to be ready for a more demanding academic experience than in college and to be prepared for intense field experiences.

"First-Timer" Career Seeker

For the young reader, however, the task of selecting a career appears particularly daunting. It is somewhat paradoxical that most of us must do something as important and with as many implications for our future as deciding on a career at a time in our lives when we may not have a great deal of "real world" experience. If you are a young person who went directly to college upon completing high school and are now contemplating going directly to graduate school, you may feel ill-prepared to make a career choice at this time in your life. It may be comforting for you to know that career changing is more likely to become the norm than the exception in our rapidly evolving world. Therefore, it is likely you will, at some point in your future, be making a career adjustment. Nevertheless, the choice of career now is important because, even though there may be career changes somewhere in your future, the *skills* you acquire in a given career ideally should be transferable to succeeding career areas. For example, social work skills such as advocacy, working across system levels, and communication are readily transferable to areas as varied as law, business management, and others.

The decision to seek a Master of Social Work degree requires careful research about the profession along with thoughtful reflection on your abilities and interests, culminating in an evaluation of the "fit" between them. In addition, it would be most useful, as much as it may be possible at this time, to consider possible alternate paths your career may take down the road. Your university career services office can assist you in evaluating your interests and aptitudes through individual advising, interest inventories, and other instruments, as well as resources to explore career options. In all likelihood, they can offer books similar to this one about other helping careers.

An option to consider is to seek employment in social work or a related field and postpone graduate work until you've had the opportunity to learn more about the field, explore related options, and test your interest. Many of the graduate programs that responded to this and the previous edition's survey for Appendix B (*In Their Own Words*) recommend, and many require, some form of paid or volunteer experience in social service prior to starting graduate work. They do so because they realize that nothing compares to actually "getting your feet wet" in the field. Only then can you make a truly informed decision on which to base the enormous personal and financial commitment a graduate education represents. Chapter 9 of this book discusses how to locate a site for gaining exposure to the profession of social work.

As a "first timer" career seeker, you are certainly not alone. According to data compiled by the Council on Social Work Education, 36.5% of full-time master's students and 16.5% of part-time master's students of social work enrolled on November 1, 2002 were 25 years of age or younger. Although CSWE does not compile statistics on whether these students had previous careers, it is reasonable to assume that students in this age group are first-time career seekers.

It is also reasonable to assume that the rest of social work master's students belong in either the category of "career changer" or "career enhancer." 19% of full-time and 27.1% of part-time master's students in the same group were between the ages of 31 and 40 years. 16.1% of full-time and 25.3% of part-time master's students were 41 years of age or older.

"Career Changer"

If you are a person who has worked a good number of years in a field unrelated to social work—in other words, a "career changer"—it would be useful to evaluate the skills you have developed in your present field and how you see those skills as forming a foundation toward a future career. The crucial general question will be whether there is a match between your goals, present skills, and social work. Can meaningful connections be made between your past work, graduate studies in social work, and future professional goals? Can the skills that you employed in the past be enhanced by social work training to achieve your goals? In short, are there specific connections between your previous experiences and education and what you hope to obtain from a graduate program to train you for practice in whatever area(s) of social work you may be contemplating?

> I used my many years in the food service industry and related those skills I gained as a manager, waitress, and so forth to social services. Often, people do not dig deeply enough to realize just how many experiences have led them to choose the path of social work.
> *Amanda Barge, MSW student*

Even though your professional experiences are outside of social work, upon graduation from a Master of Social Work program, you will have more to offer an employer than the typical graduate. The challenge will be to help the potential employer see how your previous skills make you more capable to perform the job. Ask the admissions office at the graduate schools you are considering to put you in touch with alumni who came to their school as "career changers" with a similar prior background to yours. Ask them how their previous background has enhanced their abilities as social workers and, most importantly, if they are happy with their decision to change careers to social work.

"Career Enhancer"

If you have worked in the field of social work or in a related field for many years, and are contemplating seeking a Master of Social Work degree to expand your knowledge and options in the field, the decision is somewhat simpler. By virtue of your experience, you have a clearer sense, in essence, of what you're getting into. It may be possible for you to obtain financial assistance through continuing education funds through your employer. Nevertheless, it will be important for you to carefully consider the costs of investing the time and funds for a graduate education versus the personal and professional benefits of doing so. Important variables for you to consider will be your age and expected years of practice beyond graduate school.

Social Work Career Considerations

Whatever the point in your life where you presently find yourself, there are a number of characteristics about social work as a profession that are very much worth considering.

Social work highly values a systemic perspective. The social worker must have an appreciation that people exist within multiple environments and, in turn, affect and are affected by those environments. Individuals and families exist within a social environment that involves the interaction of biological, psychological, familial, economic, legal, and cultural factors. An understanding of the person-in-environment is perhaps social work's most distinguishing characteristic. Therefore, if you are someone who prefers dealing with problems that are solvable in a predictable and linear way, such as a mathematical equation, you may find it frustrating dealing with issues that may have multiple causes and equally as many possible solutions. If, on the other hand, you are stimulated by a myriad of perspectives on any given issue, you may enjoy social work. For example, the factors contributing to housing problems, and corresponding solutions, in an urban setting may be quite different from those contributing to housing problems in a rural setting.

Social work often takes place in a multidisciplinary setting. The social worker should have an appreciation of how other disciplines such as psychiatry, psychology, and law can offer much-needed insight into meeting social service needs. Important as well is the ability to work across system levels and communicate effectively with people of different disciplines. For example, a social worker in the field of social welfare might provide family therapy at one point in the day and testify as an expert witness in court later the same day. If you are a person who does not enjoy differing views and diverse settings, social work is probably not for you.

Social workers need the ability to work independently, organize multiple tasks, and have a reasonable level of frustration tolerance. The social worker often is, so to speak, the hub of the wheel of service planning and delivery. At the direct service level, she often coordinates the entire process from the point of initial referral to completion of needed services and, if appropriate, outcome assessment. At the administrative or policy-making level, social workers are at the forefront of identifying needs, formulating programmatic solutions, overseeing the implementation of programs, and evaluating programmatic outcomes. Initiative and self-motivation are important in conceiving needed courses of action for enlisting the collaboration of sources within and outside social work to facilitate change. People who enjoy predictability in their workday will often not find it in social work. People who enjoy fresh and varied challenges, on the other hand, will feel at home in the field of social work. At the same time, however, it should be noted that many of the challenges are so formidable that a solution may not be available, because of cost or other barriers. Therefore, a social worker's day often also includes frustrations associated with seeing needs that cannot be met completely, and, in some cases, not at all.

Social workers must be sensitive to the cultures represented in the service population. A lack of understanding of customs, beliefs, and behaviors of various cultures can easily result in erroneous conclusions and recommendations. An understanding of different cultures, however, can yield optimally appropriate results in that a cultural lens provides perspective and accurate meaning to observations. A person who does not appreciate differences and does not thrive in a diverse environment will find social work difficult. The social worker must be keenly aware of his own cultural bias and not allow it to form the basis of assumptions about people whose cultural background may ascribe different meanings to similar contexts. For example, communicating in a direct and blunt fashion may be valued in one culture but seen as impolite and tactless in another.

Excellent verbal and written communication skills are necessary for any social worker. Whether communicating with clients while providing counseling, with other systems while advocating client needs, or with foundations while securing support, the social worker must be able to express ideas and concepts clearly and succinctly. Tactful and clear communication skills must be exercised at all times. By the same token, the worker must possess the ability to write reports accurately and completely. For example, judges often make difficult and important decisions about parental rights and custody issues based on reports submitted by social workers.

Social workers must feel empathy for clients and their experiences. It is very likely that some, or even many, of the previous experiences with service providers were less than satisfying for the client. Therefore, the social worker often is, in essence, initially judged based on the client's previous experiences—good and bad. Making a connection that results in the client's investment in the treatment process will require overcoming whatever obstacles exist as a result of past experiences. In addition, the social worker must be aware that being in need of social services is inherently a difficult position. Whereas the social worker cannot remove all the discomforts a client experiences, the worker's ability to treat the client with respect and empathy can go a long way toward making the experience more tolerable and fruitful.

Knowledge of community resources is invaluable in assisting the social worker in identifying sources of service. Regardless of the type of service the social worker delivers or administers, clients often have multiple needs. Sources for referrals might include public and private agencies, as well as community organizations. An understanding of resources, their services, and criteria for service can help the social worker in meeting client needs. The ability to come to know, understand, and mobilize other services for clients is vital to a social worker. A social worker should enjoy networking and contacts with many people.

The characteristics listed above are certainly not the only ones useful in social work. Many of the skills, as well as the diverse knowledge base guiding the practice of social work, are not exclusive to social work; rather, social work is a dynamic profession that, from its beginnings, felt totally comfortable utilizing whatever knowledge proved useful, regardless of its origin. Therefore, social workers can be said to be generalists who interface comfortably with many professions and disciplines including psychology, anthropology, medicine, public policy, economics, philosophy, and many others. Whatever knowledge base social workers utilize, all are agents of change. Social workers are not ivory-tower observers of society; they are active agents in the shaping of society. Social work practitioners endeavor to improve the social condition for everyone. The challenges, frustrations, and rewards of a career in social work are as varied and all-encompassing as the ambitious goals of the profession.

Helpful Hints

Do...

- consider the skills you already have and how they apply to social work.

- consider how the skills you will acquire in MSW training will apply to possible future career choices.

- consider realistically how an MSW will expand your career options.

(continued on next page)

(continued from previous page)

Don't...

- overlook taking advantage of vocational aptitude tests that may confirm social work is right for you or reveal other alternatives to explore.

- forget to take advantage of career advising available at your present or former college or university.

- leap into a social work degree program until you are satisfied that social work is a good fit with your personality, skills, and career goals.

Chapter 2

General Criteria for Evaluating MSW Programs

As of February 2005, there were 166 accredited graduate programs of social work in the United States and an additional 19 in candidacy. The number of accredited programs in February 2002, September 1999, June 1997, and June 1996 (previous editions of this *Handbook*) were 146, 132, 121, and 117, respectively. The number in candidacy in those same years was 25, 20, 18, and 12, respectively. There was an increase of 49 accredited MSW programs between 1996 and 2005. That significant increase of 42% in accredited programs over the course of only nine years, coupled with the fact that an additional 19 are currently in candidacy for accreditation, suggests that universities believe that the profession of social work will continue to experience expansion.

The Council on Social Work Education (CSWE) has been the accrediting body for graduate and undergraduate social work programs in the United States since 1952, when it succeeded the American Association of Schools of Social Work in that role. CSWE accreditation ensures that all programs establish and maintain high standards of professional preparation for entry-level practice in the profession of social work. In addition to its role as the sole accrediting body for undergraduate and graduate social work programs, CSWE also is very active in promoting "quality social work programs and professional development of faculty, administrators, practitioners, and students" (CSWE Annual Report 1999-2000). CSWE is also active in advocating for legislation supporting education in the profession.

As of March 2005, there were 25 graduate programs of social work in Canada, with one of those programs in candidacy. More than half of the programs achieved accreditation in the previous twenty-five years and three of those in the previous five years.

The accrediting body for graduate and undergraduate social work programs in Canada is the Canadian Association of Schools of Social Work—CASSW or Association canadienne des écoles de service social—ACESS. CASSW-ACESS is a voluntary, national charitable association of university faculties, schools, and departments offering professional education in social work at the undergraduate, graduate, and post-graduate levels. In 1967, it succeeded the National Committee of Schools of Social Work, which had begun in 1948. The mission of CASSW-ACESS is "...to advance the standards, effectiveness, and relevance of social work education and scholarship in Canada, and in other countries through active participation in international associations."

CASSW-ACESS fulfills its mission through a range of activities, including the accreditation of social work education programs. Its Board of Accreditation may grant candidacy status to a program for a period of up to five years. After successful candidacy, it can grant full accreditation for a period of seven years or conditional accreditation for periods of two or four years. All accredited schools of social work are reviewed every seven years.

There are accreditation standards for the First University Level (undergraduate BSW level), as well as for the Second University Level (graduate MSW level). The BSW program is normally four years of full-time study, or three years in Quebec. The Second University Level allows for two program designs. One is for students who have completed a First University Level program in social work and the second for students who hold other baccalaureate degrees.

As you review the curricular content of various schools of social work in both the United States and Canada, you will find striking similarities. The reason for the similarities is that CSWE and CASSW-ACESS prescribe specific content areas that must be addressed by all accredited social work programs. In 2003, CSWE expanded the content areas from six to eight. Formerly, the areas were human behavior in the social environment, social welfare policy and services, social work practice, social work research, field work, and additional requirements. Currently, the eight content areas are values and ethics, diversity, populations-at-risk and social and economic justice, human behavior in the social environment, social welfare policy and services, social work practice, research, and field education. CASSW-ACESS has instituted similar changes, introducing a new format for its Standards of Accreditation in May of 2004.

Choosing an Accredited School

As you consider schools, it is most important that you make sure they are accredited or in candidacy by CSWE (in the United States) or CASSW-ACESS (in Canada). Schools that are accredited by CSWE or by CASSW-ACESS have gone through a rigorous process to ensure that they meet the minimum standards for social work education and that their graduates are prepared to practice social work at a professional level.

Some schools may state that they are "in candidacy" for CSWE or CASSW-ACESS accreditation. Candidacy is a precursor to full accreditation, and schools must have met certain requirements to be admitted into candidacy. Schools that are in candidacy by CSWE are working toward accreditation and have shown that they have the potential to achieve that status. Assuming that the school completes candidacy and receives full accreditation, students who attend the school while it is in candidacy will receive accreditation of their degrees once the school is accredited, if the degree is earned under the same curriculum that receives accreditation. If you are considering a school that is in candidacy, ask when the school expects to receive accreditation and whether the curriculum you will receive your degree under is the curriculum under which the school expects to receive accreditation.

For CSWE, the movement from candidacy status to accreditation status varies. Ten of the 15 programs listed as "in candidacy" in this *Handbook's* June 1996 edition were accredited by the next edition in June 1997. The other five were still in candidacy as of June 1997. Of those five, only one remained in candidacy as of

February 2002. Of the 20 programs listed in candidacy status in this *Handbook's* 1999 edition, 14 had achieved accreditation, five continued in candidacy, and one was no longer in candidacy by the February 2002 edition. Of the 25 programs in candidacy as of the 2002 edition, 22 have achieved accreditation, while three continue in candidacy as of February 2005. Data are not available to provide similar information for movement from candidacy to accreditation for CASSW-ACESS.

If you are considering attending a program that is in candidacy status, it is important to learn as much as possible about when the program expects accreditation and to evaluate as much as possible its prospects for achieving it. Programs in candidacy status that participated in this edition's "In Their Own Words" survey (Appendix B) were asked to report the date when accreditation is expected. The program's failure to achieve accreditation could have serious implications for the marketability of your diploma. There was recently the case of a program that did not achieve accreditation as expected. Its graduates found themselves unable to sit for the state licensing exam and to qualify for many jobs that require it. Grants that fund many programs have as a requirement that staff in those programs be licensed.

Having an accredited degree is important for a number of reasons. Besides ensuring that your education meets minimum professional standards, you need an accredited degree in order to be eligible for most social work licenses. Check with your state or province licensing board to find out which accreditation(s) it accepts. An accredited degree will also enhance your employment opportunities, and some professional associations (such as the National Association of Social Workers) require it in order to join or receive full membership privileges.

Licensing and Certification

Being able to obtain a social work license is important, because most states or provinces in the United States and Canada require a license in order to practice as a social worker. Moreover, being licensed enhances your professional credibility. A few states now allow workers with degrees other than in social work to be licensed for general or clinical practice. People holding degrees in related fields such as guidance and counseling, family studies, and clinical psychology, among others, can sit for examinations to become a Licensed Professional Counselor or other similar designations.

Most states, however, require a master's in social work. At present, all fifty states, the District of Columbia, eight Canadian jurisdictions, Puerto Rico, and the Virgin Islands allow holders of master's degrees in social work from accredited schools to be licensed or certified as social workers at a variety of levels of practice. Of those, many require a doctorate or master's in social work (none require the doctorate above the MSW), while 37 also allow licensure or certification for holders of bachelor's degrees from accredited programs of social work. Eleven accept a bachelor's degree in a related field with varying amounts of social work experience. A handful of states allow certification of holders of associate's degrees, one or two years of college, as little as a basic high school education, or merely hands-on experience.

The master's degree from accredited graduate programs of social work remains the standard for professional independent practice. Most states now have multiple levels of licensure or certification. States that allow certification or licensure of holders of degrees other than the master's do so at levels of practice requiring only basic skills. For example, Alabama reserves its highest license of Private Independent Practice (PIP) for holders of doctorates or master's degrees in social work, whereas those holding only a bachelor's in social work may only be licensed at the Licensed Bachelor Social Worker (LBSW) level. An example of certification and licensure with less than a bachelor's degree is the Registered Social Work Assistant, or SWA, in Ohio.

Even if the state or province in which you intend to practice allows social work licensing with a related degree, consider that we live in a highly mobile society and someday you may relocate and find yourself in an area that does not allow licensing of holders of degrees other than social work. In addition, one of the unique aspects of the profession of social work is that the master's degree is considered the terminal degree. Therefore, you can rest knowing that by obtaining a master's degree in social work, you will be in a position to practice anywhere in the country.

As mentioned earlier, no states require a doctorate in social work in order to be licensed or certified. In fact, less than five percent of holders of master's degrees seek a doctorate. Those obtaining doctorates in social work (Ph.D. or DSW) most often conduct social research or teach in a variety of settings. A more comprehensive discussion of the subject of a doctoral education may be found in Chapter 14, *The Doctoral Decision.*

Part III of this book contains a list of addresses and telephone numbers of licensing bodies for the United States and Canada. In each listing, you will also find the levels of practice recognized and the educational and experiential requirements for each level. The list also provides information on the category of examination required for each type of certification or licensure. The address and toll-free telephone number of the Association of Social Work Boards (ASWB), which administers the exams, may also be found in the same section of this book. Check with the state or province where you may be residing in the future for its specific requirements.

In addition, some states or provinces may have other certification or licensing requirements for specific types of social work practice. One good example is the practice of school social work. In the state of Illinois, for instance, the State Board of Education must certify school social workers. Another example is California, where school social workers must hold the Pupil Personnel Services Credential. In such jurisdictions, graduate students interested in school social work certification must take specific courses in the classroom and in the field as part of the master's program. Check with the licensing bodies of the states or provinces where you may be residing after graduate school about their specific requirements.

Licensing and certification of social workers vary a great deal from jurisdiction to jurisdiction. Most states and provinces have at least two levels of licensure or certification for holders of master's degrees in social work, although what they are called varies. The first level is available to anyone who has received a master's degree in social work (as mentioned earlier, a few states allow holders of master's degrees in related fields to be licensed as social workers). There is an exam required and, upon successful completion, licensure or certification is awarded. Illinois and Indiana, for example, call this level Licensed Social Worker (LSW).

The second level of licensure or certification that exists in most states and provinces requires two years of post-master's clinical supervised experience. Upon documentation of the experience and successful completion of the examination, licensure or certification is awarded. This level of licensure or certification is usually required for independent clinical practice. Most insurance companies and third-party payers require it for payment of fees for clinical services. Illinois and Indiana, for example, call this level Licensed Clinical Social Worker (LCSW). Most states and provinces also have lower levels of licensure or certification for holders of bachelor's and lesser degrees.

Most state or province licensing and certification examinations are administered by the Association of Social Work Boards (ASWB). ASWB administers four categories of exams—Bachelor's, Master's, Advanced Generalist, and Clinical. Not every state has provisions for all four categories. The Bachelor's exam is required by most states that allow certification or licensure of bachelor's level social workers. The Master's, Advanced Generalist, and Clinical exams are required in most states for MSW degree holders. The examinations are objective in form and have 170 questions (20 of which scattered throughout the exam are pre-test items not used in scoring). Candidates are allowed four hours to complete an examination.

Some states or provinces have reciprocity agreements, while others do not. So, if you plan to relocate sometime in the future, you may or may not need to undergo another licensing examination. In Part III of this *Handbook,* you will find a listing of the type of exam required by each state. ASWB (1-800-255-6880) can provide information on the exam required by any state or province and reciprocity agreements.

In the United States, in addition to state licensing, voluntary certification is provided by the National Association of Social Workers (NASW). NASW offers the certifications of ACSW (Academy of Certified Social Workers), DCSW (Diplomate in Clinical Social Work), and QCSW (Qualified Clinical Social Worker). NASW also offers specialty certifications in services in the fields of vulnerable populations at the master's or bachelor's levels (Certified Advanced Children, Youth, and Family Social Worker, C-ACYFSW; Certified Children, Youth, and Family Social Worker, C-CYFSW); health care (Certified Social Worker in Health Care, C-SWHC), substance abuse (Certified Clinical Alcohol, Tobacco, and Other Drugs Social Worker, C-CATODSW); case management at the master's or bachelor's levels (Certified Advanced Social Work Case Manager, C-ASWCM; Certified Social Work Case Manager, C-SWCM); and schools (Certified School Social Work Specialist, C-SSWS).

Must the Diploma Read "Master of Social Work"?

Although most accredited schools of social work grant Master of Social Work degrees, not all do so. For all intents and purposes, including the important issue of certification and licensing, it does not matter. Whether your diploma reads, "Master of Social Work," "Master of Social Service Administration," "Master of the Science of Social Work," or "Master of Arts" (all actual examples of degrees granted by CSWE-accredited graduate programs of social work in the United States), the only issue that matters is whether or not the granting institution is accredited by CSWE or CASSW-ACESS. The licensing agencies are not concerned with what your diploma says, but simply that it be from an institution accredited by the proper social work accrediting body.

In some instances, there may actually be some advantages, purely in terms of perception rather than substance, to the diploma reading something other than "Master of Social Work." There are a great many who will take issue with this point of view. I choose to offer it here simply to put it on the table and make readers aware of its existence.

For those of you who expect to practice in social policy, research, analysis, community organization, and other non-clinical areas, there may be advantages to having a degree other than the traditional MSW. Many of the people who review applicants for positions in non-clinical settings may not have a social work background. Some may not be fully aware that many graduate schools of social work have excellent training in research, policy formulation and analysis, community organization, and similar areas. Therefore, when they review a résumé that states the person holds an MSW, they may be inclined to dismiss the applicant as someone versed in clinical but not policy areas. If the résumé states something else, such as a Master's in Social Service Administration, the potential employer may be less likely to be misled.

On the other hand, clinical graduates of schools that grant diplomas other than the traditional MSW are not usually miscast as "non-clinicians," because they are eligible for clinical certification and licensing.

Let me quickly follow the above by warning you against making a choice of school simply on what your diploma will say. Most schools of social work, regardless of programmatic focus on clinical versus policy education, offer Master of Social Work (MSW) degrees. In fact, many of our nation's leading policy and administrative programs grant MSW degrees. If you find such a school that meets your needs as a policy student, don't hesitate to pursue enrollment. All it may mean down the road is that when, and if, you encounter a potential employer who has the misconception that MSW automatically means clinician, you will have to tactfully educate that person.

> Research different programs to see which one best suits your goals.
> *Melissa Aragon*
> *MSW student*

The reader who is extremely interested in policy issues may at this point be wondering what the advantages are of a policy education within a social work program. How does it differ from a program in public policy? In general, public policy programs tend to be broader in their approach to policy, and will be just as likely to look at a space program, for instance, as social programs. A social work-based policy program will focus only on social welfare policy.

Another typical difference is that public policy programs tend to take a quantitative approach, whereas social work policy programs tend to take a qualitative approach to the subject. Public policy programs, therefore, tend to have more extensive requirements in the area of quantitative research than social work policy programs.

Program Rankings

There are a number of rankings of graduate programs in social work and social welfare. I advise caution in letting your choice of school be driven by them. They tend to have the same band-wagon effect on some applicants that the old advertising phrase "seven out of ten doctors recommend..." has on purchasers of aspirin. Keep in mind that rankings are the end result of someone's idea of what constitutes a good program. That "someone's" ideas may be based on needs and priorities very different from your own. Beyond that, that someone's methodology for evaluating or ranking the programs may be less than perfect. Whose point of view they represent is also important.

Having made the above disclaimer, I will add that, when placed in their proper perspective, rankings can be useful. They give applicants a feel for how the school and, by extension, its graduates, are seen, at least within academe.

Rankings generally tend to be done by educators for educators and students. Just how many practicing social service professionals know the rankings or are aware that they even exist is questionable. Those practicing professionals who are graduates of the highly ranked schools know of the rankings, because their schools tend to feature the rankings in alumni publications. On the other hand, practicing professionals outside of academe who are graduates of lower-ranked or not-at-all-ranked schools probably never hear about rankings, because their schools are unlikely to feature a story on rankings in alumni publications. The mainstream press and other media, with the notable exception of *U.S. News & World Report* (more on this later), are also unlikely to feature stories on rankings of academic programs.

If you plan to remain in academe, whether by teaching and doing research in an academic setting once you have your master's or by pursuing a doctorate, the ranking of the school you attend may be more relevant. Within academia, the rankings are analogous to the price of stocks in business. The higher the ranking, the higher the "stock." There are also, from time to time, studies on the amount of research and writings produced at various schools. Within the academic world, those reports are significant. That is the stuff that tenure is made of. Overall, the academic ranking of the program you attend may or may not assist you in securing employment.

Two well-known rankings on social work programs are worth mentioning. They are very different from one another in the methodologies they employ.

The more empirically sound of the two is *The Gourman Report: A Rating of Graduate and Professional Programs in American and International Universities* (Gourman, J., Sixth edition, Revised. Los Angeles: National Education Standards, 1997). Gourman offers rankings based on specific criteria including, among many others, the age and experience of the institution, qualifications of the faculty, curricular content, and support services and physical facilities. It offers a good starting point for those interested in programs of national prominence.

The second ranking is that of *U.S. News & World Report.* The inclusion of schools of social work in the magazine's annual education issue began in 1993. A partial listing of *U.S. News & World Report's* current rankings of schools of social work (ranked in 2004) may be found on the Internet at http://www.usnews.com/usnews/edu/grad/rankings/hea/brief/sow_brief.php.

The methodology employed in determining rankings consisted of a survey of opinions of senior faculty and deans of schools of social work. To what extent the respondents' loyalty to the schools they attended or where they are employed played a part in their responses is anyone's guess. Given that the magazine is so widely distributed and known, the results of the survey may become widely accepted by the general public, despite the weak methodology.

Financial Aid

The levels of financial assistance vary greatly from program to program. Generally speaking, the level of aid is higher at private programs than at programs in public universities. Some state-supported institutions award little or no student aid.

Ask each school you are considering to give you figures on the amount of aid awarded the previous year's incoming class. They should be able to provide you with a range, mean, median, and mode. If the school is state-supported, it should be able to provide you with figures for in-state versus out-of-state students. Also ask for the percentage of students who receive aid.

Another excellent source for this information is *Statistics on Social Work Education in the United States*, published annually by the Council on Social Work Education (CSWE). Along with a great deal of other information, it includes tables outlining the types of aid actually awarded by each program and the number of students that received each type of award. It can be obtained for $18 plus shipping/handling at CSWE's Web site (http://www.cswe.org).

Types of Aid

The types of aid available in the United States and Canada are similar. For information regarding Canadian programs, the best source is the school itself.

According to the Council on Social Work Education, as of November 2002, the most predominant form of financial aid awarded full-time master's students was in the form of student loans (awarded to 36.1% of students). Other types of aid awarded included school or university grants (30.9% of students), work study (1% of students), state or local government grants (6.7% of students), federal child welfare grants (4.9% of students), and research or graduate assistantships (3.5% of students).

Most schools award a combination of need-based aid and merit-based aid. The former is purely based on an applicant's financial situation and what his expected income will be while a student. Generally speaking, if an applicant has not been claimed as a dependent on his parents' income tax return for the year preceding admission, the parents' income will not be considered. Ask the specific schools you are considering for their policy on parental income.

Merit-based aid is not at all based on the student's financial status but rather on the student's application rating relative to other students being admitted in the same group. The strength of the admission committee's rating is the sole determinant.

Many schools also have specialized scholarships specifically for students of color and other groups. Some have fellowship money for students admitted to certain specialty programs (refer to "Specialty Programs" in Chapter 5 of this book).

I advise students not to make their initial decision of schools to consider solely on the basis of the tuition amounts. Instead, I advise selecting schools based on their programs and their relevancy to your learning goals and professional objectives. I do believe you should include among the schools to which you make application for admission a balance between state-supported schools and private schools. Follow to the letter each school's requirements and deadlines for submission of the financial aid application.

Alternative Scholarships

Before you go to all lengths to attempt to secure outside sources of scholarships, fellowships, and alternate funding, inquire of the schools what effect outside scholarships will have on the school's award to you. Most schools will reduce their award to you by an amount equal to the outside award. The rationale is that your financial need is less as a result of the outside aid. One way to look at this is that all your extra efforts to secure outside scholarships will benefit the school instead of you. There is also a more altruistic, and possibly beneficial, way to look at this. By bringing a portion of your own aid from an outside source, you free up aid the school has available for use by other applicants. For this reason, with all other factors being equal, your application may be marginally preferable, because it gives the school the added flexibility.

Graduate Assistantships

If your undergraduate academic record is exemplary, a graduate teaching assistantship may be a possibility. The key determining factor will be the match of your college major and the undergraduate offerings at your graduate school and its host university. If your undergraduate major is social work and the school where you will be attending the MSW program also has a BSW program, there may be graduate assistantships available. The reason is that as a master's student with a BSW background, you may be able to assist in undergraduate (i.e., BSW) classes.

If your undergraduate major is something other than social work, there may or may not be opportunities to assist in BSW classes, because there may be a preference given to graduate assistants who are BSW holders. There may be, however, assistantship options in other parts of the host university. If the university has an undergraduate program in your major, there may be assistantship opportunities for you. For example, if your undergraduate major is in child development, there may be opportunities if the university has an undergraduate program in that field.

Not all graduate schools of social work have a BSW component. In those schools, assistantships for master's students are not available within the school simply because there are no undergraduate classes in which to assist. Assistantships in those settings are usually reserved for doctoral students who have a master's background to assist in the master's classes. Nevertheless, there may be an undergraduate program that matches your college major in the host university that may offer opportunities for you.

If there are no teaching assistantships available to you, you may want to inquire about research or other types of assistantships for master's level students. These may involve working several hours a week with a professor on a research study or other special projects.

In any case, graduate assistantships for master's students are more difficult to obtain than for doctoral students. The latter have the benefit of a broader academic background when compared to master's students. The benefits, however, merit a serious search. In state-supported schools, graduate assistantships often offer a full tuition waiver. In addition, they may include a stipend ranging from a few hundred dollars to as much as several thousand dollars per academic year. The benefits in private institutions are generally less generous, but worthwhile nevertheless.

The financial aid office of the school(s) of your interest is a good beginning point for exploring graduate assistantship options.

Applying For Financial Aid

Some schools make it more complicated than others to apply for financial aid. Some request as little as checking on the application whether or not you are interested in being considered for scholarships and loans. Other schools, on the other hand, provide you with lengthy lists of the scholarships available and their eligibility requirements. You are asked to determine from the list which scholarships you qualify for and asked to submit specific essays and other materials for each scholarship you select.

Most schools have their own scholarship, loan, and work study applications. Usually, those forms are not a part of the initial admission application packet; rather, they are provided to those applicants who accept offers of admission.

Most schools in the United States use the Free Application for Federal Student Aid (FAFSA) in determining the need-based portion of financial awards. You can obtain that form at the financial aid office of your undergraduate institution or from the graduate schools where you apply for admission. The FAFSA is generally not available until late December and should be filed as soon as possible after the beginning of the year. You cannot file it earlier than January 1, because the data requested is based on your income for the year ending December 31. The FAFSA can also be submitted online. For further information, visit "FAFSA on the Web" at *http://www.fafsa.ed.gov/*.

Helpful Hints

Do...

- make sure the schools you are considering are accredited or in candidacy for accreditation by CSWE or CASSW-ACESS. Accreditation will determine whether or not you can be licensed as a social worker.

- check with the state or states where you may be residing in the future for their general social work licensing requirements, as well as for licensing in specific social work specialties, such as school social work. (See Part III for a listing of state licensing boards.)

- explore programs in public policy and public health and compare them carefully to MSW programs if your primary area of interest is policy.

- pursue all available forms of scholarships.

Don't...

- overlook schools whose diploma states something other than "Master of Social Work." What matters is whether or not a school is accredited by the Council on Social Work Education or the Canadian Association of Schools of Social Work, not what the diploma states. Some of the finest social work programs offer degrees that say something other than "Master of Social Work."

- let a school's ranking play the most important role in your choice of school.

Chapter 3

Comparing Academic Programs

Even though all graduate programs of social work must meet certain common requirements in class and field work content in order to qualify for CSWE or CASSW-ACESS accreditation, each retains a flavor and mission all its own. Many of the requirements of the first year of graduate study, for instance, are very similar across programs. Yet, each school has a particular perspective that translates into the particulars of how those requirements are met. A school's orientation may be more evident in the nature and variety of courses offered beyond the first-year requirements. The same may be said if the school offers specialty programs, such as maternal child health and health care. All schools have a particular perspective that can, for the sake of our discussion, be seen as being located somewhere along a continuum that ranges from a focus on the micro (clinical) aspects of social work to the macro (policy/administration) aspects of practice.

The Clinical to Policy Continuum

At one end of the continuum are schools that specifically focus on a clinical perspective. They have as their mission the training of social work professionals for the provision of direct services to individuals, families, and groups. Although programs at this end of the spectrum provide some policy-related courses in conformance with CSWE or CASSW-ACESS requirements, by and large the focus even in those courses is on policy as it affects clinical practice and not much beyond. There are advantages and disadvantages to this focus.

If you are specifically interested in clinical practice and intend to be a clinician throughout your career, you may want to seek this type of school. Faculty at this type of program are generally extremely well versed in the direct service aspects of social work. In addition, the variety of clinically-oriented electives tends to be broader at clinically-focused schools.

On the other hand, one point to consider is that even if at this time in your professional development you intend to be a clinician at the direct service level throughout your career, things may change down the road. You may later decide that you would like to explore other areas of social work. You may later discover an area of non-clinical practice that you did not know existed or an area may develop in the future that does not exist at this time. A strictly clinical education, as good as it may be in its own right, may not prepare you for all future options.

Even if not by your own choosing, circumstances may place you on a track away from direct practice. You may, for example, find yourself with an opportunity to be a supervisor or a program director in the same setting you may have originally entered intending to be a line service provider.

Many excellent schools that have a clinical focus also provide excellent classes in staff supervision, program management and development, budgeting, and related topics. Look for these types of course offerings in the school's catalog if you are leaning toward schools with a heavy emphasis on micro social work. You would serve yourself well by considering social program management classes in rounding out your clinical education. Many an excellent clinician has found himself in a supervisory position through unanticipated circumstances and wished he had more training in supervisory skills, program planning, and budgeting.

At the other end of the continuum are schools that focus heavily on policy aspects of social work including administration, policy analysis, research, and community organization.

Although most schools offer a clinical component, schools at this end of the spectrum are "top-heavy" on the policy side. Even with a clinical area of concentration, the selection among clinical electives will generally not be as broad as in the strictly clinical programs. The selection of classes on the social policy aspects of social work, however, will likely be quite good. What may be lacking in clinical classes will be made up by the opportunity to elect classes in social policy analysis and research, community organization, and management of social service organizations.

If you are at heart a clinician yet are attracted to schools with a fair amount of policy offerings, don't despair. If the clinical offerings are necessarily narrower because of the number of policy offerings, look at other programs and schools that may exist in the university at large. Does the university have good human development or family studies programs? If it does, are you able to enroll in those classes without extensive red tape and have the classes count for credit in the social work program?

Most schools tend to fall somewhere along the continuum between the extremes of purely clinical and mostly social policy. Looking at the relative balance (or imbalance) between specific class offerings in areas of clinical concentration versus policy concentration will give you a good clue as to where a school stands. The backgrounds of the faculty are also good clues. Does the school profess to have a good clinical program and yet have an imbalance of policy faculty over clinical faculty?

Many programs do an excellent job of providing a nice balance between the macro and micro aspects of social work, and others do not. In an era of increasing competitiveness in recruiting among schools, you should look beneath the recruiters' claims into the real substance of each school's program offerings and the training of the faculty charged with carrying out the programs.

Regardless of its place along the continuum, each school has its own particular model of education. Let's look, in turn, at how you can assess each program's strengths and weaknesses, regardless of whether you are interested in a clinical focus or policy focus.

Models of Clinical Social Work Education

Many people who enter the profession of social work do so out of a desire to provide direct services in areas such as child and family services, mental health, and related settings. Whereas all schools of social work subscribe to the social work mission of clinical service, they do so in various ways.

Some schools place a heavy emphasis on a particular theoretical model of clinical practice. Some schools have a definite bias toward, for instance, the traditional psychoanalytic models. Others, on the other hand, are more inclined to focus on behavioral, systemic, or other approaches to practice. Still others offer a more eclectic array of various approaches.

My recommendation is to seriously consider the more eclectic models of clinical education. One reason is that the field changes rapidly. A heavy emphasis on one given approach may leave you unprepared for whatever changes occur in the future. Unless you have a good deal of clinical experience prior to graduate school and, based on that experience, you have a definite model that interests you, I believe a broad foundation in several approaches will serve you best in the long run.

Keep in mind that a graduate education serves its purpose best when it lays a solid foundation for future growth. It is not at all uncommon for seasoned clinicians with years of post-master's experience to seek specialized training through avenues ranging from institutes for psychoanalysis to institutes for family therapy. In fact, maintaining licensure or certification in any given state requires clinicians to have continuing education.

Some examples of clinical concentration areas you will find among graduate programs in social work include:

- Children and Youth Services
- Social Work Practice With Families and Children
- Interpersonal Practice With Individuals, Families, and Groups
- Alcohol and Other Drug Abuse

- Social Work Practice in School Settings
- Health and Mental Health
- Social Work and the Aging
- The World of Work

In addition to concentration areas, many schools require students to select an area of practice on which to focus. Examples include:

- Casework
- Group Work
- Family Therapy

Some schools also provide selections of courses intended to develop specific professional skills such as case management, public speaking, and grant writing.

One way to determine a school's focus is to inquire about the percentage of students in a given area of concentration. For instance, in a school that offers both micro (clinical) and macro (policy/administration) fields of study concentration, it would be useful to learn the percentages of students in each area. If the number of students is fairly evenly distributed at perhaps no greater than a 60%/40% split in either direction, the program is probably fairly well-balanced.

Still another important component to explore in a clinical program is the types of field work placements available. More specifics on this important topic are discussed in Chapter 4 of this book.

Models of Macro Social Work Education

The approaches to macro social work education vary a great deal. They are often as unique as are the faculties of the various institutions. There are those programs that view social policy strictly from the perspective of social workers. In those programs, faculty are, for the most part, trained in social work. Other schools, however, have multiple disciplinary perspectives present on their faculties. Such schools are just as likely to have faculty trained in economics, public policy, public health, and law as they are to have faculty trained in social work.

The policy course offerings will be a good reflection of the faculty's training and interests. If you have particular interests in specific policy areas such as international social work policy, healthcare policy, immigration policy, or Latin American affairs, to name a few, a thorough review of the course offerings and faculty publications would serve you well.

Another important area of exploration is, interestingly enough, the offerings of other graduate and professional schools that are also part of the host university of the social work program. If the university has programs in public policy, law, international studies, business, or other areas of your interest, there may be the opportunity to round out your education outside of the social work program. Of course, you need to find out how available classes outside of the school in other areas of the university will be to you and whether they will count as credits toward your degree. If the given university does not have programs in the particular areas of your interest, find out if cooperative arrangements exist with neighboring institutions. If this is the case, you definitely want to explore implications to cost, financial aid, and the total number of courses required for graduation.

Examples of macro concentrations you are likely to come across in your search of a program are:

- Social and Economic Development
- Community Organization
- Management and Planning
- Fund Raising
- Research and Evaluation
- Social Welfare Administration
- Social Policy and Planning

Selecting Your Area of Concentration

An important question to ask of schools is at what point in the program will you be required to declare your selection of area of concentration (i.e., clinical with an emphasis on children and family treatment, or administrative with an emphasis on community organization).

The selection of an area of concentration is important because it will determine the emphasis of your graduate education. It should be noted, however, that it will not necessarily limit your job opportunities beyond graduation. As mentioned earlier in this book, all schools have a common core of foundation courses as required by the Council on Social Work Education or CASSW-ACESS. Therefore, all MSW holders, regardless of their school of graduation, have a core set of social work skills. The concentration adds a specialty to that core. For example, I was a clinical concentration student, yet I have held policy and administration positions, as well as clinical ones.

Some schools do not expect students to declare a concentration until shortly before completing the program's general requirements. The strength of that approach is that students are better prepared at that point than at the start of the program to make an informed selection. By that point, the general requirements will have given students a good background and foundation in both the clinical and administrative/policy aspects of social welfare.

Other schools, on the other hand, require students to declare their concentration as early as the time of making application for admission. Inquire of those schools if it would be difficult for you to alter your selection if you should change your mind as a result of what you learn from the general requirement courses.

Whether a school asks you to declare your concentration in the application for admission or not, it should not be difficult to change your selection if you do it before your concentration phase begins or even soon after beginning work on your concentration. Most schools either ask explicitly in the application what your intended area of concentration will be or infer it from your biographical statement. The reason the information is important to the school during the application phase is that it allows the school to balance the numbers of students who expect to be in the various concentrations the school offers.

Recent Developments

If your area or areas of interest lie in issues that are of relatively recent vintage, you may find few schools that offer concentrations matching those interests. For example, the issues of domestic and family violence, as well as sexual abuse, have gained national attention in recent years. As a result, there have been a number of legislative developments at the federal and state levels that have an impact on those issues. Because of the extensive preparations often required in altering established curricular concentration areas, few formal concentrations have as yet been developed. Many schools, however, have begun offering elective courses in those areas and are in the process of expanding their offerings.

Whatever your interests are, you would do well to ask what plans are in development and arrange to speak with faculty spearheading the projects. You may uncover opportunities to become involved in emerging programs as a paid student employee or research assistant.

Helpful Hints

Do...

* examine where a school lies on the clinical to policy continuum.

* consider a balanced education among clinical and administration/policy choices.

* explore the real expertise of the faculty, based on their writings.

* find out at what point in the program you will need to declare a concentration.

* inquire how difficult it is to change concentrations.

* consider the school's academic relationship with other departments within the university, as well as with other universities and colleges in the area.

Don't...

* assume all schools are the same.

* assume your choice of concentration is not important.

* assume your choice of concentration is all-important.

* expect that if your area of concentration is micro practice that you will always be a clinician, or if it is macro social work that you will be limited to working as an advocate, supervisor, or administrator throughout your career.

Chapter 4

Field Work Options

The field work component will be a very important portion of your graduate education. In this book, the terms field work, practicum, and internship are used interchangeably as they often are by MSW schools. Field work allows the student to integrate class theory into practice, develop the skills and values central to effective social work practice, and develop a professional identity. The match between your individual learning goals and professional objectives and the field work site and field work instructor can either make your graduate experience challenging, fruitful, and enjoyable, or quite the opposite.

The field work instructor is usually a practicing professional who holds an MSW and several years of post-master's experience. The field work instructor is generally an employee of the host agency who supervises the intern (MSW student) in addition to his other duties. For example, an intern in a school will often be supervised by a field instructor who herself is a school social worker in that school. Graduate schools of social work, realizing the importance of the field work instructor, are generally very selective and provide training for field instructors. The field work component is a highly valued piece of a graduate social work education.

The Field Work Setting

One important factor to explore in your selection of a graduate program is the availability of practica in the setting of your interest. Most schools of social work have sites available in a variety of social service settings. Settings typically available include:

- Medical and Psychiatric Hospitals
- Residential Treatment Facilities
- Mental Health Clinics
- Planning and Coordinating Councils
- Councils on Aging
- Governmental Agencies
- Labor Unions
- Community Programs
- University Research and Demonstration Projects
- Family Service Agencies
- Corporations
- Veteran Facilities
- Courts
- Child Welfare Programs
- Correctional Facilities
- Schools
- Work Rehabilitation Centers
- Employee Assistance Programs

Most programs of social work require students to participate in two separate field work sites through the course of the master's program. A few programs require one continuous practicum in one site with phases of progressive exposure and involvement through the duration of the master's program.

An important question to ask is whether you have the opportunity to select your field work sites or if they are assigned. Most of the schools that require two practica assign the first practicum site based on your stated interests and goals in your application, conversations with you, and/or written questionnaires completed after you have accepted the offer of admission. Most of these schools allow students to select their second practicum from a list of approved sites.

On the surface, you may feel uncomfortable with not having the opportunity to choose your first practicum. There are, however, some advantages. The first practicum, in those schools that select it for you, will probably not be what you would have chosen. In fact, it may be quite unlike anything you might have considered.

Nevertheless, assuming the field work staff does a good job, it may turn out to be a very worthwhile experience.

I will tell you of my own experience my first year in graduate school as an example. I wrote in my biographical statement that I was very interested in pursuing a career in the field of family therapy, principally around issues related to behavioral problems of children. I also wrote in my field work questionnaire that I wanted to be placed in a family agency, where I would be involved in providing individual treatment to children and families.

My assigned field work site was at a public school in a bilingual program. I was not pleased by my assignment, because I had no interest in ever being a school social worker. In addition, I knew the setting would not allow for family treatment. Nevertheless, I remained in that site throughout my first year of my graduate program.

Two years after obtaining my master's, I secured a position as a child and family therapist in an outpatient program of a community mental health center. A great many of my referrals came from schools, and I often needed to participate in Individual Educational Program staffings. My experiences as a school social work intern during my first year of graduate school were very helpful. Only then did I realize what a wonderful placement a school had been for my future goals.

> Make sure to keep your mind open to all different fields in the social work profession.
> *Michelle del Toral*
> *MSW student*

A first-year practicum carefully selected by the graduate school's field placement staff based on your career goals can be most beneficial. It may not be your dream of dreams, but it may contribute in a very positive way to your development. It can provide you with experience in a setting you would probably not otherwise ever know, on a time-limited basis, under the protected status of student with a limited caseload and good supervision.

My own practicum experience the first year, as well as that of most students I've known through the years, was a positive one. Despite not having the opportunity to select the first practicum, most graduates state, albeit with the benefit of hindsight, that it was a worthwhile experience. A few, however, state the opposite.

What If I Need To Change Sites?

A question to explore in selecting a graduate program is the degree of flexibility in changing field work sites if the first selection does not work out. Field work directors may not want to offer details, for fear of opening the floodgates of students wanting to change sites. Nevertheless, asking the question and getting a feel for the approachability of the field work personnel is important. A few students at various institutions each year find themselves having to make up field work time in the summer as a result of not switching sites in time to fulfill required hours.

Typical Structures of Field Work Programs

The first portion of the field work experience is generally designed to provide the student with exposure to the profession and the development of a sound generalist foundation for practice. The advanced portion of the field work experience is designed to develop skills in the student's area of concentration. Examples of skills for development include those required of administrators of social welfare organizations, researchers and analysts of social programs, supervisors at the clinical or macro levels, clinicians in various settings, community and grass-roots organizers, and macro planners.

There are different models for structuring the field work component, depending on the school and whether the student is attending a full-time, part-time, advanced placement, or other program.

The most typical model for a full-time program of study consists of one field work practicum during the entire first year of full-time study and a different practicum during the entire second year of full-time study. Each year, depending on the school and the field of concentration selected by the student, field work can consist of anywhere from fifteen to sixteen hours per week (two full-time days) to twenty-one to twenty-four hours per week (three full-time days).

There are variations on the two field sites model. They include one continuous placement with increasing responsibility, block field work placements during summers, and full-time placements during selected terms of the school year.

Paid Field Placements

The vast majority of field placements do not provide a stipend. More specifically, paid first-year field placements are virtually non-existent. There usually are, however, a very limited number of second-year field placements that provide a modest stipend.

According to the Council on Social Work Education, as of November 2002, of 19,210 master's students placed at an internship site, 1,702 (8.9%) were receiving some form of stipend from the internship agency. Among those, the highest percentage were social welfare agencies (25.4%). They were followed by state or local government agencies (23.7%).

Selecting a Field Work Site

The second practicum is generally selected by the student from a list of pre-approved sites provided by the school. The selection typically takes place late in the first year. It usually includes interviews to allow students and agencies an opportunity for mutual evaluation and selection.

A good source of information as you select your second practicum is the student, or students, placed there in the current year. Most schools have a directory of field site assignments. The second-year student who is currently at a site you are considering can give you excellent insight on the site and on the field work instructor. Don't neglect to ask the student questions about the safety of the site and its neighborhood. There may be times you attend field work after dark, and your safety may be an issue. Also ask more mundane questions, such as the variety of places nearby to eat and how much time you will usually have for meals.

There are important questions to explore in selecting your second-year field work site. How does the mission of the agency and the clientele it serves fit your goals? For example, if your goal is to work with clients from low-income communities, a field work site at a private practice setting largely serving middle-class to affluent clients would not be a good match. For a clinical student, the match between his interests and the agency's theoretical perspective will be important. A student primarily interested in a systemic approach to treatment should not select an agency with a predominantly psychoanalytic approach to treatment (unless, of course, he wants exposure to that model). For a policy student, the match between the agency's areas of focus and his own interests is crucial. A student interested in health issues will not benefit from placement in a municipal department largely responsible for urban planning.

Field work placements, particularly those in a student's final year of graduate school, frequently become full-time employment for the student after graduation. As you explore settings for your second field placement, ask yourself if the potential site is a place where you would like to work. Is the agency size such that there are likely to be openings when you graduate? If it isn't, is your work in that agency as an intern likely to bring you in contact with other agencies that may become potential employers?

Assessing Potential Field Instructors

The fit between you and the potential field work instructor can make all the difference. During your interview for your second-year field site, attempt to learn as much as possible about the field instructor in that agency. Don't have an interview with a person other than the person who will be your field instructor should you be offered and accept that particular placement. You want to get a feel for the chemistry between that person and you.

Most people who become field instructors do so voluntarily without additional pay from their agencies. Most are genuinely committed to the profession and seek to convey their knowledge to future professionals. In addition, most schools provide training for field instructors and closely monitor field sites. The case can be made, therefore, that there are no bad field instructors. There are, however, bad matches of field instructors and students, and such matches can have chaotic results.

There are a number of things you want to learn about your potential field instructor. What is that person's supervisory style? Some instructors employ a confrontational and challenging style. For instance, they might confront the student with a hypothetical situation and ask what the student would do. They might also challenge the student's methods in an attempt to have the student thoroughly explore the reasoning and possible consequences of his actions. Other instructors tend to be more supportive and do much more "hand holding." Others fall somewhere in between. None of these styles is necessarily intrinsically good or bad. The important issue is the degree of comfort you have with the potential field instructor's particular style.

Do the instructor's other duties allow for consultations at times other than scheduled supervisory times? Some instructors prefer not to be approached with questions and concerns at times other than scheduled meetings. Is your learning style such that it would be hampered by not having the instructor available as needed? Other instructors have no problem being available whenever the need arises. Which style suits you best is the important question.

How long has the person been a field instructor? If you are the first field work student the person has ever had, there may be some rookie mistakes you may be subject to (but maybe not). On the other hand, if the person has been a field instructor for a great many years, is he set in his ways and not very flexible?

What other specialized training does the instructor have? For a student interested in family therapy, for instance, it would be beneficial to have a field instructor with post-graduate training in family treatment. For a student interested in health administration, a field instructor with a certificate in this field would be an excellent match.

Additional Field Work Factors to Consider

There are additional questions related to field work that you may want to explore. An important item is the mechanism for communication between the school and the practicum agency. At some schools, the instructor for the methods class is also assigned the role of field liaison for the students in his class. At other schools, there is a full-time staff person fulfilling liaison duties. The liaison function is important because it monitors the quality of field work experiences. It also intervenes should any problems arise. If the mechanism is a slow one, precious time will be lost should the need arise for alternate placement. The delay could result in the postponement of the student's expected graduation date.

Another item that may be worthy of exploration, depending on your interests, is the possibility of doing a block full-time placement in the summer between years in lieu of your second-year practicum. Most schools require that practica take place concurrently with class work during the academic year. The reason is a sound one, particularly for clinical students. There is a better opportunity to apply class theory to the field and vice versa if the two are taking place simultaneously.

Some schools, however, allow students to do block placements either during the summer or in other unique ways. Some even allow them in cities other than where the school is located. For instance, the School for Social Work of Smith College, through its Block Plan, offers eight-month block field placements across the nation and beyond, allowing students to become immersed full time in the experience. Another example is the Wurzweiler School of Social Work of Yeshiva University in New York City, which has participating field work sites in over twenty states, four Canadian provinces, and in Israel and Taiwan.

You may also want to ask if the program allows students to find their own field work sites over and above the options provided by the school, especially if you have a unique area of interest. Through the course of your first year, you may come to know of a setting that matches your interests and goals. Will the school work with you and that agency in arranging your second practicum? The potential site will still need to meet the requirements of the school in terms of the qualifications and level of experience of the field instructor, the type of supervision that must be provided, the caseload assigned an intern, and agreement to other school guidelines. I located my own field work site for my second year of graduate school, and it was a great experience. Other students have successfully created their own practica in sites not previously approved by their schools.

Helpful Hints

Do...

- explore the variety of field work settings each school offers.

- ask to what extent you have a role in determining your field work placements.

- ask how difficult it is to change field work sites if things don't work out.

- ask if there are paid field placements available (probably not too many, but worth asking).

- explore the match between your goals and experiences at the setting.

- ask if the agency is likely to have job openings when you graduate. If it isn't, is your work in that agency as an intern likely to bring you in contact with other agencies that may become potential employers?

- explore the possibility of a summer block placement.

(continued on next page)

(continued from previous page)

Don't...

- underestimate the importance of the field work component to your graduate education.

- dismiss varied experiences in field work settings. They may open your eyes to new possibilities.

- neglect the opportunity to have an interview with the person who will be your field instructor, so you can assess the "chemistry" between the two of you.

- feel it is inappropriate to ask the instructor about her supervisory style, flexibility in supervision, and other characteristics.

Chapter 5

Special Issues

There may be special issues you will want to consider when looking for a school of social work. If you are currently employed and wish to continue working, you may be interested in a part-time MSW program. If your undergraduate degree is in social work, you may qualify for advanced standing. If your career goals are very specific or unique, there may be a joint degree or specialty program that will help you meet those goals. Finally, the faculty of a particular school may have special expertise in a particular area of practice that is of interest to you, and this may influence your decision.

Part-Time Programs

An increasing number of graduate schools of social work in the U.S. are offering part-time programs. According to the Council on Social Work Education, part-time students comprised approximately 40.5% of students enrolled in the Fall of 2002. The Council on Social Work Education requires that students of part-time programs meet the same requirements as full-time students. The differences between full-time programs and part-time programs lie not in content and requirements, but in their structures. Therefore, everything in this *Handbook* regarding classroom and field requirements applies to part-time programs as well as full-time ones. Typically, part-time programs take three years or more to complete, whereas full-time programs are usually two years in duration.

The availability of classes during off-work hours varies greatly from program to program. Some programs allow students the option of attending classes either during the day or evenings, but have a complete course of offerings that allows part-time students to complete all their required class work in the evenings.

Be aware, however, that the choices of electives in these programs may be more limited than in the day program. There are simply fewer evening hours than day hours to schedule electives, and it may not be cost-effective for a school to schedule a highly specialized elective at two different times, given that the total number of students taking the course is low. If you have the option of taking electives in other departments and schools of the university, explore whether those programs hold classes in the evening.

Some part-time programs offer classes during the evenings and weekends. Still others require at least a portion of the required classwork to be done during the day on Monday through Friday. Will your employer allow you the flexibility to attend day classes occasionally if the need arises?

The option of completing field work requirements during off-work hours also varies greatly among programs. Some are able to arrange field sites totally in the evenings or in some combination of evenings and weekends. The options for field sites in those programs, however, may be a great deal more limited than in day full-time programs. This is particularly true for students in administrative and policy concentrations of study. Most administrative and policy agencies do not have evening and weekend hours, so the choices are extremely limited. For clinical students, on the other hand, choices are much broader, because most clinical programs have evening hours to accommodate their clients.

It is for those reasons that a great many part-time programs do not offer field work on a part-time basis. Rather than restricting their students to an extremely limited pool of field work options, they opt to require students to do a full-time block field placement over the course of several weeks or to do a placement several full days per week for one or more terms. The issue of your employer's flexibility as to your work hours should be settled before you apply to a graduate program and accept an offer of admission.

Some programs allow part-time students who are employed in social service settings to do one of their required internships at their place of employment. Normally, requirements include that the practicum be in a program other than the one in which the student is employed. For example, if you are employed as a medical social worker in a hospital, you may be able to do your practicum in another department of the hospital, such as the outpatient adult psychiatric unit, the substance abuse unit, or another unit different from the one in which you currently work.

Another requirement may be that the person who acts as your field work supervisor be someone other than the person who is your job supervisor. In addition, that person must hold a master's degree in social work and meet the school's requirements of post-master's experience. The employer must agree to other school regulations.

The rationale for these and other requirements schools may have in allowing you to have a practicum at your place of employment is two-fold. One is that it is important that your roles as an employee and as a student be clearly differentiated. The other is that your practicum should provide a worthwhile learning experience, rather than reiterating what you already know from your job. Otherwise, you could simply end up working additional hours doing what you normally do in your job, learning nothing new, and not being compensated for the extra time. Check with the schools of your interest regarding this option and their requirements.

There are other queries you should make in exploring part-time programs. In an era of increasing financial pressure from their host institutions to be self-supporting, many schools of social work have recently entered the part-time market.

There are financial reasons that motivate schools to develop part-time programs. One is that part-time students who are employed often qualify for less financial aid from the school because they have income from full-time employment or because their employers offer tuition assistance. Inquire of the school to what extent financial aid is based on merit (the strength of your application relative to others offered admission in your group) and on need (your family income). If financial aid is based mostly on need, chances are your award will be minimal to non-existent, because you will have income from your employment.

Unfortunately, some schools have not fully considered accommodations to meet the special needs of students in the newly developed part-time programs. The hours of operation of their library, computer facility, or even dining facilities, for instance, may not have been expanded to adjust to the needs of students who are employed during the day. Administrators may still be on a nine-to-five schedule and unavailable to evening students for questions on registration, class selections, and financial aid.

Inquire about those issues before making application and considering accepting an offer of admission. As someone employed full time, attending classes part time, and attending field work part time, in addition to your personal responsibilities and commitments to your family and significant others, you already have enough on your plate. Having to wrestle for basic services with school officials will be an added burden worth avoiding.

Another factor to explore is that of the faculty who teach in the evening program. Many schools employ part-time instructors to teach in the evening program. Their regular full-time faculty may be involved only marginally, or not at all, in evening classes. Part-time faculty may or may not be capable of delivering the same level of education as full-time faculty. On the other hand, part-time faculty at some institutions may actually be much more connected to the issues of actual practice than full-time faculty, who may be primarily involved in writing and research. In addition, the availability of part-time instructors for student contact outside of class may be very limited.

Advanced Standing Programs

A great many graduate schools of social work in the U.S. offer advanced standing to incoming students who hold a Bachelor of Social Work (BSW) degree from an undergraduate program accredited by the Council on Social Work Education (CSWE). In Canada, CASSW-ACESS accreditation standards also allow for a shortened program for students holding an accredited BSW degree. The number of credits granted vary anywhere from approximately the equivalent of one semester to an entire year. Therefore, it is possible for holders of a BSW to earn a Master of Social Work in as little as only one academic year of study beyond the BSW.

According to the Council on Social Work Education (*Statistics on Social Work Education in the United States: 2002, p. 34)*, 65.7% of applications for advanced standing came from individuals who held a baccalaureate social work degree from an institution other than the one to which the application was made, and 23.5% of advanced standing applications were from graduates of BSW programs under the same auspices as the prospective master's program. Applicants in the latter group were much more likely to be accepted and enroll than applicants in the former group. A total of 993 (67.3%) of 1,476 applicants to their same host school subsequently enrolled, whereas only 2,137 (51.9%) of 4,116 applicants to other programs enrolled.

Schools with advanced standing programs typically reserve only a portion of spaces in an incoming class for advanced standing students. Competition for those spots among aspiring advanced standing applicants is very stiff. The mean undergraduate GPA of accepted advanced standing students is often higher than that of the conventional incoming class. If you are considering making application as an advanced standing student, seek that data from the institution, so you can assess your chances realistically.

If you apply seeking advanced standing, many schools will consider you only on that basis. That is, if you are denied admission into the advanced standing program, your application will not be considered for the regular program. That means that if you are denied advanced standing, your only remaining option to enter the same school's regular program is to reapply the following year as a conventional student. Check with the schools you are considering on their policies.

Some schools do not have an advanced standing program in terms of reducing the number of total classes a student will be required to take to graduate. Instead, a student may waive some required courses but will need to take other more advanced courses in their place. In those programs, it is possible for students holding a BSW or related degrees such as psychology, family studies, human development, and others to request to waive out of some of the graduate program's required courses. Graduate courses typically eligible for waiver are Human Behavior in the Social Environment (HBSE) and Research and Statistics in the first year's requirements.

Typically, if the waiver request is approved after reviewing the content of similar undergraduate classes, the student is required to take other graduate courses in the place of the waived courses. Some schools offer an advanced HBSE course that must be taken if the regular HBSE class is waived, while other schools allow students receiving waivers to take elective courses of the student's choice. Therefore, the length of the program is not shortened. On the other hand, the student's education is enriched because redundancy in courses is eliminated while exposure to more advanced courses is increased.

Other schools do not have an advanced standing program at all. There is a school of thought that believes it is a disservice to the student and to the profession to rush a student through a master's program in only one year. It is believed an advanced standing student's education suffers because he does not have the benefit of the first year's practicum to lay a foundation for the advanced practicum. Rather, the advanced standing student goes directly into the advanced practicum in his only year in graduate school.

If you are leaning toward obtaining your MSW via an advanced standing program, one possible way to increase your preparation for the advanced practicum is for you to take some time to work full time in human services before going on to graduate school. Without this added experience, the advanced standing program student who goes directly from high school to college to an advanced standing program is at a clear disadvantage. Check with the schools you are considering for their policies on the maximum time allowed between earning a BSW and acceptance into their advanced standing programs. Some allow for a maximum time of five years and others have more strict standards.

The advanced standing program student must select an area of concentration right away because he will bypass most, if not all, of the program's general requirements, which are normally fulfilled before work on the selected area of concentration begins. Thus, he will not have the benefit of further exposure to, and exploration of, various aspects of social work that comes about during the general requirement phase of studies.

It can be argued that students who declare a selection of area of concentration after undergoing the general requirements phase do so in a much more informed way. Keep in mind that some schools, however, require all students to declare their area of concentration as early as the time they make application for admission.

The prime advantage of the advanced standing concept, of course, is that up to a year of school is saved for the student. If time is very much of the essence for you, you may want to consider it. On the other hand, you may also want to weigh what you will lose. Attending a conventional graduate program will allow you the opportunity to be exposed to a great deal more. The ultimate result, I believe, will be a better experience for you.

Joint Degree Programs

A good number of accredited graduate programs of social work offer joint degree opportunities. Most common offerings include joint programs with schools of law, schools of divinity, schools of business, schools of public or health policy, schools of gerontology, schools of urban and regional planning, and schools of education. There are also a few programs available in less traditional areas, such as dual degrees in social work and dance therapy, for instance. If you are interested in these possibilities, you have your job cut out for you. You should undertake a thorough investigation of the other program in whichever discipline you choose as carefully as you are exploring the social work program. Appendix B, *In Their Own Words*, contains information on joint degree programs from participating schools.

Applicants for admission to joint degree programs are normally required to apply to each school independently. A crucial factor in the admissions decision will be the extent to which the applicant makes a case for seeking the two degrees. How have the applicant's background and experiences in both fields tested and shaped her interests? How will the applicant's future professional plans benefit from dual training? Normally, an applicant must meet the individual entrance requirements of both programs.

There are a number of factors to consider about joint degree programs. Foremost is the fit between the two programs of study. Chances are that a number of one program's required courses will be counted as electives by the other program and vice versa. That means that you will not have as many electives in either program as non-dual degree students. You need to consider what you will be missing. If the two programs are highly complementary, the loss is minimal versus the time you save.

Joint degree programs normally save time for the student versus pursuing each program separately. For example, an MBA/MSW joint program might take three academic years of full-time study to complete. Were the two programs to be taken separately, each would take two years for a combined total of four years. Having some courses count for both programs is how the compressed time period is achieved.

Another factor to consider is whether splitting your time between two programs of study will allow you enough exposure outside of the classroom to the faculties of the two schools. A very important part of a graduate education rests on the mentoring relationships you will develop with faculty. If the two programs share some of the faculty, these relationships may be enhanced.

The source of your financial aid will vary depending on how much time you are enrolled in each program. For example, if two thirds of your classes are in program A and the other third in program B, your financial aid will probably be prorated accordingly. How will this affect your financial aid packet? If the two programs have fairly similar financial aid policies, there may not be much of an impact. If one has a much lower level of financial aid, you may need to consider additional employment or other sources of funds during the periods of time the majority of your coursework is in the program with the lower level of aid.

The best source of information is current students. Ask to be put in contact with students who are currently in the joint degree program you are considering.

Specialty Programs

In addition to joint degree programs, many schools offer specialty programs. Whereas these types of programs do not generally offer a degree in addition to the Master of Social Work, many offer a certificate that, depending on the nature and reputation of the specialty, can be very valuable. Beyond the specialty program's inherent benefits to your knowledge and professional development, a certificate can be a nice addition to your résumé, because it is an added credential. Appendix B, *In Their Own Words*, contains information on specialty programs from participating schools.

Specialty programs are offered in a variety of areas, such as urban practice, health administration and policy, rural practice, practice with populations of color, lesbian-gay-bisexual-transgender studies, family support, multiethnic practice, Jewish communal service, maternal child health, Native American studies, international social welfare, and aging.

At some schools, there are special application procedures to participate in a specialty program. In addition, there may be a fellowship attached for each of your years of study. Normally, once the next academic year's incoming class is selected, additional information is sent to incoming students regarding specialty programs and special application procedures.

Advantages to participating in a specialty certificate program include the specialized and usually state-of-the-art training, the additional credential, exposure to faculty in your particular area of interest, and, in some cases, fellowship funds. You should inquire, however, if receiving additional funds through the fellowship will decrease the need-based portion of your financial aid. If fellowship funds reduce other aid by the same amount, you really have not gained any funds.

There are a number of possible disadvantages to participating in specialty programs. One is that you usually will have few to no elective classes. The classroom portion of a regular master's program usually consists of the courses in general requirements, courses in a specific area of concentration, and electives. Because of accreditation requirements, students in specialty programs still have to fulfill the school's general requirements and the requirements for their selected area of concentration. Therefore, the courses of the specialty program usually take the place of the electives. If the specialty program is a good match with your interest, you will not lose by giving up electives.

If, on the other hand, you are considering a specialty program more for the possible additional funds than for the program content itself, think again. You are only in a master's level social work program once, and you want to make full use of the resources that will help you achieve the growth you will need to practice in the social work field of your choice. Whatever financial aid you may gain will be more than offset by your missed opportunities of elective courses if the specialty program doesn't truly match your interests and goals.

Faculty

The composition of the faculty also brings specific qualities to a school and how it approaches the business of educating its students. Whether you are interested in micro or macro social work, a critical issue will be the match between the type of training you are looking for and the faculty's interests and levels of experience. Explore carefully the training, background, and experiences of the faculty. Most schools include in their catalogs a list of faculty and their research interests and recent publications.

Investigate the school's faculty-student ratio. However, look also into the percentage of faculty typically on sabbatical or teaching only a part-time load or not at all as a result of research and writing commitments. The de facto faculty-student ratio may be substantially different from the reported ratio.

Does the composition of the faculty and activities reflect the school's stated mission? Most schools have beautifully crafted mission statements that speak eloquently about service to the underrepresented and vulnerable of our society. Yet, there is sometimes a discrepancy in what a school says and what a school does. Is the faculty involved in projects to serve surrounding communities through service as consultants or agency board members? To what extent does the school support faculty, students, and staff in community involvement?

If you are considering schools in cities you do not know, ask what percentage of the faculty live in the immediate area around the campus. The answer will be a good measure of the quality of the neighborhood's safety and general environment.

Does the faculty as a group represent the populations social workers are pledged to serve? Much has been

> Don't be afraid to ask questions to verify the school's program will meet your interests and needs. Do their faculty participate in organizations that support the ethics of the profession?
>
> *Mary Hess*
> *Human Services Program Chair*

written as of late about the wonders and benefits of "diversity." It has become a fashionable word to include in school catalogs and curricula. Yet, many of the schools most often quoting the concept lack diversity in their own faculty and administration.

Regardless of our level of training, experience, and expertise, our perspective is colored by our cultural lens. It is a most important part of a social work education to have the benefit of exposure to perspectives of faculty of various cultural backgrounds and sexual orientations. By the same token, it is important to have genuine diversity among the administrators who set policy on issues of curriculum and student services, including admissions and levels of student financial aid.

Another of the great benefits of a graduate education is the opportunity to interact with faculty beyond the classroom. How available are faculty to informal exchange with students, whether or not the given student is enrolled in their classes?

Those of you particularly interested in attending a school where faculty are heavily involved in ground-breaking research and publishing need to be particularly inquisitive. You may see in a school's catalog the name of a faculty person whose writings have inspired you during your undergraduate years. You will do well to ask how much actual teaching that person does, as well as how available that person is to discussions with students beyond the classroom.

Major schools are in intense competition with one another as to the percentage of faculty who publish in a given year. Therefore, some of each school's most notable faculty may be involved only marginally in actual teaching. Some notable faculty take one- or two-year sabbaticals on occasion to pursue research and writing. Will the faculty of your interest be available at the school for teaching and other contact with students during the time of your graduate education? A name on a catalog's faculty listing won't do you much good if you never actually meet the person.

It is also important to know who actually teaches the classes. Do the professors on the faculty list actually teach the classes, or are classes conducted by doctoral students? I am not at all stating that your education will not be served well by doctoral students. Many are very knowledgeable, have outstanding abilities to convey class material, and are very committed to their students. Nevertheless, you need to know what to expect, so you can develop an informed opinion about the school.

A related question is relevant to those who will be attending evening or other alternative programs. Is the faculty that teaches in the full-time program the same faculty that teaches in the alternative program? You may have been attracted to the school because of its renowned faculty and find once you are there that your classes are taught by adjunct part-time instructors. Once again, let me make clear that I am not stating that teaching by adjunct part-time faculty results in an inferior education. In fact, an argument to the contrary can be made, because many part-time instructors work during the day in real-life social service settings and bring vast practice experience to the classroom. Again, the issue is your ability to arrive at an informed decision about the school.

Recent Developments

The last few years have seen attempts on the part of many colleges and universities to offer programs online. In our survey of programs ("In Their Own Words," Appendix B), Florida State University reports having "the only CSWE accredited, fully Web based, advanced-standing MSW program in the nation." There are also a good number, however, that are beginning to offer a limited number of electives online. All programs that participated in this edition's "In Their Own Words" survey were asked whether they have online offerings.

Helpful Hints

Do...

- ask if the part-time program will require any full-time work, such as a day field placement.

- ask if all courses in the part-time program are available in the evenings or weekends, or if you will need to take some courses during business hours.

- ask if library and other support services are available evenings and weekends.

- ask if admissions requirements are more selective for advanced standing programs than for conventional programs.

- consider joint-degree programs if your plans include a second degree. They can be time-savers.

- explore carefully the training, background, and experiences of the faculty.

(continued on next page)

(continued from previous page)

- investigate the school's faculty-student ratio.

- ask what percentage of the faculty live near the campus. The answer will be a good measure of the quality of the neighborhood's safety and general environment.

- inquire about the racial and ethnic diversity of the faculty.

- find out how available faculty are for informal exchange with students.

- ask who actually teaches the classes. Are they taught by faculty members or graduate assistants?

Don't...

- assume the faculty in the part-time program are the same as that of the full-time program.

- if given the option, assume that doing a field placement at your full-time place of employment is the best option.

- assume going part-time will result in less graduate expense.

- assume advanced standing programs, because they save time, should be your first choice.

- assume that if you apply for advanced standing and are rejected that you will automatically be considered for the conventional program.

- apply for a specialty program simply because it may offer additional aid.

- assume you will have access to well-known faculty. They may not be teaching or may be on sabbatical.

Chapter 6

Support Services for Students and Graduates

An important area that is often overlooked by students while exploring schools is that of support facilities and services. Good support facilities and services can make your time in graduate school more enjoyable and fruitful. Some support services, such as career placement, can make a big difference to your success when you graduate and throughout your career. Poor support facilities and services, on the other hand, can have a very negative impact on your graduate life and career.

Visiting The School

I strongly advise against making a final decision about a school without a site visit. I've visited a number of nationally ranked schools that have extremely poor physical facilities lacking, in some instances, basics such as adequate heating and cooling capabilities. Don't underestimate the impact of discomfort on your ability to concentrate on school work.

With proper notice, most schools' admissions offices can make arrangements for you to sit in on classes and meet with students and faculty during your visit. Ask to meet with students from similar backgrounds and circumstances as you. If you are married and will have small or school-age children, for instance, speaking with a current student about child care, schools, and other similar issues will be helpful. If you are from a small community and the school is in a large city, speaking with a student from a similar background about adjustment and safety issues will be beneficial.

Think of your visit as a test drive of the school. You certainly wouldn't buy an automobile without a test drive. The monetary and time investment in your graduate education is certainly much greater, and its impact on your future longer lasting, than any car you will ever purchase.

Are the classrooms and seating comfortable? Are they adequately heated or cooled? Is the school accessible to people with disabilities? Even if you do not have a disability, it is important to know. You may suffer an injury while a student that places you in a wheelchair during a period of time (it happens!). Even if the chances of your personally having even a temporary disability are remote, the fact that a school has, or doesn't have, provisions for the disabled says something about a school. It speaks to its commitment to various populations and much more.

Safety

Another important issue is that of safety. What provisions are made for the safety of students? Depending on the schools you are considering, their locations, and how familiar you are with the neighborhoods and cities, safety may or may not be a concern. If you are considering schools in major cities that you are unfamiliar with, talk to current students at the schools.

Have any students been victims of crimes on campus? Some university police departments issue weekly or monthly crime alerts detailing the locations and nature of recent incidents on campus. The Jeanne Clery Disclosure of Campus Security Policy and Campus Crime Statistics Act requires colleges and universities in the United States that receive federal financial aid to disclose information about crime on and near their campuses. You can find a searchable database of reported crime statistics online at: *http:// www.securityoncampus.org/schools/cleryact/*

What provisions does the university take to safeguard its students? Some schools have free van or bus service for students to and from their dormitories and apartments during certain hours of the night. If you are thinking of living off campus and will not have a car, ask about the safety and reliability of public transportation.

Getting your social work education in a large city has some advantages. Large urban areas make excellent laboratories for the student of social welfare. They often have a wide array of cutting edge social service programs that can be excellent practicum sites. You need to weigh those benefits against the risks of higher crime normally associated with large urban areas.

Library Services

Another area to look into is that of library services. Does the school have its own library? If so, how well-stocked is it with books and periodicals? Is there a full-time librarian and other qualified staff available during all operating hours? Do the library's operating hours match those of the building? An open building with a closed library is of limited use. Is there electronic access to library materials?

If the school does not have its own library, how well-stocked is the university's main library with social work matter? What other school or program libraries are available to you? If your area of interest is clinical, a good psychology library on campus will be very useful. If your interests lie in policy, is there a public or health policy library available to you on campus?

Does the library have cooperative arrangements with other universities for sharing materials? If so, how long does it take to actually receive materials from sister libraries? Even better, do the libraries have state-of-the-art computers that allow you to access materials from other libraries online?

Computer Support

Does the school have its own computer center available for student use? Are its hours adequate and accessible to you? What is the technical support at the center? Is it staffed all of the time or only part of the time by qualified personnel who can meet your needs? How current are the computers and related equipment? What mechanisms are in place to keep it current?

If you have your own computer, you may want to investigate the compatibility of the school's computers and your own. Compatibility would allow you the flexibility to transport your data on disk and work on it either at home or at the school.

If you are planning to buy a computer, also ask about compatibility. In addition, inquire if the university has a computer store that offers reduced prices to students. Some, but not all, university computer stores easily beat even the lowest retail computer prices. It still pays off to comparison shop.

It may also be possible to obtain a low-interest student loan for the purchase of your computer. After all, it won't be often in your post-student life that you will obtain such favorable interest rates.

Housing

Some schools have housing on campus, while others do not. On-campus university housing usually consists of graduate dormitories and, in most instances, also graduate apartments. The quality of housing varies a great deal.

Therefore, I strongly recommend asking to view dorms and apartments. Some are new and very well-equipped with appliances, other furniture, and air conditioning. Others are nothing less than Spartan. Depending on the school's location, rents can be quite high. If you are from a relatively small community and the school is in a large urban area such as Chicago, Los Angeles, Boston, or New York City, the costs may astound you.

The same can be said about off-campus housing. School catalogs usually have an estimate of living expenses for single and married students, breaking down the typical costs of room and board, health insurance, books, local commuting expenses, and other miscellaneous expenses.

Bookstores

The cost of textbooks is higher than ever and expected to soar even higher. Whatever steps you can take to minimize textbook expenses will be helpful to your budget. Visit the university bookstore and evaluate its prices. Typically, university bookstores are at the high end of the price spectrum.

Inquire about alternative stores. Some universities have independent cooperative bookstores on or near campus that allow you to buy stock at minimal rates (perhaps $15 to become a member). Once you are a member, you can enjoy anywhere from ten to fifteen percent off the regular prices (which are usually less than university stores). Once you leave school, you can sell your stock back to the store and recover your investment with accrued appreciation.

Another alternative is to shop at online bookstores. General bookstores (Amazon.com, Barnesandnoble.com, and Borders.com, among others) sell virtually every book in print. Others, such as Textbooks.com and ecampus.com, specialize in textbooks and offer used books and buyback options. You can shop and compare prices at these bookstores at any time, day or night. Shopping online will mean that you need to plan for a time lag between the time you place the order and the time you actually receive the books. You may need to inquire of professors well ahead of time about the required texts, so you can have them in time to begin the new term. As mentioned earlier, the amount of required reading in graduate school is voluminous. Having to begin your required readings a week into the term will pose an additional challenge that can be avoided with proper planning.

Some textbooks are now available in electronic formats, as well. You may want to compare these with their print counterparts.

Health Services

Most of the larger universities have comprehensive outpatient and inpatient health services for students. Other universities have arrangements with local healthcare providers. Most schools require students to carry health insurance and waive the requirement to buy the university's coverage for students who show proof of alternative coverage. Still other schools require all students to pay a health fee to cover most types of outpatient services but will waive the requirement to purchase university major medical coverage with proof of alternative coverage. Costs and requirements vary greatly among schools, and it is best to make individual inquiries.

Other Facilities

Miscellaneous other facilities worth evaluating during your campus visit include dining facilities and their prices; recreational facilities, including athletic fields, swimming pools, and whatever other activities interest you; and community offerings such as museums, concert facilities, theaters, and other entertainment. The option of enjoyment can bring a nice balance to the academic challenges of a graduate education.

Advising Services

The availability and accessibility of advising services can play a critical role in your ability to get the most out of your graduate education. By and large, the first third or so of your graduate education will involve few decisions. During that period of time, your classes will be predetermined by requirements of the Council on Social Work Education. Your first field practicum will probably be assigned to you, as discussed in Chapter 4.

It is only after you begin working on your selected area of concentration that you will have choices to make in terms of class selection. Later in your first year, you will probably also have the important task of selecting your advanced practicum.

It is from that point forward that you will need knowledgeable and accessible advice. Will there be advisors within the school with backgrounds in social work to inform your decisions?

One model for advising used by schools is to divide students among faculty. Faculty are then required to serve as advisors to their assigned students. One weakness of this model is that the levels of commitment on the part of faculty to the role of advisor will vary greatly. In addition, unless a conscientious effort is made to match student and faculty interests, a given faculty person, even if invested in assisting his advisees, may not have the needed expertise.

In actual practice, many students in schools that employ that model simply seek advice independently from faculty and administrators they've come to know as sharing interests. If the school allows the flexibility, the system works. If there isn't the flexibility, the system is haphazard at best.

If there are not advisors within the school, will you have to resort to advisors at the university level who may or may not know and understand social work? Advisors at the university level are usually generalists who must advise students in numerous disciplines. Some are very knowledgeable about social work, while others have only superficial knowledge of our profession.

Job Placement Services

In the long term, the school's job placement services may be one of the most important factors to consider. As complicated and time-consuming as it is to do justice to selecting the right program for your studies, it is most important not to neglect this aspect of your search.

Some schools have job placement services of their own, while others rely on the university job placement office to provide services to students, soon-to-be graduates, and alumni.

At one end of the spectrum are those schools (not many, unfortunately) that have a full-time job placement director with a good support staff. Those schools generally provide a comprehensive range of services to social work students seeking part-time and summer employment; students about to graduate and seeking their first post-master's full-time job; and alumni exploring changes, re-entering the job market, or seeking information on licensing and continuing education.

Services afforded students in schools with the in-house comprehensive model of job placement include assistance in locating part-time jobs within the university or elsewhere in research and demonstration projects. While a graduate student, I was fortunate to have a 20-hour-per-week position in a university demonstration project aimed at the reduction of gang violence. In addition to supplementing my extremely tight budget, the experience was very beneficial.

A well-staffed and well-operated job placement office may also have very good files on fellowship opportunities, such as the Presidential Management Internship and paid summer internship opportunities.

This type of job placement office may also provide comprehensive training to students on job search skills, including résumé and cover letter writing, salary negotiation, interviewing skills, and self assessment as they apply specifically to the profession of social work. It may also be involved in aggressively soliciting job listings and on-campus interviews by local, regional, and national employers. It might also hold an annual or semiannual Career and Jobs Day and publish a printed or online jobs bulletin on a regular basis.

At the other end of the spectrum are graduate programs that rely solely on the job placement office at the university level for all their job placement needs. With increasing budgetary constraints across academe, this model may become more and more prevalent. The strength of the model for the university is that centralized services are more cost effective. The primary weakness is that the specialized needs of social workers may fall between the cracks. Nevertheless, some university job placement offices have counselors on staff who are very knowledgeable about social work and do an excellent job on behalf of social work students and alumni.

Some schools fall somewhere between the two ends of the continuum of comprehensive services housed at the school and no services at all housed at the school. They may have some services at the school level, including perhaps individual career counseling, but rely on the university office to provide social work students with generic job search skill training applicable to many disciplines.

The extent to which the school provides job services to alumni should be explored. Most schools are smart enough to realize that it makes financial sense to provide services to alumni, because happy alumni tend to make larger, more frequent gifts to schools. A good job placement office is available fully to alumni free of most charges, with the possible exception of minimal subscription costs to cover the cost of producing and mailing jobs newsletters and similar items.

Continuing Education Program

Determine if the school has a continuing education program. The extent to which a school offers its resources to practicing MSW professionals is a good measure of that school's commitment to improving the quality of social services in its own community and beyond.

As mentioned earlier, your education will be far from over once you attain the Master of Social Work degree. Whether your professional focus is on policy and administration or on direct service, you will need to update your knowledge base frequently. Continuing education offers the opportunity for learning the latest approaches to the professional challenges that you will face. In addition, the opportunity to interact with other professionals by means of a workshop or seminar can be a rewarding experience that can serve to renew your professional outlook. Remember the old adage, "Take care of yourself so you can take care of others."

If you intend to practice clinical social work, the need for continuing education takes an added practical quality. Most states now require Licensed Social Workers (LSW) and Licensed Clinical Social Workers (LCSW) to submit evidence of a specified number of continuing education hours per year at the time of application for license renewal. The number of continuing education hours each state requires varies.

If the schools you are considering have a continuing education program, ask if the courses are approved to be applied toward continuing education licensing requirements in your state. Also, ask if alumni of the school are eligible for a discount when enrolling in the school's continuing education programs. Over the course of your professional career, savings can add up to a great deal.

If the school has a continuing education program, ask if students in the MSW program can enroll in workshops or seminars. Generally, such courses are not counted toward degree requirements, but a few schools are flexible enough to allow students to obtain some form of credit toward the MSW by taking continuing education classes.

Whether or not you obtain credit toward your MSW, continuing education courses can be a valuable addition to your professional growth. For example, a good one-day workshop on grant writing can be a valuable experience for anyone contemplating that sort of work. Does the school provide a discount to current MSW students who choose to enroll in a continuing education class? Some schools offer as much as fifty percent off to their students.

It may seem premature now to be thinking of continuing education courses. After all, you are only at the stage of selecting and applying to MSW programs. Yet, if you make your school selection based on a thorough understanding of what it can and cannot offer you down the road, your post-MSW relationship with your future school can be very fruitful.

Alumni Involvement

Another very effective method for schools to provide job placement services to their students, soon-to-be graduates, and alumni is to enlist the assistance of the school's alumni association. The judicious and selective use of alumni mentoring networks can yield large dividends to the school in terms of cost-free volunteer assistance and for job seeking students and alumni in terms of valuable contacts and job leads.

Another excellent use of alumni is in the provision of individual and group mentoring opportunities for providing real-world visions of career options to students. Ask the schools you are considering about the extent of alumni involvement with students. If you will be relocating upon graduation or at another time, will the school provide you with directories of alumni residing in or near your new city? They can be valuable sources for job leads and general information about the area.

On the other hand, beware of schools that attempt to have alumni provide services that only a full-time staff should provide. Although committed and well-intentioned, alumni are volunteers who have their hands full at their places of employment. They cannot be expected to provide job services and the like without adequate support from paid staff of the school. In our current economic climate, schools may try to trim their budgets by placing unrealistic expectations on their alumni.

Remember also that you will someday be an alumnus/a. If the school shows a tendency to overuse alumni, you may be on the receiving end of that down the road. On the other hand, judicious use of alumni as resources can be very satisfying to the alumni, students, and school.

How Successful Are Job Services?

Ask to see data on the success rates of the school's job placement services. The school should be able to provide you with information on job placement rates of recent graduating classes. Data usually include the length of time of the job search, the average salary obtained, the types of settings where graduates obtained employment, and the locations of the jobs obtained.

If the school does not have data or is vague in its response, ask what methods the school uses in evaluating the efficacy of its job placement efforts. If you still do not receive some level of information, think over your options of schools carefully.

Achievements of Alumni

The job placement data on recent graduating classes should give you a sense of how recent graduates do in the short run. It is also important to get a sense of how the school's graduates achieve in the long run. Can the school provide you with information on typical career paths of graduates in various areas of concentration?

Can the school put you in contact with alumni practicing in the area of social work of your interest? A candid conversation with an alumnus may include questions such as his assessment of how well the program prepared him for the type of work he does. You may also want to find out how graduates of the school are perceived in the field. Are they thought of primarily as clinicians, administrators or policy specialists, or some combination? If he had to make a choice again about a graduate program, would he still attend the same school? Of course, take the answers as coming from someone who is clearly biased on behalf of the school. After all, it is unlikely the school will give you the name and phone number of a dissatisfied alumnus. Nevertheless, the conversation should be helpful to you.

Helpful Hints

Do...

- evaluate library facilities.

- check that state-of-the-art computer facilities are available. They are a most important part of your education because you will need those skills wherever you go in the future.

- look at the quality, proximity, and safety of housing.

- inquire about the availability of alternative bookstores. They can save you a great deal of money when compared with campus bookstores' often exorbitant prices.

- inquire about recreational opportunities in the area ("All work and no play...").

- check the availability of advising and job placement services.

Don't...

- overlook support facilities and services.

- make a final decision about a school without visiting it.

- overlook safety issues.

- think you won't get sick, or possibly suffer an accident, while a student. Check out the cost and quality of healthcare and insurance.

- forget to inquire about alumni achievements and involvement. They can be valuable resources while you are a student, in your job search upon graduation, and beyond.

Part II

*What
Schools Look For
In Applicants*

What Schools Look For In Applicants

The mechanism by which schools of social work review applications varies. For purposes of discussion, the term "Admissions Committee" is used throughout this Handbook to refer to the group of people charged with the responsibility of reviewing applications. In some schools, administrators and faculty rotate serving on the admissions committee for a term of several academic years. As many as one third of the faculty may be on the committee at any point in time. In this model, the committee members may be asked to read applications and rate each applicant according to predetermined standards on a rater's form. A few schools include second-year master's students on the committee as actual readers of applications with rating responsibility at par with faculty members. Sometimes two separate raters review each application independently and the admissions director or another administrator makes the final decision based on the ratings of each applicant relative to the applicant pool. A variation on this model may be that the admissions director makes decisions for applicants who are either clearly not qualified or clearly qualified for admission and sends all other applicants to committee. Another model may be that the admissions director makes all admissions decisions, without the aid of a committee. Whatever model of review a school employs, most employ a dual lens in evaluating applicants.

Most programs of social work attempt to answer two questions regarding each applicant. The first is, "Does the applicant show evidence of academic preparation and the ability to succeed in a graduate program?" Once that question has been answered affirmatively, the school asks, "How has the applicant tested his or her interest in the field of social service, and what potential contributions can the applicant make to the profession?"

Part II will look more closely at these two areas and offer strategies you may employ to enhance your preparation for application to MSW programs. Additional suggestions are presented to help you succeed in those programs and beyond.

Chapter 7

Evidence of Academic Preparation

In general, schools of social work attempt to evaluate the applicant's academic preparation and potential for graduate study in several ways. One way is to look at the applicant's performance as reflected in the undergraduate grade point average (GPA). Beyond that, admissions committees use letters of reference from academic sources to obtain a picture of the candidate that may not emerge from the GPA. Some schools attempt to evaluate potential for graduate work by requiring applicants to submit scores from standardized tests, such as the Graduate Record Examination (GRE) or the Miller Analogies Test (MAT), while other schools make tests optional. A few schools require personal interviews. The large number of applicants makes interviews for every applicant impractical. Most schools, therefore, invite only selected applicants for interviews.

Although not often considered as such by many applicants, the supplementary statement (referred to by various names including, among others, biographical statement or statement of purpose) also serves to gauge academic preparation, because it serves as a sample of the applicant's writing. The supplementary statement's importance cannot be overemphasized, both as a writing sample and as a vehicle to expound on the factors that contributed to an interest in the field, actual experiences, and educational and professional goals. General aspects of the supplementary statement are discussed in Chapter 10 of this book. Questions typically found in statement instructions, and how to best address them, are detailed in Chapter 11.

The Undergraduate Record

Let's look first at the undergraduate record. The degree to which schools are interested in a particular undergraduate major field of study varies. Most seek applicants with a broad and solid liberal arts background. A good way to ascertain a school's position is to ask for figures on the percentages of different undergraduate majors among recently admitted applicants. At one major school, the "big three" undergraduate majors admitted each year are psychology, sociology, and social work. It is not uncommon, however, for over sixty percent of each incoming class to have undergraduate majors in such diverse fields as nursing, criminal justice, communication, and business.

The Undergraduate Major

Having majored in social work in college does not necessarily place an applicant in a position of advantage. It should be noted, however, that undergraduate social work majors may have an advantage in that their undergraduate curriculum includes a field work placement. This aspect will be discussed at greater length in Chapter 9.

The Undergraduate GPA

More crucial than the undergraduate major itself is the applicant's performance, whatever the area of concentration. In addition to evaluating the candidate's overall grade point average (GPA), many schools compute the applicant's post-sophomore GPA. Indeed, many schools place more weight on the post-sophomore GPA than on the overall GPA. It is thought that the last two years of college are a much better indicator of the candidate's academic ability and potential for graduate study.

Performance in the first two years of college is often affected by experimentation with different majors and by a period of adjustment to college. Many a college career has begun with a well-intentioned effort in a major that proves outside of a student's interests and abilities. The result can be mediocre to poor grades. By the same token, living away from home for the first time or readjusting to an academic environment after years in the work-a-day world can also result in less than optimal academic performance.

By the last two years of college, the reasoning goes, the candidate has negotiated the adjustment to college and has settled into a major field of study. In addition, course work in the last two years is more advanced and more comparable to graduate study. Many introductory college courses, although of prime importance in preparing students for later work, are not particularly challenging in the areas of verbal and written expression and critical thinking. Many examinations in introductory survey courses are objective and do not require the ability to synthesize, analyze, and present a coherent written essay response as is often the case in more advanced classes.

Therefore, it is generally presumed that work in the last two years of college requires the development of analytical and communication skills. Those skills are critical in graduate social work education and in professional practice.

This is not to say, however, that the first two years of college are disregarded. The overall GPA is also considered, but usually not to the degree of the post-sophomore GPA. I state this to caution readers who may be in the early part of their college careers and may be tempted to think they can afford to do less than their best now. A good foundation now will increase the chances of good performance later.

A second word of warning: As an admissions officer, I was often asked by genuinely bewildered applicants why they had been denied admission when their GPA in their major was high. More often than not, the answer was that their GPA outside their major was mediocre to poor. Although your performance in your major field of study is important, so is your performance elsewhere. Do not make the mistake of thinking that grades in some courses are "irrelevant" to your graduate school application.

Those readers who are attending, or attended, an undergraduate institution that emphasizes analytic and communication skills throughout its curriculum may take issue with my statement that the first two years of college are not generally thought of as particularly challenging in the areas of verbal expression and critical thinking. Be assured that admissions committees of most schools take into account the quality of the undergraduate institution the applicant attended. Those applicants who challenged themselves by attending undergraduate institutions with particularly rigorous programs generally will not be at a disadvantage if they have a slightly lower GPA than applicants who attended less demanding programs.

On the other hand, applicants will generally not be at a disadvantage regardless of the perceived quality of their undergraduate school. Admissions committees realize that an applicant's choice of undergraduate program is often influenced by financial or personal factors. The need to stay close to one's family as a source of financial support, for example, places geographic limits beyond the applicant's control. The real issue is how well the applicant performed.

Undergraduate Narrative Evaluations

There are a number of undergraduate institutions that have moved away from letter grading systems to narrative evaluations. If the college you attended subscribes to that type of evaluation, you will not have a GPA, because there will be no grades to compute.

Get started on the application process early.

Melissa Hawk
MSW student

The primary step you must take is to be a very early applicant. Inquire of the graduate schools what is the earliest possible date you can submit your application. I recommend this because very few people apply early. Therefore, assuming the school reviews applications on a rolling basis (as most do), there will be few applications to read early in the review cycle. The admissions committee will be able to take its time in reading your narrative evaluations.

If, on the other hand, you make application late in the year or, worse yet, on or near the final deadline, the committee will have many more applications to read. The chances of your application being given the time it requires will be very low.

Undergraduate Electives

I stated earlier that the particular major is not as important as the level of academic performance. Nevertheless, it is important to provide the graduate admissions committee with evidence of some "rhyme and reason" behind your course selection. The major and other course selections should support your proposed field of concentration for graduate study. For example, if you propose to focus on clinical social work, a foundation in undergraduate clinical psychology or clinical social work course sequences is advisable.

On the other hand, if you anticipate a focus on social administration or on broader policy aspects of social welfare in graduate school, your undergraduate record should indicate some preparation in the areas of macroeconomics, political systems, and related subjects. Master's programs seek students who have made a conscientious effort to inform themselves thoroughly before making a choice of graduate study.

Some schools require or strongly recommend a minimum of 60 semester hours in the liberal arts. Some add the stipulation that at least 30 of those hours be in the social and behavioral sciences. A good foundation in the humanities might include courses in English, languages, literature, fine arts, philosophy, and religious studies. Courses in the areas of the social and behavioral sciences might include American government, anthropology, behavioral disabilities, economics, geography, history, legal studies, ethnic studies, child development, and psychology.

Classes in Research and Statistics

Whatever your intended graduate focus, it is important to have preparation in the area of research and statistics. Most graduate schools of social work require, or at a minimum strongly recommend, an undergraduate course in research and statistics.

If you have been out of college for some time and you had courses in research and statistics, check with the graduate schools you are considering to see if (a) they have a requirement for research and statistics courses and (b) if they do, if there is a time limit for having taken the course. Some schools require that the course be taken within the five or seven years preceding matriculation to graduate school. The reasoning is two-fold: unless the person has been involved continuously in research, it is unlikely the concepts have been retained. In addition, the field of research and statistics evolves at such a rapid pace that many concepts become outdated, or at least altered, fairly quickly.

Many undergraduate programs in the social sciences offer a two-course sequence in research and statistics. Social science research courses are preferable to business-oriented courses. The quasi-experimental nature of social science research is much more applicable and relevant to graduate study in social work than the more pure research found in the natural sciences and business. In addition to a level of familiarity with research and statistics, many graduate schools of social work require at least one course in human biology.

A word of comfort is in order at this time. Many potential applicants to graduate programs in social work find the prospect of graduate level research and statistics somewhat intimidating. I count myself among that number, as I think back to my days in graduate school. Be assured that, although demanding and certainly not to be taken for granted, research and statistics classes at the master's level are not intended to make researchers out of students. (That's what doctoral programs are for.)

Rather, their intent is for master's level practitioners to acquire an understanding of research practice and methods, so they may be informed professionals capable of discerning between solid and not-so-solid data they will undoubtedly encounter in their careers.

Helpful Hints

Do...

- assume your grades in *every* undergraduate class are important.

- take steps to make your choice of undergraduate major and other course selections support your proposed field of concentration for graduate study.

- have a good mix of liberal arts, social and behavioral sciences, and humanities courses in your undergraduate record.

Don't...

- assume having an undergraduate major in social work is mandatory.

- assume grades in non-social work courses are irrelevant.

- neglect to take classes in research and statistics while an undergraduate.

Chapter 8

Potential for Graduate Work

Besides convincing admissions committees that you are academically prepared for graduate work, you must show them that you have the potential to succeed in graduate school and in the social work profession. This chapter will address some of the ways admissions committees assess this potential—through academic letters of reference, test scores, and interviews. Also refer to Appendix B, *In Their Own Words*, for comments from the schools themselves in the form of tips for applicants and comments on common applicant mistakes.

Academic Letters of Reference

In this chapter, I will comment only on academic references and save remarks on professional references for the chapter on exposure to the profession of social work. A good rule of thumb on the types of references is to have half the letters submitted from academic sources and the other half from professional sources. This recommendation is in keeping with the general rule that committees on admission are looking at your application through the dual lenses of academic preparation/potential and exposure and suitability for the profession of social work.

Number of Letters

All graduate schools of social work require applicants for admission to submit letters of reference. The number of letters required varies by school, ranging from three to six. Some give applicants some latitude in the number of letters. For example, a school might request a minimum of four and a maximum of six letters of reference.

It is very important that you keep track of the specific requirements of the various schools to which you make application. An "MSW Application Tracking Sheet" is provided in Appendix D of this book to assist you. One school I am familiar with disqualifies a number of applicants every year because of incomplete applications. It is the only school in its region to request a minimum of four letters of reference, whereas all the other area schools require only three letters. Invariably, a number of applicants fail to send in a fourth letter and find themselves with incomplete applications. It may seem too obvious a point to mention, yet it is worth recommending you keep careful track of the timely submission of all the required materials to each school.

> Keep track of what is required in the application process and the application timetable. It's easy for time to get away from you.
> *Deborah Kesling*
> *MSW student*

If a school gives you an option as to the number of letters to submit (i.e., a minimum of four letters and a maximum of six), don't assume you will be at a disadvantage if you submit fewer letters than the maximum allowed. If the school needed or wanted the maximum number, it would have said so; take it at its word. In general, it is better to be very judicious about the types of references and their sources. I've seen applicants who would have been much better off with one less reference that offered vague or unkind comments.

Sources of the Letters

Academic references are more relevant if they come from professors in social work classes or related fields, such as psychology or sociology. Letters from professors who taught you research and statistics are highly recommended. In addition, letters from professors who have a good knowledge of your analytical and writing abilities are useful.

Without disputing the value of other classes to a comprehensive education, letters from professors of art, theater, and other fields that are less related to social work are not your best choices, unless you majored in one of those fields. Given that most MSW faculty who comprise admissions committees may not be familiar with those fields, you may have to do some educating of admissions committees in your biographical statement about the academic demands of your undergraduate major.

Request letters from professors who have a good grasp of your academic abilities through multiple classes. It is not a good idea to request letters from professors that you only had for one class, perhaps an introductory class, several semesters ago. The professor may not remember much about you but may be too embarrassed to admit it. The result will be a reference that is vague, lacking in enthusiasm, and fails to provide any meaningful insight to the admissions committee.

I have been asked many times if references from alumni of the graduate school to which you are applying are preferable to non-alumni. The answer is they may or may not be. On the surface, it would seem that alumni are a good source, because they can comment from firsthand knowledge of the school on their perception of your suitability for the program, as well as your potential for success in the program. On the other hand, how their comments are received by the school will depend on how the school views the particular alumnus/a. His or her opinions may be highly valued or they may not hold much meaning. Unfortunately, in most instances you will not be in a position to know the last factor. My recommendation is not to let whether or not a person is an alumna be the primary reason for selecting her as a reference.

Timing Your Request

It is very important, and simple common courtesy, to allow your references plenty of time to write the letters. Composing a good reference requires time to carefully consider your strengths and potential. Many applicants do not allow enough time—and place themselves, and their sources, in the uncomfortable position of last-minute reminders by phone and other means. The results are letters that are never what they could have been.

Take into account the source's schedule and other responsibilities. For example, asking a professor to produce a letter of reference in one week's time during midterms or finals is highly unreasonable. Asking him to take time from holidays is also not a good idea. In general, allow a good four weeks or more during periods that are not unusually hectic.

Under the right circumstances, most professors consider it a pleasure and a privilege to write letters of reference. After all, they were in your shoes at some point in the past. Despite your best efforts at asking at the right time and allowing plenty of time, there will be sources who do not respond promptly. In those circumstances, delicacy and tact are your best allies.

Keeping Track of Letters

In an effort to cut back on administrative expenses, many graduate schools of social work are moving toward an "applicant-managed" application. What that means is that the applicant collects all the application materials and submits them together to the school. If this is the case, your reference sources will be giving you their completed references. This is usually done in a sealed envelope, sometimes supplied by the school in the application packet, that is signed across the seal by the author of the reference.

It is important to make it very clear to your reference sources what they are to do with the completed reference. Given that the applicant-managed model of application is fairly recent, many of the professors in the field today may not be familiar with it. Therefore, they may believe that they need to mail their completed references directly to the school.

If they do that, it may cause some confusion for the school and more work for you. If it does happen, contact the school immediately to explain the situation and verify that the letter was received and that it will be held until you send in the rest of your application. Write down the name of the person you speak with, and when you submit your application, include a letter referencing the conversation and the name of the person with whom you spoke.

One possible way to avoid confusion is to give your sources stamped self-addressed envelopes they may use to return the reference to you. If the schools you are applying to require the sources to send the letters directly to the school, it is also a good idea for you to provide a stamped, addressed envelope.

If You Can't Locate Professors

If it has been several years since you graduated from college, it may be difficult to impossible for you to locate your former professors. If you do find them—depending on how much time has elapsed—they may not remember much about you. Do your best to locate at least one of your professors. When you do, tactfully remind her of your experiences in her class. She may be flattered that you remember her and, consequently, be hesitant to mention she does not remember you. She will appreciate any hints you offer. If you are compulsive enough to have kept your college papers, offering to send a copy of a paper you wrote for one of her classes would be most useful.

Don't despair if you are unable to contact any former professors because it has been a long time since you left college. Admissions committees understand your predicament. I suggest a brief explanatory footnote in the place on the application where you list your reference sources. Briefly bring to the committee's attention that you were unable to locate former professors because of the passage of time. If it has only been two or three years or less since you finished college, however, the committee may not be as understanding.

If you are unable to provide academic references, you can still provide what I call "pseudo-academic" references. Current or former employers in settings that require academic skills will serve this purpose. Positions that require the ability to analyze complex problems, formulate solutions, and use exceptional verbal and written communication skills are good options.

Letters From Relatives

I'll make one final note on letters of reference. Letters from relatives should not be used. Period. Although not all schools make it explicit that letters from relatives are not allowed, I highly advise against their use. Even if the relative is in a professional position to comment knowledgeably on the applicant's academic and professional abilities, the fact that the opinions are being rendered by a relative casts a shadow of doubt.

I have seen marvelous letters of reference from relatives that are simply dismissed by the committee. In addition, the committee may wonder if the person is of such limited ability and academic or professional exposure that he cannot locate other people who can offer references.

Standardized Test Scores

Some graduate schools of social work require applicants to submit scores from the Graduate Record Examination (GRE) or the Miller Analogies Test (MAT). Other schools give applicants the option of submitting scores. Still other schools do not require scores for admission, but either require them or strongly recommend them for scholarship applicants. Contact the schools you are interested in to learn their specific requirements.

In those cases in which applicants have a choice about GRE or MAT scores, applicants who are confident that their undergraduate record reflects their abilities often opt not to submit scores. On the other hand, applicants whose undergraduate records were affected by personal circumstances often opt to submit scores as a way to strengthen their applications. The wrong decision can hurt any applicant regardless of his GPA. If your GPA is high, do not submit scores unless they are also high. If your GPA is low but so are your GRE or MAT scores, don't submit scores; there is no need to add to the evidence against you.

If you find you need to submit standardized test scores, do not take the task lightly. I strongly recommend you explore preparatory courses or, at the very least, invest in a self-guided preparatory manual. I feel strongly about this subject, because I have seen well-qualified candidates "shoot themselves in the foot" with poor scores. Poor scores on the GRE or MAT can cast doubt on even the best of college grades. Allow yourself plenty of rest the night before the exam and approach it calmly and methodically.

When to Request Scores

Do not request that your scores be sent to any graduate school before you know how well you scored. It will cost more to order reports later, but it will be well worth the expense. By so doing, you will have the opportunity to make informed decisions on whether or not to submit scores to those schools that make scores optional. If your GPA is high, don't risk hurting your chances of admission with low GRE or MAT scores if you can help it. I have, on occasion, seen instances when applicants with very high GPAs were denied admission because they made the tactical error of submitting low scores to schools where scores were optional.

To make a better decision on whether or not to submit GRE or MAT scores, inquire what the range, mean, median, and mode were for the most recent admissions cycle at the schools that interest you. For the more competitive, nationally-ranked schools, if your GRE scores average below 650 on the test sections and your GPA is in the vicinity of 3.2 or above on a 4.0 scale, it is probably best not to submit scores if you have the option.

Timing of the Test

When you take the test is also important. I suggest taking it late in your third year of college or early in your fourth year. By so doing, you have time to make the critical decisions of whether or not to use the scores or attempt to retake the test.

Taking the test early will also insure you meet the schools' application deadlines. Many an otherwise qualified applicant has been disqualified because she took the test late and scores did not reach graduate schools by their deadlines.

Interviews

The large number of applicants has made it impractical at most schools to make a personal interview a required part of the admissions process. Some schools reserve the right to invite selected applicants for interviews. Generally, the applicants invited to interview are few and usually are invited because they may present a unique profile. For example, it may be someone who appears an excellent candidate in all aspects but one. Grades might be excellent but the quality of experiences questionable, or the applicant might be a "career-changer" who the admissions committee wants to meet to get a better sense of the reasons for the change. Check with the schools of your choice on their interview policies.

Informal Interviews

Having said that, let me add that in actuality, interviews take place regularly. Even though a school may not grant formal interviews, applicants who make a visit to campus and meet with school officials can use the opportunity as a sort of interview. During my time in admissions, I often met with prospective applicants I found particularly impressive. In such instances, I would write a memorandum to the admissions committee highlighting my impressions. Please note that I would not write a memorandum for every prospect that visited—only for those who projected qualities that I felt were not reflected in the written application materials.

If you will be visiting a school, I suggest preparing thoroughly and formulating well thought-out questions. The questions for your school visit in Appendix E provide a starting point. In addition, review the interests and publications of the faculty (generally found in the school's catalog) and identify those with interests similar to your own. Ask if it would be possible to meet with the faculty members you identify. If it is possible to meet with faculty, read some of their work and be prepared to discuss it intelligently. Be aware that the faculty member(s) may not be available. Normally, meetings with specific faculty members are reserved for applicants to doctoral programs. If you do get the opportunity, take full advantage of it at the levels of (a) learning more about the school and (b) possibly increasing your chances of admission.

One particular case comes to mind that illustrates the benefits of this strategy. An applicant visited the school and met with a faculty member. The faculty person was so impressed with the applicant's grasp of the field and his future goals that the faculty person wrote a memorandum to the admissions committee on the applicant's behalf. The applicant was offered admission, despite a marginal GPA. It is unlikely he would have been admitted without the added factor of the memorandum from the faculty member. The applicant went on to excel in the program and became a respected student leader among his peers.

Should you be offered and accept admission, there is another possible advantage of having met with a faculty member. Often, particularly at schools with very prolific researchers, the faculty member you meet with may be working on a research project that employs students. You will have a distinct advantage over other prospective student employees. Often, student positions are never openly listed, because researchers fill them from students they know. Aside from providing you with a nice source of income while you are a student, a job in research will round out your résumé a good deal better than a job, say, stacking books in the library.

Helpful Hints

Do...

- strive for a balance in reference letters by having half of the letters submitted be from academic sources and the other half from professional sources.

- keep careful track of the timely submission of all the required materials, including letters of reference, to each school.

- be very judicious about the types of references and their sources.

- if they are needed, take standardized tests early enough to review scores before deciding whether or not to submit them to schools.

- treat any contact with any school representative as an interview. Make no mistake about it, it is.

Don't...

- ask for references at the last minute. Be respectful of the person you are asking.

- be too concerned if, as someone who attended college many years ago, you cannot locate professors to seek references.

- submit letters of reference from relatives.

- submit standardized test scores until you know what they are.

Chapter 9

Exposure to the Profession

The term "graduate school" is used throughout this book, and is generally widely used, in reference to schools of social work. In reality, schools of social work are not "graduate schools" in the traditional academic sense. Instead, they belong more in the classification of professional schools. Much as schools of business train for professional practice in the world of business, schools of law train for the professional practice of law, and schools of medicine train for the professional practice of medicine, schools of social work provide training for the professional practice of social work. Of necessity, the training is not purely academic. Schools of social work are not preparing individuals for purely academic endeavors. They are training professionals for delicate practice with living human beings, and these professionals bring backgrounds and needs as varied as the clients themselves.

Therefore, it is important, and indeed inescapable, that the admissions process include an evaluation of factors much broader than simply academic merits. The demonstrated ability to perform academically is crucial but it is only a beginning point. The ability to integrate the theoretical knowledge base into compassionate and effective practice is the measure of the social work professional. Beyond scholarly ability, the applicant must show evidence of a sensitivity to human needs and the ability to interact with diverse groups of people across a span of system levels.

Without this added dimension, the highly academically qualified applicant falls short. The weight given to experiential factors is normally the same as that given to academic factors in admission decisions at most MSW programs. When asked in a 1999 survey by *The New Social Worker* magazine what advice they would give potential applicants, one of the most frequent responses of recent graduates and current students at MSW programs was to obtain plenty of field experience. They cited that experience is helpful at multiple levels—(1) schools look for evidence of firsthand knowledge of the field, (2) the experience helps students integrate class material, and (3) experiences help clarify if social work is indeed the profession they prefer.

> Make sure you get experience in the field before you apply for graduate school. It will help you get accepted and will help you realize if social work is the appropriate field for you.
>
> Lisa Lusczynski
> MSW student

The settings where aspiring MSW applicants can gain experience are as varied as the options in the field of social work itself. Before discussing the settings themselves, it will be useful to identify the general principles valuable for social work practice that you should seek to be exposed to before applying to schools of social work. I hope that an understanding of the principles will allow you to identify settings I may not mention. Nevertheless, later in this chapter I will offer specifics on potential settings, how each may relate to your particular goals, and suggestions for locating them.

The Basic Principles of Social Work

Historically, the profession of social work has concerned itself with serving those who would not otherwise be served. In its infancy over 100 years ago, social work was concerned with universal social security, child labor, and similar issues affecting the disenfranchised and powerless. To be sure, the passage of time has brought increased sophistication in terms of the theoretical foundations and methods utilized, but the basic mission remains the same: to help individuals improve their social functioning and status.

In its very name, the profession recognizes the need to view the individual in his social context. Social workers seek to understand the interplay of various systemic factors affecting individuals.

For example, the *Statement of Purpose* of the School of Social Service Administration of the University of Chicago states, in part, "Individual distress occurs in a social context involving the interaction of biological, psychological, familial, economic, and cultural factors."

Issues Addressed by Social Work

The issues addressed by the many types of social work being practiced today are as broad and varied as our society. Many challenges faced by social workers lie in the areas of child welfare, housing and homelessness, poverty, violence, psychiatric disorders, developmental disabilities, physical disabilities, substance abuse, sexuality, legal, and a host of other issues.

Keep in mind that the real world is never as neatly divided as categories in any book would lead you to believe. In the real world, categories often overlap and distinctions are easily blurred. So is the case in the real world of professional social work practice. For the purpose of our discussion, I will focus on the major areas of child welfare services, housing and homelessness, and psychiatric and substance abuse treatment. The issues of poverty, violence, and legal system involvement cut across all categories to one extent or another.

Child Welfare

The category of child welfare services, for instance, can encompass a wide variety of job functions and settings. As with all categories, the range of functions can be classified virtually anywhere along the continuum from purely direct service to purely administrative or policy oriented. Whatever their specific function, social workers in the field of social welfare are primarily concerned with the well-being of children and adolescents.

Clinical positions in child welfare include hospital social workers focusing on maternal and child health, case managers for women and children infected and affected by the HIV virus, therapists for wards of the state with emotional and behavior problems, therapists in Employee Assistance Programs specializing in child and family issues, family crisis intervention counselors, school social workers, counselors in family preservation programs, caseworkers in state departments for family and children services, therapists for child physical and sexual abuse offenders, child abuse investigators, protective services workers, foster home developers, and domestic violence counselors.

Settings for child welfare clinical practice include community mental health centers; domestic violence shelters; hospitals/clinics; private clinical practice; state departments of child and family services; private companies and corporations; Head Start programs; psychiatric centers; nonprofit organizations; county, state, and other governmental agencies; residential treatment centers; churches; community crisis centers; court systems; public schools; foster care agencies; and public health programs.

Administrative and policy positions and settings in child welfare include administrators of community mental health centers; strategic planners on child welfare services at the local, state, or federal levels of government; policy analysts for grassroots agencies reviewing systemic community child welfare problems and gathering data for lobbying efforts; directors of child welfare initiatives at foundations allocating funds to create and sustain comprehensive, integrated, community-based service systems for children, youth, and their families; grant and proposal writers consulting with community organizations; community education coordinators in community programs providing programs on sexual abuse prevention, truancy prevention, gang prevention, and similar topics; trainers and facilitators for public child welfare workers; investigators/researchers in college or university-based centers for children studies; coordinators of adoption services in public or private agencies; and administrators of organizations for purposes of lobbying on children's issues.

Housing and Homelessness

Clinical positions and settings in the area of housing and homelessness include workers at homeless shelters, workers at shelters for victims of domestic violence, examiners and licensers of emergency and long-term foster homes, workers at senior housing centers, and social workers at extended care facilities.

Administrative and policy positions and settings in the field of housing and homelessness include administrators for housing and economic development councils, foundation grant officers specializing in housing initiatives, community reinvestment specialists at financial institutions, administrators at shelters for the homeless, and administrators at shelters for victims of domestic violence.

Psychiatric and Substance Abuse Treatment

For well over the past thirty years, the vast majority of mental health services in the United States have been delivered by social workers. Only in the recent past have states come to recognize social workers as independent practitioners through legislation that makes provisions for licensure, certification, or registration of social workers. By 1993, all states and the District of Columbia had laws in those regards.

Social workers practice as clinical therapists, family therapists, clinical supervisors, mental health workers and therapists, substance abuse counselors, psychiatric social workers, and in many other related positions. The settings include community mental health centers, hospitals and clinics, private clinical practice, child and family service agencies, day treatment programs, psychiatric centers, domestic violence centers, councils on alcoholism, and many other clinical settings. By the same token, social workers can be found in administrative and policy-making positions in all clinical settings.

Cross-Over Issues

Because of the fundamental nature of the social work profession and the population it is pledged to serve, most social workers are in some way dealing with issues of poverty, violence, and the legal system. For example, clinical social workers providing therapeutic services in community mental health centers have many clients with multiple concerns, including poverty, violence, and substance abuse across system levels. Some clinical positions more directly related to issues of poverty include employment services coordinators at private and public agencies, vocational counselors, human rights spokespersons, and community organizers in poverty-stricken communities.

Some administrative and policy positions and settings more closely related to issues of poverty include administrators of public housing projects, administrators of economic development entities in the community or at foundations, and planners for city departments of planning and development. Workers at correctional institutions also deal more directly with issues of violence as do workers in courts, at shelters for victims of domestic violence, in state agencies for the prevention of child and adult abuse, community crisis intervention centers, and hospitals.

Locating a Site for Gaining Exposure to Social Service

It is hoped the above overview of areas of practice and settings of social workers will provide you with a starting point. Carefully evaluate where your interests may best be served. If you are more attracted to direct work with individuals, groups, and families, seek a clinical site. If, on the other hand, you find the broader aspects of program planning, fund raising, and program evaluation intriguing, seek an administrative or policy setting.

It is important that you recognize that if your level of experience is minimal, the level of autonomy and direct involvement you will be allowed will be equally minimal, regardless of the setting. Nevertheless, firsthand exposure, even if only at the level of observer, will be beneficial to your growth and in demonstrating to social work schools your commitment to the field.

Once you've tentatively identified your potential settings of interest, there are some excellent sources for beginning the search. Your local United Way office will probably have information on agencies that seek volunteers. In fact, most chapters of the United Way publish a listing of volunteer opportunities. They are in an excellent position to know, because many community agencies receive United Way funding. You can call the United Way of America at 703-836-7112 or go to *http://national.unitedway.org* to get the telephone number of your state or local United Way chapter.

Another good source is your college or university's career and placement office. Agencies and organizations that seek volunteers realize that college students make excellent volunteers because of their educational levels and sincere enthusiasm. Agencies are wise to cultivate good relations with their community's educational institutions.

If your college or university has a community relations office, so much the better. Many educational institutions have come to recognize how important it is to be thought of as a good neighbor and devote considerable resources to that goal. A good community relations office will have listings of volunteer opportunities in the community and may even offer stipends to students who participate in selected projects.

> Job shadow a number of social workers in different positions to get a feel for the range of positions available later. It helps to have an idea of what you're preparing for.
> *Elizabeth E. Seebach, Ph.D.*
> *Clinical Psychology Professor*
> *Univ. of WI–LaCrosse*

If you're in the United States, another good source is your state chapter of the National Association of Social Workers (NASW). NASW has chapters in all fifty states, as well as New York City; Metro Washington, DC; Puerto Rico; the Virgin Islands; and an International chapter. You may reach the national office of NASW toll-free at 1-800-638-8799 to learn how to contact your state or local NASW chapter.

A word about NASW is appropriate here. NASW is the national organization for social workers in the United States. It has been instrumental in achieving tremendous progress in the provision of social services through legislation at the national, state, and local levels. NASW was a driving force in achieving certification or licensure of social workers in every state.

I highly recommend that you explore the benefits of NASW membership. Rates are extremely reasonable for students. As of February 2005, regular membership dues are $178/year; the student rate is $45/year. Those who join NASW as students also qualify for a reduced transitional rate for a period of time after graduation. I know of no better way to stay abreast of developments in the field of social work than through membership in NASW. It should be noted, however, that you must be a current student in a Council on Social Work Education accredited social work degree program or a program eligible for candidacy to be eligible for student membership in NASW. Other categories of membership require an accredited degree, other than associate membership, which requires that you be employed in a social work capacity and have at least a bachelor's degree in a field other than social work. I should mention that I have been an active member of NASW for many years, and my recommendation of NASW is purely voluntary.

If you're in Canada, an excellent source is the Canadian Association of Social Workers (CASW). To become a member, you must join the provincial/territorial organization of the province or territory where you reside or plan to live. A listing of all organizations may be found at the CASW Web site (http://www.casw-acts.ca/). The CASW Web site is the authoritative source of information on the profession of social work in Canada.

Selecting the Site

Once you've identified several possible sites that accept volunteers, it will be time to carefully assess which will be most beneficial for you. One factor to consider is the reputation of the agency or institution. If it is a national organization, it will be known to many schools of social work to which you make application for admission. If it is a local or regional organization, it may only be known to schools within your region.

This is not to say that small local agencies will not be excellent settings. One way to overcome the factor of the agency not being known to schools when you apply is to ask the person from the agency who writes you a reference to include a brief statement of the agency's mission and services.

You may also want to inquire of the local Better Business Bureau (BBB) about any consumer complaints the Bureau has received about the agency. Unfortunately, there are some agencies that undergo periods of extreme unethical practices under a bad administration. I know of at least one agency that had a former top level officer placed in a witness protection program in exchange for testifying to corrupt practices. The same agency has recovered nicely over the years and currently has an excellent reputation, thanks to new leadership. Having served as a volunteer or intern in an agency during questionable times may not be good for you.

It does not hurt to look ahead. Your graduation from an MSW program may seem far away at this time, but it will be here before you know it. Therefore, consider whether the agency is large enough to be an employment possibility for you in the future. I know of several colleagues who have risen through the ranks at agencies where they once volunteered as college students.

What Will You Be Doing?

Of more immediate concern, of course, is the question of what your duties will be as a volunteer. Be candid with the agency about your future educational plans in social work. Whereas you should be realistic about the things you are capable of doing at this time, you should also expect to be in a position to at least be exposed to learning experiences.

A position that keeps you filing membership records in a back room, for instance, will do little for your professional growth. On the other hand, opportunities to assist staff in community education programs on issues such as parenting or child abuse prevention, even if initially only in arranging the classroom, registering participants, and observing the program, will be very beneficial.

Seek Learning Opportunities

Most agencies provide continuing education for their staff as part of their licensing and funding source requirements. Some agencies provide workshops either in-house or send their employees to outside seminars and conferences. Ask if as a volunteer or intern you will be afforded the same opportunities. They can greatly contribute to your knowledge of the field and your professional growth. In addition, being able to document in your MSW applications for admission that you have participated in social work-related continuing education will be a big plus.

Who Will Supervise You?

Another very important aspect to consider is the background of the person you will be working for. Although not a must, it would be very helpful to work for a person with a background in social work or in a related field, preferably at the master's level. Working with a social worker will familiarize you with the perspective that guides our profession.

Down the road, a letter of reference from the supervisor of your volunteer experience as you apply to master's programs will serve you well. Letters from social work professionals have added credibility, because they can comment on the person's suitability for a graduate social work education and the profession from the perspective of one who has experienced it.

Your Conduct On Site

Once you select a volunteer site and are on the job, be sure to approach all work with the agency with the same high level of dedication and diligence as if it were a full-time paid position. The profession of social work is small, and one's reputation is one's calling card. Most social workers in a given region, and in some cases across regions or even nationally, come to meet each other at seminars, workshops, conferences, or other events. Many serve on boards of directors of several agencies or even at some graduate programs of social work. Begin cultivating a sound reputation now, and it will serve you well later.

Helpful Hints

Do...

- keep in mind that weight given to experiential factors is normally the same as that given to academic factors in admission decisions at most MSW programs.

- seek experiences in social work settings that will contribute to your development.

- attempt in your volunteer experiences to work for people with a background in social work or in a related field, preferably at the master's level.

Don't...

- fail to approach all volunteer work with the same high level of dedication and diligence as if it were a full-time paid position.

- forget to request a letter of reference from your supervisor and other professionals (especially social workers) familiar with your work in volunteer settings.

Chapter 10

The Biographical Statement: An Overview

All graduate schools of social work in Canada and the United States request that applicants submit a biographical statement. The essay may also be referred to as a supplementary statement, personal statement, admissions essay, and by other similar titles. Whatever each institution chooses to call it, its purpose is the same. It is intended as a vehicle for the admissions committee to learn more about the applicant than mere grades on a transcript, standardized test scores, or letters of reference can convey. It is your opportunity to give the school a broader perspective of your background, experiences, and educational as well as professional goals. This chapter is intended to give you an overview of the biographical statement, while Chapter 11 provides more specifics on the typical questions found on instructions for biographical statements and how to formulate your responses.

How To Approach Writing Your Statement

I recommend that you perform a thorough self-assessment before writing your statement. Make a list of all jobs, volunteer positions, and internships you have ever held. In short, take an inventory of any experiences that somehow contributed to your interest in social work. Review Chapter 9 of this *Handbook,* which discusses social work settings. Don't neglect to also list classes that you may have taken that contributed to the development of your interests. For some people, even an individual field trip taken as part of a class may have been significant. In Appendix F, you will find a worksheet that will help you organize your efforts in writing the biographical statement.

Chances are you've had some experiences in settings that you may not have previously considered related to social work. I've often met with students who tell me of jobs in research, legal offices, and other settings and then proceed to state they have no social work experience. They are surprised when I mention that certain types of research are very beneficial to aspiring social workers.

Even if the research was not directly related to social welfare issues, the exposure to the act of research is very useful. The aim of social research courses in MSW programs is to make students aware of the essentials of good research and the benefits of good research to an informed professional practice. Applicants seem equally surprised that an experience in a legal aid agency can serve as valuable exposure to clients who are at a crisis point in their lives and very much in need of assistance coping with many social systems around them.

Once you've made as comprehensive a list as possible, identify the skills you developed as a result of each particular experience. Chapter 9 discusses social work skills and may help you in this process. Keep in mind that the most important aspect in the experience is not necessarily the setting itself.

The most important elements are the skills you develop that are transferable to other settings. For example, the skills developed in interviewing clients are transferable to many other settings. People who seek services at a legal aid agency typically are experiencing financial difficulties, either of a temporary or chronic nature. They are also at a point in their lives when they are experiencing a life event of considerable stress, such as a divorce, eviction, or other event. They require an interviewer who can ease their anxiety and be empathic enough to allow them to express their needs at their own pace. Those skills are transferable to virtually any crisis setting.

A review of your experiences will be helpful not only in making an inventory of the skills you may have begun to develop, but also in identifying the areas of social work where you may want to go in the future. That awareness can help you immensely in determining which of the programs you are considering can best train you to achieve your goals.

By this point, you should be in an excellent position to make a strong case in your statement about why your experiences and goals are a good fit with the particular school's programs. For example, if your experiences have been in a pediatric hospital setting, you have probably begun to develop skills in the areas of assessing the impact of the onset of childhood illness on the family system. A careful evaluation of those skills can serve as a good foundation for assessing a school's maternal and child health program. In turn, the process can move to making a solid case for the suitability of the program to your educational and professional objectives.

It is difficult to overstate the importance of presenting a thoughtful and deliberate case of your reasons for wanting to be a social worker and for wanting to attend the particular program in your biographical statement. All other aspects of two applicants competing for a place in the class being equal, the person with the better biographical statement will win out. In the schools with more competitive admissions, most applicants have excellent undergraduate records and stellar references. What often separates them is the biographical statement. It often weighs as much or more than the undergraduate record and the references combined.

How Schools View Your Statement

Admissions committees view the biographical statement at a number of levels. At one level, the statement offers committees an understanding of how the applicant developed his interests in social work, and how he has tested his interests through employment, internships, and volunteer or personal experiences. By so doing, the statement gives the committee a sense of the degree to which the applicant's decision to pursue a career in social service is grounded in a solid and realistic view of the profession. Statements that do not accomplish this are generally of the "I've-always-been-a-people-person-and-I-want-to-work-with-people" type.

The statement also gives the committee a good understanding of the reasons behind the applicant's desire to pursue training for practice in a particular aspect of the profession. This is most important because admissions committees attempt to assess not only the applicant's suitability for the program, but also the program's suitability for meeting the person's educational and professional objectives.

At another level, the schools view the biographical statement as a sample of the applicant's writing. The ability to express oneself clearly and succinctly in written form is essential to success in a graduate program of social work. Most of the work graduate students of social work do consists of papers and essays and only a few objective tests. Furthermore, schools of social work believe that good writers are good thinkers. The ability to analyze problems and formulate sound and realistic solutions is central to being a social work student and professional.

At still another level, admissions committees view the biographical statement as a measure of how well the applicant follows instructions. You will serve yourself well by carefully following application instructions as they pertain to the biographical statement's format, areas of content, and length. It is not inaccurate to say that every word in every sentence of the instructions on any school's application was the subject of much thought and debate in admissions committee meetings. Committees expect applicants to be equally thorough and thoughtful in following those instructions. An applicant who neglects to do so is projecting an image of a sloppy and careless student graduate schools would rather do without.

The Cardinal Sins of Statement Writing

I strongly advise against using the same statement for the various schools to which you are making application. To be sure, you definitely should apply to more than one school. You should, however, write individual statements that conform to each school's re-

quirements. It is tempting, in our age of computers and word pro-
cessors, to simply alter a few items (such as the name of the school)
and submit the same statement to all schools.

Each school has unique characteristics and programs. Tailor
each school's statement to how your development and goals fit
with each particular school's programmatic focus. Admission committees are quick to spot statements that speak eloquently about
wanting to pursue a particular specialty that is not available in the
school.

The most extreme
case I've seen of the
"mass production" of a
statement was the case
of an applicant who ap-
plied to school "A" and
made a reasonable case
why "A" was the best
school for his goals, only

> If you have a BSW, be clear about
> not simply filling your application
> with the right social work lingo—
> committees will want to see that
> you have a clear understanding of
> how graduate work...is different.
> *Tara Tieso, MSW student*

to state in his closing remarks that he had always had the goal of
attending school "B." He clearly made the mistake of not changing the name of the school uniformly as he printed the different
versions of the same statement.

Another practice to avoid is over-focusing on personal psychological issues and treatment. Please refer to Chapter 11 of this
book for specific recommendations on the judicious inclusion of
information on personal psychological treatment. I recommend
careful thought about mentioning past treatment for two reasons.

The first reason is that the committee may interpret excessive
self-revelation as an indicator that you are seeking to enter the
profession as a means to continue working on your personal issues. Unfortunately, many practicing professionals do a great disservice to their clients by failing to distinguish their own issues
from those of the clients they treat. For the same reason, I discourage letters of reference from personal therapists.

The second reason that I discourage a great deal of self-revelation in the statement is that once your statement is in your file, it remains there through your time at the school and beyond. Most schools allow professors and even field instructors access to student files. A good rule of thumb is: don't write anything in your statement you would not want professors, administrators, and field instructors to know.

A Final General Word About Your Statement

In short, the writing of the biographical statement is not to be taken lightly. If you have an outstanding undergraduate record and vainly (and foolishly!) believe no graduate school can afford to pass you up, think again. I have seen applicants to MSW programs who have multiple graduate degrees in related fields from the nation's finest institutions be denied admission. More often than not, they are denied because they took admission for granted and did a last-minute, careless job in composing their biographical statements. A carelessly written biographical statement is a frequent mistake by applicants, as reported by the schools themselves in Appendix B, *In Their Own Words.*

In *The New Social Worker* magazine's 1999 survey of current MSW students and recent MSW graduates, many responded that the most stressful part of the MSW application process was composing the personal statement. When compared with papers you probably wrote as an undergraduate, the personal statement will appear deceptively simple. After all, most schools request only between three and five typewritten pages. The amount of introspection, exploration of future expectations and goals, and the need to match those to the particular program should not be taken lightly. Give yourself plenty of time to compose your statement thoughtfully and to have it critiqued for content and grammar.

Helpful Hints

Do...

- make a thorough self-assessment before writing your statement. Make a list of all jobs, volunteer positions, and internships you have ever held. In short, take an inventory of any experiences that somehow contributed to your interest in social work.

- identify the skills, and their application to social work, you developed as a result of each particular experience.

- make a strong case in your statement about why your experiences and goals are a good fit with the particular school's programs.

- remember that schools view the biographical statement as a sample of the applicant's writing. The ability to express oneself clearly and succinctly in written form is essential to success in a graduate program of social work.

- keep in mind that admissions committees view the biographical statement as a measure of how well the applicant follows instructions.

- remember that the writing of the biographical statement is not to be taken lightly, regardless of how marvelous your undergraduate record may be.

Don't...

- ignore experiences in settings that you may not have previously considered as social work-related.

(continued on next page)

(continued from previous page)

- underestimate the importance of presenting a thoughtful and deliberate case of your reasons for wanting to be a social worker and for attending the particular program in your biographical statement.

- write a statement that simply says, "I've-always-been-a-people-person-and-I-want-to-work-with-people."

- use identical statements for the various schools to which you are making application.

- over-focus in your statement on personal psychological issues and treatment.

Chapter 11

The Biographical Statement: The "Questions Behind the Questions"

Now that you have a general idea of the purposes of the biographical statement and how to approach it, let's turn our focus to the specifics of this aspect of your application.

Length, Content, and Format

Instructions provided by most, but not all, schools state a range for the length of the statement. In general, the length requested is from two to four typewritten, double-spaced pages. If a school you are considering does not specify length, it is a good idea to stay within the 2-4 page range. Whether a school provides limits or not, the length of the essay is a measure of the applicant's ability to be concise, yet thorough.

Most, but again, not all, schools provide a list of questions for the candidate to answer in the statement. A list of typical questions, and how to approach them, follows later in this chapter. If a school to which you are making application does not specify questions, it would be a good idea to follow the general questions listed in this chapter.

The format (i.e., the organization) is generally not specified in the instructions. The reason is that schools want to give applicants latitude in determining how to present their essays. The applicant's

f you will, a gauge of their writing ability. Most appli-
to write the statement as a narrative listing of their
the questions. Other applicants choose different and
varied approaches. Whichever approach you select, it will be important that you address all of the points requested in the application instructions. It will be equally important to have a suitable introduction and conclusion.

Introducing Your Statement

How you choose to introduce your essay is very important. Some applicants begin the statement rather suddenly with details about their undergraduate concentration and how they came to be involved in social work. Although this approach may be factual and even substantive, it is much more advisable to begin with a well thought-out introduction (i.e., telling the reader what is ahead). This may seem somewhat unnecessary, because the readers on the admissions committee know full well what is ahead. After all, every applicant is given the same instructions. Other applicants choose to begin with a clever introduction, such as a quote or situation vignette from their lives or work experiences. There is a danger in attempting to be too clever. I suggest a more traditional, solid approach. Whichever way you select, a good beginning is crucial at several levels. One is that, in addition to content, the admissions committee looks for evidence of writing ability. At another level, a good beginning that engages the reader's attention is important to help your statement stand out among the many the committee reviews.

For example, you may choose to begin with a general introduction as follows:

Although my undergraduate concentration was in Juvenile Justice, I decided to explore the social work field beginning in my junior year. An internship that was to result in a job offer upon graduation served as a foundation to many later experiences professionally and as a volunteer in civic and other organizations.

By having an introduction that foreshadows what is ahead, you are arousing the interest of the reader to learn how your internship sparked your interest and what happened thereafter.

Typical Statement Questions

All schools provide applicants with some form of instructions for the personal or biographical statement. Most actually list a number of questions that should be addressed. Some, however, do not provide questions and limit the instructions to length of the statement and give the applicant a wide latitude as to what to include in the statement. Although the questions and their specific wording vary from school to school, in general, they fall into several categories. The categories are:

- Describe your social work experiences and why you have selected social work
- Describe your educational goals and expectations
- Describe your short- and long-term professional goals
- Provide evidence of your capacity for graduate work
- Describe why you seek a graduate social work education at this point in your career

Question 1: Describe Your Social Work Experiences and Why You Have Selected Social Work

This portion of your essay should not read like a résumé in narrative form. Given that most applications already have a section on your volunteer, internship, and paid experiences, you do not need to repeat them here.

I felt my essay really had a significant impact on my admission. I would suggest that in students' essays, they focus on specific experiences they've had in a human service field, and what they learned from that.

Amanda Barge
MSW student

The question behind this particular question is really, "Do you know what you're getting into?" That is to say, how well thought out is your decision to seek a graduate education in social work? A good way to respond to the question is to elaborate on why you chose social work versus other similar professions. For example, someone interested in clinical work with individuals, families, and groups could accomplish the goal by either obtaining an MSW or a doctorate in clinical psychology. In answering this question, that particular individual would have to make the case for why she chose social work over psychology. She might say, for instance, that even though both disciplines offer clinical preparation, the social work option is more attractive to her because of its emphasis on the person-in-environment as opposed to the more individualized psychological perspective.

Write about the other graduate school options you considered along with social work and why you selected social work. Your response will give the committee a clear picture of your understanding of social work. Be clear and to the point. Avoid platitudes such as, "I believe, as does the profession of social work, in the inherent worth of every individual." Instead, get down to the basics of why you think a social work education is better suited for your goals than alternative graduate programs.

You should highlight how you came to learn about social work. Were there specific individuals within the profession who gave you exposure to the profession? Were there particular scholastic or work experiences that fueled your desire to enter the profession of social work? Identify the values that were inherent in those experiences and how they match the values you bring to the profession. In other words, the committee wants to determine if your career goal is well-grounded. Many people write that they are "people people," love working with people, and so they want to be social workers. Anyone can make that statement, but not anyone can fully answer the question posed.

Highlighting Your Experiences

It is most helpful to weave into your narrative specifics about your role within each organization and what you learned from each experience. If space limitations make it necessary to leave out some of the general information about each organization, don't be concerned. The committee is much more interested in *your* experiences and what *you* bring to the school and the profession as a result of *your* experiences than it is in knowing, for example, that a given agency sponsors a New Year's Eve community celebration.

Personal Treatment and Family Experiences

Many individuals' first experiences in social work are as clients. While there is no need for you to provide specifics on your treatment, it is important that it be clear to the committee that whatever issues led you to treatment have been resolved and that you seek entry into the profession to assist others and *not* because you seek to help yourself. Admissions committees are cautious about people who bring their own agenda to the profession. You should be clear that you do not seek entry into the profession to further resolve your own issues.

While a discussion of your own psychotherapy, for example, is relevant, it should avoid excessive self-revelation that may make the admissions committees wonder about your emotional stability. On the other hand, it is quite appropriate to present your own treatment as a tool to learning more about yourself as a fundamental prerequisite to helping others. Also, it reveals a willingness to look at yourself.

> Put a LOT of thought into the personal statement. It says so much about you.
> *Melissa Aragon*
> *MSW student*

A great many applicants select social work as a result of experiences with family members. Again, presenting the situation as a learning experience without excessive revelation is the best approach. For example, it can lead nicely into how the experience led you to seek further exposure to social work as a volunteer.

If the nature of your relative's needs had a substantial impact on your time, the committee will likely ask itself to what extent it may affect your ability to concentrate on graduate work. If the situation persists, you should outline what mechanisms are in place to meet your relative's needs that will allow you time for graduate studies.

Don't Exaggerate or Give the Impression of Exaggerating Experiences

In the quest to be offered admission, it may be tempting to present experiences in a slightly more positive light than perhaps was the case. You certainly want to showcase your experiences and what you learned from them; yet, it is important to present them realistically. It is a fine line to tread. On one hand, you want to state your accomplishments so that the committee understands you bring a valuable background to the school. On the other hand, you do not want to come across as a pretentious applicant who doesn't fully recognize that she has much to learn.

It is wise not to overstate some of the claims of your experiences and accomplishments. The committee is much more interested in applicants who recognize the need for further training than in applicants whose statements indicate they feel very accomplished already.

Question 2: Describe Your Educational Goals and Expectations

The committee wants to know what you hope to gain from your graduate education in social work. Let's look at the question behind the question. The committee is attempting to learn to what extent the program options at its school are congruent with your goals. Most schools of social work have many more applicants than there are places in the class. If an applicant is unclear about her goals or expresses goals that clearly cannot be met by the school's options of study, that applicant may be eliminated from further consideration. For example, the applicant may make a logical and persuasive case for wanting to specialize in rural social work. If the particular school does not offer a rural specialty, the applicant may well be denied admission because the admissions committee believes the school is not in a position to teach the applicant what she wants to learn. Committees look very closely at the "fit" between an applicant's goals and the school's offerings and resources. For example, I recall one applicant to a leading school who had impeccable credentials, yet was denied admission. He stated his primary interest was in international social work, and the committee felt the school did not have the expertise to meet the applicant's needs.

The challenge you face in addressing this question is to demonstrate to the committee that you "did your homework" by learning about the school's options for areas of study concentrations. Clearly state how the program offerings match your goals. It is best not to make statements that appear designed to flatter the school. I advise against a statement such as, "... I would like to undergo training at the best social work department in the Southwest," or "I want to be in the best training program possible." Either of those statements may be interpreted as referring to a school's regional or national ranking. Although such schools are very proud of their rankings (and work very hard to maintain them!), they do not seem to want to be selected by students exclusively on that basis. They'd much rather be selected for the content of the programs than for the ranking itself.

It is also best to avoid platitudes such as "... they (clients) deserve a helping professional prepared through a quality well-balanced program, regardless of its rigors." The committee already knows what clients deserve. It is more interested in learning about the specific reasons you believe its specific school will help you to become a prepared professional.

It is also most important that you make it clear that you want to expand your education, and are not merely seeking a credential.

Your wording should not sound as though it belongs in the pages of a school catalog. Use your own words and say what you want to learn in graduate school that you believe will prepare you to do the sort of social work you intend to make your life's work.

Connect what you hope to learn at the school to what you hope to do as a practicing professional.

Question 3: Describe Your Short- and Long-Term Professional Goals

As much as is possible at this point, you should mention your specific goals. For instance, you may have the objective of becoming a licensed clinical social worker. It is best to avoid drifting off into general statements such as, "... sharing myself as a professional social worker" and "...wanting to have a fulfilling career as a social worker." The committee assumes all applicants want those things. You will serve your cause best by being more specific. What areas of social work are of potential interest to you? How do you see your past experiences (i.e., identify the transferable skills between what you do now and what you hope to do post-master's) and what you hope to obtain from the master's program contributing to your professional work?

Although being as clear as possible about your present professional goals is recommended, this should be tempered with a healthy expectation that other possibilities are likely to arise. Too often, applicants write as though they know precisely what their careers will be. The realization that a graduate education is likely to open her eyes to many new possibilities indicates the applicant understands she has much to learn.

Another way this question is often posed is, "What do you expect to contribute in the future to the profession?" Avoid being vague and making statements of the "baseball, mom, and apple pie" variety. That is, do not make general statements that anyone considering social work might make about wanting to help "..individuals and groups of people no matter who they are, what they do, or where they come from."

Rather than making those types of statements, you'd do better focusing on specifics. With what types of populations, around what issues, and in what settings do you intend to practice? As noted above, you do not want to come across as though you are not open to possibilities that may present themselves in graduate school. To say that you believe the graduate experience may present possibilities you may not yet be aware of would be good.

Question 4: Provide Evidence of Your Capacity for Graduate Work

This question is posed in a number of different ways. For example, you may be asked to write about a social/human problem that interests you.

The intent behind the question is to determine your understanding of a social issue and your perception of the positive and negative forces the profession of social work can bring to bear in addressing the issue. Your response will also serve as a gauge of your level of sophistication in viewing a social work issue and, therefore, your readiness for graduate work. Don't let this alarm you. The committee does not expect you to *have* a graduate-level view of the issue. It only expects you to show *potential* to undertake graduate work. Once again, your writing will be most important. Your ability to explain your position clearly while supporting your views logically and coherently will be examined closely.

Another way to pose this question is, "What does the applicant consider to be a major issue that professional social workers should be concerned with in the 21st century; what does the applicant *see* as a role and responsibility of social work in relation to this issue?"

The point behind the question is to assess the applicant's level of sophistication in viewing social problems. Once again, connecting your educational goals to the offerings of the school would be a good idea. You should select an issue that is related to the population you plan to work with after graduation. For example, if your population of choice is adolescents, you may write about family dysfunction as a result of alcohol and other substance abuse, youth and generational alienation, domestic and family violence, sexual abuse, or another relevant issue. Stay away from generalities and do some serious research on the subject. You can follow with your views on each subject as backed by the facts. Conclude with how you see social work addressing the issue.

It will be beneficial not to be too general in your choice of an issue; after all, this is only one section of your statement. For example, if your interests are in juvenile delinquency and the widening socio-economic gap, you should limit your response to one or the other. Whichever you select, be specific in defining the issue and how you see social work methods as a potential solution. Avoid digressing into side issues that do not address the question.

Do your homework in preparing to write about the issue you select. Be cautious about the claims you make. By doing so, you will avoid the possibility of having your statements disputed if the faculty committee members who happen to read your application are experts on the subject. A faculty expert on your given subject could have some problems with broad generalizations. This is not to say that as an applicant you are expected to be an expert on the subject, but it is expected that you understand your limitations.

Another way the topic of your capacity to undertake graduate work may be addressed is to inquire about the personal qualities you believe you bring to the profession of social work. It is tempting for applicants to highlight strengths while ignoring their areas that would benefit from improvement. It would add a great deal of balance for you to also highlight minimal or non-existent qualities that you hope to develop through your graduate studies and beyond. A social worker must be aware of her shortcomings and identify ways to improve them. That is, after all, what we ask our clients to do. Many applicants make the mistake of tooting their own horns so loudly that they fail to acknowledge that the real purpose of graduate school is to provide an education.

Plans for Covering Expenses

Although not always asked as part of the biographical or personal statement, most schools inquire about the applicant's plans for meeting the expenses of a graduate education. Sometimes it is one of the questions in the application itself.

It is a very important and relevant point. Many schools do not have extensive assistance available, and students will more than likely have to secure scholastic loans and even work part time while in graduate school. Your response to the question will give the committee a picture of how realistic you are about what you will need to do while in graduate school. If attending school full time, you will have to carry a full class load and also spend anywhere from sixteen to twenty-four hours per week in a field setting. Above all of that, you will probably need to work between ten and twenty hours per week to supplement your living expenses. If you will be enrolled in a part-time program, you will likely be employed full time.

If you have already secured a scholarship or grant from an independent source (such as your church, synagogue, your or a parent's employer, or another source) be sure to mention it in your statement. It will provide the school with further evidence of your commitment to a graduate education, your ability to plan, and your resourcefulness. As mentioned earlier, it may be advantageous to your application, because the funds you bring will allow the school to free up funds it would have used for you to benefit other deserving applicants.

If you worked part time during college, it would be useful to mention it. For example, "I achieved a grade point average of 3.8 while working 15 hours per week."

Question 5: Describe Why You Seek a Graduate Social Work Education at This Point in Your Career

More often than not, this question is asked only of applicants who seek a return to school after being employed for some time.

This question seeks to answer the "Why now?" question that all social workers seem to be enamored with (for good reasons). The only really poor answer to this question is to say that you want a master's so you can be promoted. Schools do not want people who are simply seeking a credential. They want people who seek an education.

If your background is in a career unrelated to social work, you need to give the committee a better understanding of (1) how you came to select your present occupation and (2) how, through your time in that profession, you came to recognize social work as your future calling. Was your interest in social work there all along, but you chose the other career for other reasons (financial security or family pressures, for example)? Your statement should answer the important questions the committee asks itself on all career changers: (a) "Why the change?" and (b) "Why now?"

As someone seeking to change careers, you have probably been away from an academic setting for some time. Therefore, your job accomplishments should also be connected to your intellectual capacities, and indirectly to your academic abilities. Some of the same skills that it took to excel in business, for example, skills involved in supervising employees, are very applicable to social work. Some of the same skills that it takes to excel in business, particularly the ones involved in business education programs, are very applicable to the academic setting.

It would be useful for you to highlight how you see the skills you developed in your present career applying to your goals in social work. A great deal will depend on how the committee views your rationale for the career change.

It is tempting for career changers to make passionate, even poetic, arguments for their wish to change careers. In some ways, by so doing they are preaching to the choir. For example, someone switching from business to clinical social work may be tempted to expound on the beauty of clinical practice. The committee does not need to know how different clinical work is from the business environment. Rather, they want to know what qualities the applicant brings to clinical work, the types of clientele she seeks to serve, and how she believes a clinical education at their particular school can help her meet her goals.

It is not necessary to make apologies for having been in another field (you'd be surprised how many people do!), yet you should make a bridge between your previous background and social work. Use examples of how you may have used your skills in volunteer social work settings or with family and friends. Beware, however, that one of the possible dangers of examples of having helped friends and family is that an applicant may unintentionally come across as someone who believes he is a "natural social worker." This sometimes makes admissions committees nervous. Highlight your awareness that you have much to learn, as you describe how you have helped family and others in the past. Doing so will eliminate the possibility of coming across as someone who thinks he is already a social worker and simply wants a credential. It will help the committee understand that you are seeking an education, not merely some letters to put after your name.

Concluding Your Statement

As mentioned at the beginning of this chapter, many applicants strive to introduce their statements in a clever and unusual way. Equally as many do the same in concluding their statements. Many close by saying how much they hope to be offered admission, how they believe they can make a difference in people's lives, and how intelligent they are (in so many words). Doing so is not necessary, because every applicant hopes to be offered admission, everyone that applies has a sincere belief that they can make a positive difference in people's lives, and all consider themselves intelligent and mature. Rather than saying those things at the end, be thorough in answering the questions, keeping in mind the questions behind the questions, and those things will speak for themselves. By the time the committee reviews your application and reads your statement, it will be the judge of those things.

Going Beyond the Instructions

Just as it is most important to address every point in the statement instructions, it is important *not* to go beyond what is requested. The old adage of "never volunteer" certainly applies to biographical or personal statements. Making application to graduate schools is a process filled with much anxiety. Many applicants attempt to ease their tension by submitting as many documents as they can think of with their applications. Normally, it is not a good idea to include copies of additional materials. One reason is that the instructions do not state you can do so. The committee may interpret it as a failure to read the directions. Another reason is that the material may hurt instead of help you. For example, applicants sometimes want to include evidence of past work, such as a grant they've authored. Committee persons who review the application may well be some of the nation's foremost experts in grant writing. Will the grant stand up to the scrutiny of such expertise? I believe it would be best not to take that chance.

Helpful Hints

Do...

- begin with a well thought-out introduction (i.e., telling the reader what is ahead).

- consider the questions behind the questions.

- write about the other graduate school options you considered along with social work and why you selected social work.

- provide specifics about your role within each organization and what you learned from each experience.

- when writing about a personal or family crisis, and aspects of the situation persist, outline what mechanisms are in place to meet continuing needs that will allow you time for graduate studies.

- clearly state how the school's offerings match your goals *without* making statements that appear designed to flatter the school.

- be as clear as possible about your present professional goals while maintaining a healthy expectation that other possibilities are likely to arise.

(continued on next page)

(continued from previous page)

- if asked to discuss a social issue, stay away from generalities and do some serious research on the subject.

- if asked to discuss the personal qualities you bring to the profession, add balance to your descriptions of your strengths by also highlighting minimal or non-existent qualities that you hope to develop through your graduate studies and beyond.

- if you are changing careers, highlight how you see the skills you developed in your present career applying to your goals in social work.

Don't...

- begin your essay with an overly clever introduction.

- make your essay read like a résumé in narrative form.

- write about personal treatment experiences without making clear to the committee that whatever issues led you to treatment have been resolved and that you seek entry into the profession to assist others and *not* because you seek to help yourself.

- overplay your experiences and risk coming across as a pretentious applicant who doesn't fully recognize that she has much to learn.

- use platitudes such as "I want to give of myself to those in need." Instead, be specific about your goals and how you plan to achieve them.

(continued on next page)

(continued from previous page)

- conclude by saying how much you hope to be offered admission, how you believe you can make a difference in people's lives, and how intelligent you are (in so many words). Doing so is not necessary.

- go beyond what is requested in the instructions.

Chapter 12

Less Than Perfect Undergraduate Records: What To Do

College can be highly demanding emotionally, intellectually, and financially. In addition, it takes place at a time in most people's lives that has more than its share of stresses. For the so-called traditional student, it comes at the tail end of adolescence, a time of much self exploration and uncertainty. For the so-called non-traditional student who is often also bearing the burden of family responsibilities, it comes at a time when the future looms equally uncertain. Therefore, it is not uncommon for undergraduate records to be less than perfect.

The patterns of uneven undergraduate records are as unique as the students themselves. Generally, however, they fall into three categories. I have often seen undergraduate records that reflect generally above-average performance with the exception of a semester or two of dismal performance. I have also seen records that simply seem to languish in a constant state that exhibits neither academic brilliance nor outright incompetence. I've also come across individuals who have forged excellent careers, yet apologetically explain that their college transcript of a decade ago (or more) is their biggest shame.

Do any of these scenarios (or a combination thereof) mean the end of all hopes for graduate study? Not necessarily. It does mean, however, that you must face the issues head-on in an honest and realistic fashion at the time of your application.

I have seen instances in which applicants rush to provide an explanation after having an application for admission denied. Many schools are reluctant to reverse their decisions except in circumstances in which the information was not available at the time of application and is absolutely compelling. Providing an explanation after the fact usually does not fall into that category, because the explanation could have been offered at the time of initial application. Understandably, schools are hesitant to reopen the process once a denial has been made, for fear of opening the floodgates of requests of appeals from other denied applicants.

Let's look at ways the above three scenarios should be approached.

The Case of Poor Performance During a Brief Period in an Otherwise Above–Average Record

Many applicants make the mistake of not wanting to call attention to a semester or two of poor performance. They carefully avoid all references to it in the hope that the admissions committee will not notice it or, at least, will overlook it. The invariable result is that the committee does notice and, in the absence of any explanation, assumes all was well and the grades in question reflect the student's inability to grasp the material.

A better strategy is to face the issue head on. I recommend what I call a GPA Addendum. It is intended to alert the graduate admissions committee to any unusual circumstances that affected the student's ability to focus on the class materials during the period in question. A good degree of judgment should be exercised in determining to what extent personal matters are discussed. For example, if financial pressures necessitated increasing the amount of work hours, and consequently lessened the amount of time devoted to studies, the family or personal factors at the root of the issue need little elaboration.

A vital part of the Addendum will be the presentation of evidence of (a) how the crisis was resolved and (b) that once the crisis was resolved the student resumed the usual above-average level of performance. Without this last part, the Addendum becomes little more than a poor excuse for deficient performance. The Addendum should be brief, perhaps no more than one-half typewritten page, and present the facts in a straightforward fashion without assuming a "woe is me" tone.

If the application contains a space where you must enter your undergraduate GPA, I recommend placing an asterisk directing the committee to the GPA Addendum. I recommend an Addendum separate from the supplementary or biographical statement, because to include it in the statement may break the flow of expression of the development of your interest in social work, your expectations for a graduate education, and your professional goals.

A sample of a brief, yet effective, Addendum follows. The applicant was offered admission to the school that was his first choice.

I was placed on academic probation during the Summer session and the Fall semester of 2000. I had personal and financial problems, which detracted from my studies. In January of 2001, I transferred from the (local) campus of my university to its (main) campus. The reduced cost of living due to facilities such as subsidized married student housing allowed me to adjust my work hours and resume full attention to my studies. I retook the classes I had in the two terms in question and after one semester I was removed from probation, having achieved a graduation GPA of 3.47 on a 4.0 scale. I went on to graduate in May of 2003 with a GPA of 3.42.

Letters of Reference

Applicants in this category may be somewhat tempted to obtain "sympathy letters of reference." Such letters are often from clergy, close friends, and similar sources. They typically contain statements of admiration for the endurance displayed by the applicant in difficult times. Although well-meaning, such sources add little of substance to the central issue of informing the committee of the applicant's academic abilities and potential for the profession.

The fact that the applicant overcame the crisis, as evidenced by a return to previous levels of academic excellence, should suffice. There is no reason to dwell on the subject. The letters of reference will be used to best advantage if they come from sources as explained earlier.

Standardized Test Scores

As mentioned earlier, applicants who have an overall above-average undergraduate record should be careful not to allow poor standardized test scores to hurt them. If your scores on the GRE sections average less than 650, you probably should not submit scores if you can help it. Even if you had a period of poor performance in college, that issue was addressed by the resumption of above average performance after the period in question.

An Average to Below-Average Undergraduate GPA

Most graduate schools of social work will require a cumulative or post-sophomore GPA of at least 2.75 on a 4.0 scale. A good number of schools require 3.0 on a 4.0 scale as a minimum.

A word of caution is in order on the meaning of a school's stated minimum GPA. The minimum GPA refers to the lowest GPA with which applicants will be considered for admission. It does not mean that an applicant with a GPA equal to the school's stated minimum is automatically granted admission. For the more competitive programs, there may be few, if any, applicants with undergraduate GPAs equaling the school's stated minimum who are actually offered admission. Rather than attempting to judge your chances of admission based on a school's stated minimum GPA, it is better to inquire of the schools the actual GPA range, mean, median, and mode for those applicants offered admission in the most recent cycle.

In general, if your GPA is below 2.75 on a 4.0 scale, you will probably have difficulties gaining admission to a graduate school of social work. There are, however, a number of strategies you can attempt.

The things you can do will depend largely on how low your GPA is, how much time has elapsed since you completed college, and what you have been doing since graduation. An added factor will be how competitive admissions are to the particular schools of your interest. In general, the higher the ranking of the school, the more competitive the admissions process. Among other factors that will have an impact on your chances of admission will be the number of graduate social work programs that compete for students in your given geographic area and the level of demand for new social workers in the given market.

Current College Seniors and Recent Graduates With a Slightly Lower GPA Than a School's Stated Minimum

If you are in your last year of college and plan to apply for admission to graduate school for next year, your options decrease to the extent that your GPA is below the school's stated minimum.

If you are only slightly below the stated limit (no more than approximately 0.15 below), you may be able to obtain conditional or probationary admission. Be aware, however, that the more prestigious schools, as well as those with extremely high numbers of applicants in relation to the spaces in the incoming class, do not normally grant conditional or probationary admission.

Schools willing to consider probationary admission will pose some stringent requirements. In addition, the number of students admitted on a conditional basis may be no more than a handful in any given school.

If you can make a case that family and work obligations affected your ability to do well in college, your case will be strengthened. By the same token, be ready to present evidence that whatever the circumstances that affected your college performance were, they will be resolved by the time you enter graduate school. If you are unable to provide reasonable evidence that the circumstances will not continue, the admissions committee will have no reason to believe your graduate work will be any better than your undergraduate work.

If your record is mediocre at best throughout college, you will also need to provide additional evidence that you possess the academic abilities necessary for graduate study. Even if someone can substantiate that detrimental circumstances existed during college, it does not necessarily follow that the same individual could have done better had circumstances been better.

Letters of Reference

Whether your overall college performance was only slightly below-average or extremely below-average, I advise against "sympathy letters of reference." As mentioned earlier, aside from retelling your tales of woe, they add little to the real issue at hand. The central question the graduate admissions committee needs answered is, "So, you had unfortunate circumstances during college, but what can you show us to prove you can do well under better circumstances?"

Therefore, I recommend letters of reference from professors where you did your best work. Such letters may show the committee that you have potential, because you managed to do well in some classes, despite your circumstances.

Standardized Test Scores

If the school allows the option, submitting credible scores on a standardized test can be a way of providing evidence of your academic abilities and potential for graduate work. Scores from the Graduate Record Examination (GRE) or, for some schools, the Miller Analogies Test (MAT) may be a way to strengthen your application given a low undergraduate GPA. A word of warning, though—as I advised earlier, it is better to wait until after you've received your scores before deciding whether to have the scores reported to the schools. True, you will spend a little more money by submitting a request after you take the test, but the expense will be worth it if it keeps average to low scores that can harm your chances of being admitted from being reported.

Each school's definition of a good GRE or MAT score varies depending on the quality of students in its applicant pool. Ask the admissions offices of the schools of your choice what are considered good scores. For the more competitive schools, a score below 650 on each category of the GRE will probably not strengthen your possibilities of admission.

Current College Seniors and Recent Graduates With a GPA Substantially Lower Than a School's Stated Minimum

If you are in your last year of college or graduated from college less than two years before your expected time of entrance into graduate school and your undergraduate GPA is substantially lower than the stated minimum of the schools you hope to attend, your chances of acceptance are low.

For such students, most schools recommend a minimum of two years of successful post-college full-time employment before applying. The two years are recommended because they will test your interest and aptitude for the profession and allow time for natural maturation.

Even after successful employment, however, the academic question will remain. Use the two years to take undergraduate or graduate courses in related fields. Obtaining above-average grades will provide graduate schools with more recent evidence of your abilities and commitment. Be aware that unless those courses are from a graduate school accredited by CSWE or CASSW-ACESS, the chances are they will not be transferable for credit once you are formally admitted as a degree-seeking student in a graduate program of social work. Check with the graduate schools you are interested in about the transferability of any classes before enrolling.

Even if you find that the classes will not transfer, they will be well worth it if they will help you disprove your previous academic short-comings.

Possibilities for classes to take include graduate level classes in social work or a related area, such as psychology or sociology, as a non-degree student, or student-at-large. If you did not take courses in research and statistics or in human biology as an undergraduate, this presents an opportunity to meet those and other prerequisites while providing evidence that you can excel academically and that you have the potential for graduate study.

Letters of Reference

The second important advantage to taking student-at-large classes is that you can obtain academic letters of reference from your professors. Good letters can go a long way in laying to rest your earlier college background.

Even with all of the above, generally speaking, if your GPA from college is 2.2 or below on a 4.0 scale, your chances of admission to a graduate program in social work will remain low.

Standardized Test Scores

You may also want to consider taking the Graduate Record Examination (GRE) or the Miller Analogies Test (MAT), if the schools of your interest provide that option, as a way to provide further evidence of academic readiness for graduate school. Be forewarned, however, that even with high grades in student-at-large courses and standardized test scores (depending on how high the scores are), your chances of admission to the highly selective schools may remain low.

If your heart is set on such a school, an alternative is to gain admission to a less selective school and excel in your first year of the graduate program (mostly, if not totally, A grades) and apply to your first choice school as a transfer student for your second year.

There are opposing arguments to this strategy. Arguments against it center mainly around the issue of the continuity of your graduate education. Although curricula in the first year of graduate programs in social work are fairly consistent among accredited schools of social work, some philosophical differences among schools lend each program its own particular focus and flavor.

One advantage of this option is that if you are not accepted as a transfer student, you can still complete your Master of Social Work at the school you attended your first year. It is also possible that after spending one year in the school that was not previously your first choice, you may decide you don't want to leave. You may have developed good relationships with the faculty and your fellow students and enjoyed the program more than you anticipated.

Distant Past Graduates With a GPA Substantially Lower Than a School's Stated Minimum

If you graduated from college some time ago, depending on how low your GPA was, your academic performance from as long ago as 15 or 20 years may still come back to haunt you.

If you have managed to forge a moderately successful career, perhaps one of the biggest obstacles you will encounter will be facing the ghost of your past. Many a highly successful and normally confident professional seems to lose composure upon touching on the subject of a distant past poor college record. In fact, many delay seeking an advanced degree to avoid battle with the old dragon of their past shortcomings. Once they decide to accept the challenge, most are successful in slaying the dragon. This is not to say, however, that victory comes without substantial effort.

Don't hesitate to apply the skills that have made you a professional success to the admissions process. Actively seek interviews with admissions personnel at the schools of your choice. Use the interview to highlight your maturity and skills and how they relate to your decision to seek graduate education, as well as ways they will contribute to your post-graduate goals. Be matter-of-fact about your college record without being apologetic. Chances are the interviewer recalls younger days when the long-term implications of a college record were not considered.

It is important to approach the interviews as a means to learn what each institution will require of you to address the academic prerequisites for admission. It is best, and more realistic, not to approach the interviews with the goal of convincing officials that your professional record is so outstanding as to negate the need to address the academic issues. If you do, the likely result will be that you leave the impression of being egotistical and lacking understanding of the unique qualities and skills necessary for academic success.

Even despite an applicant's highly successful professional record, schools will require some recent evidence of academic success. I have seen extremely successful individuals react in shock to being denied admission to graduate school because they failed to provide evidence of recent academic success. The reason graduate schools need to see such evidence is that skills required for professional success and those required for academic success are not always the same. To offer a more mundane example, even Michael Jordan—with all his athletic talents—could not transfer his success on the basketball court to the baseball diamond.

I recommend the same strategies offered in the previous several pages. One strategy is to take some graduate level classes as a student-at-large. They will provide graduate schools with recent evidence of your academic abilities. Just as important, they will serve to ease your readjustment to the role of student. If your professional position allows you independence and responsibility over others, adjusting to the role of student may be more emotionally challenging than you think. It will be a humbling experience indeed to be in a classroom with people half your age who seem, at least initially, much more capable than you.

Standardized tests such as the Graduate Record Examination (GRE) and Miller Analogies Test (MAT) are also ways to build up your academic credentials, provided the schools of your choice accept standardized test scores. The same warnings and caveats about how to prepare for standardized tests and how to decide when and which scores to have sent to graduate schools explained earlier in this book apply to you.

Keep in mind that the more highly ranked schools may be more difficult to enter. Interestingly, the highly ranked schools may also be more flexible in evaluating the unique backgrounds and qualifications of non-traditional students. You may also want to consider the option of going to a school that ranks lower in your list of preferences and attempting to transfer for your second year to the school you rank as your number one choice.

Helpful Hints

Do...

- face issues of past academic shortcomings honestly and realistically at the time of your application.

- use an addendum to your application to alert the graduate admissions committee to any unusual circumstances that affected your ability to focus on your studies during a period of poor performance in college.

- follow explanations of periods of poor academic performance with evidence of a return to previous levels of academic excellence.

- consider using standardized test scores to provide evidence of academic ability if your undergraduate record was average to poor.

- if your college record is extremely poor, consider taking graduate level classes in social work or a related area, such

(continued on next page)

(continued from previous page)

as psychology or sociology, as a non-degree student to show current evidence of academic ability.

Don't...

• avoid all references to brief periods of poor academic college performance in the hope that the admissions committee will not notice it or overlook it.

• submit "sympathy letters of reference."

Chapter 13

You're Accepted: What's Next?

You may just be getting started now, but, given the right research and preparation, the day will come when offers of admission will come to your mailbox. When they do, celebrate and pat yourself on the back for a job well done. Once the celebration is over, however, it will be time to consider your options carefully. The factors to consider will include the timing of each offer relative to offers from other schools (and which school is your first choice) and relative to the financial aid award, whether the offer is for an actual place in the class or to be placed on a school's waiting list, and whether your personal circumstances have changed and you wish to pursue deferring your admission to a future academic year.

Timing of The Offer

Most schools process applications for admission before proceeding to make financial aid awards. Therefore, you will probably receive offers of admission and be asked to accept or reject the offer before you know the level of financial aid you are awarded. Accepting an offer usually entails making a substantial cash deposit anywhere between $100 and $500 to hold your place in the class. To add to the dilemma, acceptance deposits are usually non-refundable. Basically, it is like being asked whether or not you want to buy something before you know the price.

It is a difficult decision to make. You may have an offer from the school of your dreams but you may not yet know whether you can afford to go there. If the school in question is private and the financial aid award is good, chances are that the amount you pay will be roughly equivalent to the amount you would pay at a public university in the same state. If the award is at a lower level, however, you could pay dearly for accepting without knowing the amount of the award first.

Students who find themselves in that difficult position often opt to request an extension of the time allotted to accept or decline the offer. Some schools are reluctant to grant an extension, while others do so routinely. You have nothing to lose by trying.

Waiting Lists

An added dilemma confronts students who are placed on a school's waiting list. They are told that they qualify for admission but the class is full. If the notice comes from a school you are very interested in, it is very tempting to pass up solid offers of admission from other schools in the hope that a spot opens up and you are selected from the waiting list.

Before you decide to pass up other offers, ask for more specifics about the chances of being selected for an open spot from the waiting list. Inquire how many people are on the waiting list and how many spots are expected to open. Generally, schools make more offers of admission than there are places in the class. They "overbook" the class based on past experience of the number of offers of admission that are usually declined. Therefore, spots will usually only open up for waiting list candidates if the schools underestimated the rate of decline responses.

Another question to ask is at what place you are on the waiting list. Are you the next person or tenth on the list? Chances are that the waiting list is not a list but a waiting pool. That is, people are not ranked within the group. As openings arise, people are selected not based solely on the rating of their applications but on other factors. For instance, the school may want to balance its male-female ratio or the number of students who expect to be in different concentrations and make waiting list selections accordingly.

Perhaps the most important question to ask is what effect getting a spot so late will mean to your financial aid award. Will there still be enough money left?

My best advice if you are on a waiting list is, unless you have a fairly solid idea that your chances are good to get a spot in the class, don't pass up other offers. You could wind up with no school to attend and have to start all over again the following year.

Deferring Admission

Some schools allow admitted applicants to defer the date of admission for periods of one to two years. For example, if the applicant is offered admission for Autumn of 2005, he can defer the start of school until Autumn of 2006 or even Autumn of 2007. Policies on deferral vary among schools, and it is best to consult individual schools.

If a school allows you that option, there are pluses and minuses you should consider. Having an additional year or two of full-time employment in social service will certainly benefit you. It will give you a nice foundation for graduate work. You will have more of a real-world frame to fit the theories you will learn in the classroom. During your year to two years of employment, you will enjoy the peace of mind of knowing that you have been admitted and have a place in a graduate school.

Some people use the option of deferral to spend time in the Peace Corps or in other similar programs. There are many excellent experiences you may not be able to enjoy later in your life. Having a place assured in a graduate school allows for concentrating on the experience without having to mail application materials from faraway lands where mail service may not be reliable.

A possible disadvantage to deferring admission is cost. Tuition rates have been steadily rising at rates well above inflation for a good number of years. Therefore, the cost of your education will be greater as time goes on. With a one-year deferral, the total cost of your graduate education may rise as much as ten percent and even more if you defer for two years. In addition, financial aid benefits are in a period of decline. Many educational institutions are experiencing periods of financial difficulties, and this is being reflected in financial aid policies.

Chances are that financial aid packages will be smaller as the years progress. Full-tuition scholarships even for the most gifted applicants are, for the most part, a thing of the past. The gap between ever-increasing tuition rates and decreasing financial aid packages is likely to grow wider. Unfortunately for most students, the gap must be bridged through educational loans and other personal and family resources. Purely on economic grounds, I suggest attending graduate school as soon as possible.

Many schools, on the other hand, do not allow students to defer admission. Some schools in this group may allow reapplication for a period of up to two years without requiring a reapplication fee. In addition, the reapplication procedure may be much simpler than was the case for the original application. For instance, the application form may be much shorter. Resubmission of transcript and other information that will remain unchanged may not be necessary. A brief update to your biographical statement indicating your activities since the time of the original application and perhaps one or two additional letters of reference may suffice.

A very important point is not to take readmission for granted. It is not uncommon for reapplicants to be denied admission, even though they may have been offered admission the first time. For any given school, the quality of the applicant pool varies somewhat from year to year. If a person was a marginal applicant, a slight increase in the quality of the applicant pool could cause a denial.

In addition, many unpredictable and highly subjective factors may come into play. When all is said and done, the fate of an applicant may rest on factors as unpredictable and subjective as who happens to be the person or persons on the admissions committee who read the application. Members have different perspectives and, in some cases, may view the same applicant in very different ways. A more thorough discussion of admissions committees may be found in the introduction to Part II of this book.

Accepting the Offer

Once all is said and done and you've made the final choice of school, it is time to accept the offer. If you were thorough in your contacts and visit, the admissions office probably knows you by now. In accepting the offer, I recommend that you display the same sense of thoroughness and professionalism that you showed in your search. The mechanics of accepting the offer may be as simple as checking off a line on a form sent to you by the school. If that is the case, you should definitely comply with the instructions and complete the form. Nevertheless, I recommend you also include a cover letter indicating your acceptance, addressing any remaining items, asking whatever questions you may have about what is next, and thanking the office of admissions for its assistance through the application process. You would be surprised how few people thank admissions staff and how much it is appreciated. A nice brief letter as follows would be appropriate:

I am in receipt of your letter dated March 16, 2006 offering me admission to your Autumn, 2006 entering class as well as a Dean's Scholarship in the amount of $6,000.00 (renewable per your requirements).

I am very pleased to accept your offer and enclose a check in the amount of $400.00 as deposit on tuition. I have requested my undergraduate institution to send official final transcripts directly to you at the close of my last semester this June.

Thank you very much for all your kind assistance and patience during the application process and your hospitality during my visit. I look forward very much to being a student at your school.

A question often asked by students who are soon to begin graduate school is if there are any books or other materials they should be reading before beginning school. My response surprises many of them. I encourage them to relax and enjoy their summer (or whatever time remains before classes begin). The application process is rigorous, filled with many important decisions, and provokes much anxiety. Now that you have lived through it, you deserve a hearty congratulations and some time for yourself. The time remaining is much better spent relaxing than in attempts to further prepare for school. If you weren't prepared, the school would not have accepted you. There will be plenty of reading to do once school begins. There is no need to jump into the frying pan before your time.

If you are relocating to your graduate school from another city, I recommend you arrive at least four to seven days before the beginning of school. Doing so will allow you the opportunity to become familiar with your new surroundings and get to know a few people on campus. Adjusting to the pace of graduate school will be more manageable if you've had the opportunity to get to know the basics of your new setting before classes begin.

Most schools host some kind of welcoming reception, picnic, or other event. In many cases, the event represents a substantial expense for the school. In today's climate of shrinking budgets, schools still recognize the importance of a good beginning for new students. Don't underestimate the importance and the many benefits of attending. It will allow you to meet faculty, staff, second-year or more advanced students, and your fellow classmates. The relationships you begin to form will be an invaluable support through graduate school and, in many cases, throughout your career.

Helpful Hints

Do...

- consider what the "true cost" of a particular school will be by looking at your net cost after financial aid is known.

- follow to the letter all financial aid requirements and deadlines.

- ask precisely what it means if you're placed on a school's "waiting list."

- consider the pluses and minuses if you are considering deferring admission.

- send a cover letter with your acceptance.

- make time for yourself before school begins.

- (if you are from out of town) arrive to campus a few days early.

- CONGRATULATE YOURSELF!

Don't...

- let the cost of a given school be the sole determinant of whether to seek admission.

- jump at the first offer of admission; consider other offers (and how each compares in financial assistance).

- forget to thank admissions staff.

- underestimate the importance of making friends among faculty, staff, and other students.

Chapter 14

The Doctoral Decision

For most purposes, the master's is considered the terminal degree in the profession of social work. In 2002, according to the Council on Social Work Education, the number of students enrolled in doctoral social work programs was 2,400, approximately 7.3% that of students enrolled in master's programs. Nevertheless, even if at this point you are only at the stage of contemplating seeking a master's degree, there are factors you should know about the doctoral option.

What Can You Do with a Doctorate That You Cannot Do with a Master's Degree?

The short answer to that question is "not much." The more complete answer, of course, is much more complicated. Let's focus on the short answer first. Master's trained social workers (for purposes of this chapter, defined as master's level social workers who do not also have doctoral training) are found in all areas of the profession, including direct practice, administration, teaching, and research. In short, there are no areas of practice reserved exclusively for doctoral degree holders. The more complicated answer involves the fact that having doctoral training most certainly enhances the ability to practice and advance in certain practice areas.

Most notable are the areas of research and teaching. Whereas master's trained social workers engage in both of those activities, their counterparts with doctoral training generally hold an advantage. Most doctoral programs of social work have as their primary mission to prepare researchers. Master's programs, on the other hand, have as their mission to train practitioners. Therefore, doctorate holders generally have a more thorough knowledge of research methods than their master's trained counterparts. Research and teaching go hand in hand, particularly in the larger academic settings.

Council on Social Work Education figures for 2002 highlight the importance of a doctorate to achieving tenured status. In schools with master's and baccalaureate programs, of those members of the faculty with tenure, 47.3% held the tenured rank of professor, 44.4% held the rank of associate professor, and 8.3% held the rank of assistant professor. Of tenured professors, 96.4% held doctorates. Of tenured associate professors, 92.8% held doctorates. And of tenured assistant professors, 77.1% held doctorates. In schools with only baccalaureate programs, the figures were lower but still significant. In those programs, of the 30.9% that held the tenured rank of professor, 73.5% held doctorates. Of tenured associate professors, 62.6% held doctorates. Of tenured assistant professors, 39.3% held doctorates.

If your full-time goal is academia, you should consider doctoral training. On the other hand, if you wish to teach as a supplement to a more practice-oriented professional life, a master's degree will suffice.

These figures may make you feel that many years of schooling lie ahead if your goal is academia. The prospect may appear particularly daunting if you are at an early point in your career, either about to finish college or recently graduated, and are exploring master's programs.

It may help for you to know that most doctoral students have spent a good number of years working at the master's level before returning to school. In 2002, the average age of male social work doctoral students taking coursework was 36.4 years of age for full-time students and 41.9 for part-time. The average age for females was 38 for full-time and 40.9 for part-time.

The Cost of a Doctoral Education

For full-time doctoral students, the larger cost of a doctoral education is the income they forego from full-time employment. Whereas 36.1% of master's program students in 2002 reported having student loans, only 10% of doctoral students took student loans. The difference is that doctoral students are more likely to receive funds from their institutions and schools of social work, including tuition assistance and/or stipend support. In 2002, 54% of all social work doctoral students received financial aid in some form, including grants, loans, and other types of support. Schools of social work granted aid to 18.8% of doctoral students, whereas universities granted aid to 14.4%.

What Do You Look for in a Doctoral Program?

Unlike master's programs, doctoral programs are not accredited by the Council on Social Work Education in the United States or by the Canadian Association of Schools of Social Work in Canada. Therefore, there is a much wider variation in the content, focus, and overall quality of programs. That means that students shopping for a doctoral program must be much more careful.

With some variations, most doctoral programs focus on research. The focus of the research is likely to vary according to (a) the overall emphasis of the school and (b) the expertise represented on the faculty. As noted in the discussion of master's programs elsewhere in this book, most schools have developed a particular perspective over time. There are schools, for instance, that focus heavily on policy and administration aspects of social work, while others have a clinical perspective. The historical focus of the school affects the school's selection of faculty, which, in turn, preserves and enhances the school's focus. Therefore, a key factor to explore is the match between your area of interest and that of the schools you are considering.

A beginning master's student does not need to know precisely her intended area of social work practice. After all, a master's student has most of the first half of the master's program to explore social work through the core curriculum required by the Council on Social Work Education or CASSW-ACESS. A doctoral applicant, however, is expected to have a fairly clear idea of her intended area of research. Although most doctoral programs begin with a block of courses, there are usually only a handful of required courses. The rest are selected by the student in preparation for the dissertation phase. The first task for a prospective doctoral applicant is to define as clearly as possible the subject area that is to be the main thrust of her doctoral studies.

Once an area is identified, a close review of faculty interests among various schools is in order. Does the school have a core of faculty conducting research in the area of your interest? If so, read as much of their work as possible. My advice to prospective doctoral applicants to the School of Social Service Administration of the University of Chicago while I was assistant dean there was to behave as a doctoral student while an applicant. That is, do your research. Know the work of the faculty and whether it matches your interests.

The next step is to visit the schools you are considering and meet with faculty to discuss their work and your interests. Are they willing to work with doctoral students as advisors or chairs of dissertation committees? Look beyond their scholarly qualities to their human qualities. Are they people with whom you would enjoy working? The most successful doctoral experiences result from mentoring relationships developed with faculty. Also inquire about their research plans for the next four to six years. Do their plans include a change of focus that may not match your needs? Do their plans include extensive periods on sabbatical or as visiting faculty elsewhere? Many doctoral educations are prolonged because students must work long-distance with dissertation committee members.

Meeting with current doctoral students is also critical. Do they find the faculty and overall climate of the school supportive of doctoral students? Many schools devote their resources to enhancing baccalaureate and master's programs to the detriment of doctoral programs. Doctoral programs generally cost money for schools, whereas baccalaureate and master's programs generate money. Most doctoral programs are small, accepting anywhere from only eight or 10 to perhaps 20 new students each year. Add to those numbers the fact that students take only a handful of common courses and quickly disperse into courses specific to their areas of interest and disperse further into their respective dissertation areas. That means that the doctoral experience can be a lonely one. Are there associations of doctoral students within the social work program or the university at large? Do not underestimate the importance of a supportive group of peers.

In short, what a doctoral applicant should look for in a school is as diverse as the population of prospective applicants. The best advice is to know exactly what you seek and look for a program that best matches your goals.

What Do Doctoral Programs Look for in Applicants?

Aside from a clearly defined area of interest as described above, doctoral programs look for evidence of academic preparation and potential for advanced studies, professional maturity, and a commitment to research. With some variations, applications require undergraduate and graduate transcripts, a personal statement, samples of writing (preferably research), and letters of recommendation. The key factor to highlight in all of these is evidence of experience and potential for research.

Academic preparation is measured by the quality of the applicant's academic performance in the master's and baccalaureate programs. A brilliant graduate record does not necessarily negate a poor undergraduate record. In fact, baccalaureate achievement is often seen as a better predictor of doctoral performance than the graduate record. An argument for this view is that advanced undergraduate courses are more purely academic than MSW courses, which tend to be more practice oriented. Evidence of above average achievement in research and writing is fundamental.

Seeking a doctoral degree in any field represents an enormous commitment. Most social workers do not choose to do it because, as noted earlier, the MSW is sufficient for most purposes. A few, however, undertake the task. When viewed in terms of the representation of doctoral degree holders in academia, the impact of these relatively few is great on the profession. Beyond teaching itself, their impact on informing practitioners through their research is also great. Whereas most top-level administrators in public and private social agencies are master's trained, most recognize the importance of seeking doctoral consultants from academia and elsewhere.

Helpful Hints

Do...

- have a clearly defined area of interest.

- read thoroughly the writings of faculty in programs you are considering.

- meet with faculty to evaluate their interest in and availability for working with doctoral students.

- meet with current doctoral students to learn firsthand the pluses and minuses of each particular program.

Don't...

- overlook the human element of faculty (is the "chemistry" right between you?).

- fail to realize research is the name of the game in doctoral programs.

- underestimate the time cost of undertaking a doctoral education.

Part III

Sources For Your Search

SOURCES FOR YOUR SEARCH

This section is intended to provide you with resources in locating a program that meets your needs. It is also intended to provide you with sources to inform you about the requirements in the state or states where you may be residing after completing graduate school.

The first portion of this section is a listing of graduate social work programs in the United States and Canada that are accredited or in candidacy for accreditation. For programs in the United States, the accrediting body is the Council on Social Work Education. For Canadian programs, the accrediting agent is the Canadian Association of Schools of Social Work. Schools that are in candidacy are indicated by an asterisk.

The second portion of this section is a compilation of the results of a survey that was sent to the accredited schools and schools in candidacy for accreditation in the United States. Seventy-three schools responded to the survey, providing insight into what they see as unique aspects of their schools and important points for applicants to consider. Similar insights may be obtained about Canadian schools at the Web site of the Canadian Association of Schools of Social Work (http://www.casswacess.ca/xASSOC/as1.htm) in the directory of MSW programs.

In visiting the Web sites of the various schools, it is also every bit as important to visit the Web page for the host institution. As noted earlier in this Handbook, understanding the host institution can yield insight into the school itself. All schools' Web sites have a link to their host university Web site. If the school you are considering does not currently have a Web site listed here, it would be helpful to locate the host university's Web page. Many schools may not have a Web site at the time of the writing of this book but may have one by the time you are reading it. A list of all U.S. university and college Web pages may be found at Yahoo (http://dir.yahoo.com/Education/Higher_Education/Colleges_and_Universities/United_States/). A listing of Web site addresses of Canadian schools may be found at the Web site listed above for the Canadian Association of Schools of Social Work.

The next part of this section consists of a list of boards for social work licensing and certification for all fifty states, the District of Columbia, Puerto Rico, ten Canadian jurisdictions, and the Virgin Islands. Knowing the licensing or certification guidelines of the states or provinces where you may be residing after graduate school will help you make a more informed decision about the program that will best prepare and qualify you for the type of social work you intend to practice.

Qualifying examinations in most states and territories are administered by the Association of Social Work Boards (ASWB). This organization is the best source of information for questions on reciprocity among states and the categories of examination required by each state. Each state listing includes the levels of practice licensed and the education, experience, and examination requirements for each. In Canada, the Association canadienne des travailleuses et travailleurs socioux or Canadian Association of Social Workers (ACTS/CASW) provides assessment of foreign credentials for those wishing to practice social work in Canada.

This is followed by an Application Tracking Form you may wish to use to record information on each school to which you are making application as you proceed through the application process.

Finally, this section includes a list of questions to ask when you visit schools, a worksheet for the biographical statement, and a listing of sources of further information.

Use these materials to organize your efforts as you make your way through the application process.

Appendix A

Graduate Social Work Programs in the United States & Canada

The following is a list of graduate social work programs in the United States as of February 2005. The listed schools are accredited by the Council on Social Work Education (CSWE) or in candidacy for CSWE accreditation. (Those in candidacy are marked with an asterisk.)

Alabama

Alabama A&M University
Social Work Department
Normal, AL

University of Alabama
School of Social Work
Tuscaloosa, AL

Alaska

University of Alaska Anchorage
School of Social Work
College of Health and Social Welfare
Anchorage, AK

Arkansas

*University of Arkansas
School of Social Work
Fayetteville, AR

University of Arkansas at Little Rock
School of Social Work
Little Rock, AR

Arizona

Arizona State University
School of Social Work
Tempe, AZ

Arizona State University West
Department of Social Work

College of Human Services
Phoenix, AZ

California

California State University, Bakersfield
Social Work Program
Bakersfield, CA

*California State University, Chico
School of Social Work
Chico, CA

California State University, Fresno
Department of Social Work Education
Fresno, CA

*California State University at Hayward
Social Work Program
Hayward, CA

California State University, Long Beach
Department of Social Work
Long Beach, CA

California State University, Los Angeles
School of Social Work
Los Angeles, CA

*California State University, Northridge
Social Work Program
Northridge, CA

California State University, Sacramento
Division of Social Work
Sacramento, CA

California State University, San
Bernardino
Department of Social Work
San Bernardino, CA

California State University, Stanislaus
Social Work Department
Turlock, CA

*Humboldt State University
Department of Social Work
Arcata, CA

Loma Linda University
Department of Social Work
Loma Linda, CA

San Diego State University
School of Social Work
San Diego, CA

San Francisco State University
School of Social Work
San Francisco, CA

San José State University
College of Social Work
San Jose, CA

University of California at Berkeley
School of Social Welfare
Berkeley, CA

University of California at Los Angeles
Department of Social Welfare
School of Public Policy and Social
Research
Los Angeles, CA

University of Southern California
School of Social Work
Los Angeles, CA

Colorado

Colorado State University
School of Social Work
Fort Collins, CO

University of Denver
Graduate School of Social Work
Denver, CO

Connecticut

Southern Connecticut State University
Graduate Social Work Program
Department of Social Work
New Haven, CT

University of Connecticut
School of Social Work
West Hartford, CT

Delaware

Delaware State University
Master of Social Work Program
Department of Social Work
Dover, DE

District of Columbia

Catholic University of America
National Catholic School of Social
Service
Washington, DC

Gallaudet University
Department of Social Work
Washington, DC

Howard University
School of Social Work
Washington, DC

Florida

Barry University
School of Social Work
Miami Shores, FL

Florida Agricultural and Mechanical
University
Department of Social Work
Tallahassee, FL

Florida Atlantic University
School of Social Work
Boca Raton, FL

Florida Gulf Coast University
Division of Social Work
College of Professional Studies
Fort Myers, FL

Florida International University
School of Social Work
Miami, FL

Florida State University
School of Social Work
Tallahassee, FL

University of Central Florida
School of Social Work
Orlando, FL

University of South Florida
School of Social Work
Tampa, FL

Georgia

Clark Atlanta University
Whitney M. Young, Jr., School of Social
Work
Atlanta, GA

Georgia State University
School of Social Work
College of Health and Human Sciences
Atlanta, GA

Savannah State University
Department of Social Work
College of Liberal Arts and Social
Sciences
Savannah, GA

University of Georgia
School of Social Work
Athens, GA

Valdosta State University
Division of Social Work
Valdosta, GA

Hawaii

University of Hawaii at Manoa
School of Social Work
Honolulu, HI

Idaho

Boise State University
School of Social Work
Boise, ID

*Northwest Nazarene University
Department of Social Work
Nampa, ID

Illinois

Aurora University
School of Social Work
George Williams College
Aurora, IL

Chicago State University
Department of Social Work
Chicago, IL

Dominican University
Graduate School of Social Work
River Forest, IL

Governors State University
College of Health Professions
Masters of Social Work Program
University Park, IL

Illinois State University
School of Social Work
Normal, IL

Loyola University of Chicago
School of Social Work
Chicago, IL

Southern Illinois University Carbondale
School of Social Work
Carbondale, IL

Southern Illinois University Edwardsville
Department of Social Work
College of Arts and Sciences
Edwardsville, IL

University of Chicago
School of Social Service Administration
Chicago, IL

University of Illinois at Chicago
Jane Addams College of Social Work
Chicago, IL

University of Illinois at Urbana-
Champaign
School of Social Work
Urbana, IL

Indiana

Indiana University
School of Social Work
Indianapolis, IN

University of Southern Indiana
Social Work Department
Evansville, IN

Iowa

St. Ambrose University
School of Social Work
Davenport, IA

University of Iowa
School of Social Work
Iowa City, IA

University of Northern Iowa
Master of Social Work Program
Department of Social Work
Cedar Falls, IA

Kansas

Newman University
Social Work Program
Wichita, KS

University of Kansas
School of Social Welfare
Lawrence, KS

Washburn University
Department of Social Work
Topeka, KS

Wichita State University
School of Social Work
Wichita, KS

Kentucky

Spalding University
School of Social Work
Louisville, KY

University of Kentucky
College of Social Work
Lexington, KY

University of Louisville
Raymond A. Kent School of Social
Work
Louisville, KY

*Western Kentucky University
Department of Social Work
Bowling Green, KY

Louisiana

Grambling State University
School of Social Work
Grambling, LA

Louisiana State University
School of Social Work
Baton Rouge, LA

Southern University at New Orleans
School of Social Work
New Orleans, LA

Tulane University
School of Social Work
New Orleans, LA

Maine

University of Maine
School of Social Work
Orono, ME

University of New England
School of Social Work
Portland, ME

University of Southern Maine
Department of Social Work
Portland, ME

Maryland

Salisbury University
Department of Social Work
Salisbury, MD

University of Maryland at Baltimore
School of Social Work
Baltimore, MD

Massachusetts

Boston College
Graduate School of Social Work
Chestnut Hill, MA

Boston University
School of Social Work
Boston, MA

*Bridgewater State College
Social Work Department
Bridgewater, MA

Salem State College
School of Social Work
Salem, MA

Simmons College
School of Social Work
Boston, MA

Smith College
School for Social Work
Northampton, MA

Springfield College
School of Social Work
Springfield, MA

Wheelock College
Division of Social Work
Boston, MA

Michigan

Andrews University
Department of Social Work
Berrien Springs, MI

Eastern Michigan University
MSW Program
Ypsilanti, MI

Grand Valley State University
School of Social Work
Grand Rapids, MI

Michigan State University
School of Social Work
East Lansing, MI

University of Michigan
School of Social Work
Ann Arbor, MI

Wayne State University
School of Social Work
Detroit, MI

Western Michigan University
School of Social Work
Kalamazoo, MI

Minnesota

Augsburg College
Department of Social Work
Minneapolis, MN

College of Saint Catherine/University of
Saint Thomas
School of Social Work
St Paul, MN

University of Minnesota-Duluth
Department of Social Work
Duluth, MN

University of Minnesota-Twin Cities
School of Social Work
St. Paul, MN

Mississippi

Jackson State University
School of Social Work
Jackson, MS

University of Southern Mississippi
School of Social Work
Hattiesburg, MS

Missouri

Saint Louis University
School of Social Service
St. Louis, MO

Southwest Missouri State University
School of Social Work
Springfield, MO

University of Missouri-Columbia
School of Social Work
Columbia, MO

University of Missouri-Kansas City
School of Social Work
Kansas City, MO

University of Missouri-St. Louis
School of Social Welfare
College of Arts and Sciences
St. Louis, MO

Washington University
George Warren Brown School of Social
Work
St. Louis, MO

Montana

*University of Montana
Department of Social Work
Missoula, MT

Nebraska

University of Nebraska at Omaha
School of Social Work
Omaha, NE

Nevada

University of Nevada, Las Vegas
School of Social Work
Las Vegas, NV

University of Nevada, Reno
School of Social Work
Reno, NV

New Hampshire

University of New Hampshire
Department of Social Work
Durham, NH

New Jersey

Kean University
Department of Social Work
Master of Social Work Program
Union, NJ

Monmouth University
Social Work Department
West Long Branch, NJ

Rutgers, The State University of New
Jersey
School of Social Work
New Brunswick, NJ

New Mexico

New Mexico Highlands University
School of Social Work
Las Vegas, NM

New Mexico State University
School of Social Work
Las Cruces, NM

New York

Adelphi University
School of Social Work
Garden City, NY

Columbia University
School of Social Work
New York, NY

Fordham University
Graduate School of Social Service
Lincoln Center Campus
New York, NY

Greater Rochester Collaborative MSW
Program
Rochester, NY

Hunter College of the City University of
New York
School of Social Work
New York, NY

*Long Island University—C.W. Post and
Brooklyn
Collaborative MSW Program
College of Management
Brookville, NY

New York University
Shirley M. Ehrenkranz School of Social
Work
New York, NY

Roberts Wesleyan College
Master of Social Work Program
Rochester, NY

*State University of New York,
Binghamton University
Division of Social Work
School of Education and Human

Development
Binghamton, NY

State University of New York at Stony
Brook
School of Social Welfare
Stony Brook, NY

State University of New York, University
at Buffalo
School of Social Work
Buffalo, NY

Syracuse University
School of Social Work
Syracuse, NY

University at Albany, State University of
New York
School of Social Welfare
Albany, NY

Yeshiva University
Wurzweiler School of Social Work
New York, NY

North Carolina

East Carolina University
College of Human Ecology
School of Social Work
Greenville, NC

*Fayetteville State University
Department of Social Work
Master of Social Work Program
Fayetteville, NC

University of North Carolina at Chapel
Hill
School of Social Work
Chapel Hill, NC

University of North Carolina at
Charlotte
Master of Social Work Program
Charlotte, NC

University of North Carolina at
Greensboro/North Carolina A&T State
University
Joint Master of Social Work Program
Greensboro, NC

North Dakota

University of North Dakota
Department of Social Work
Grand Forks, ND

Ohio

Case Western Reserve University
Mandel School of Applied Social
Sciences
Cleveland, OH

Cleveland State University/University of
Akron
Joint Master of Social Work Program
School of Social Work
College of Fine and Applied Arts
Akron, OH

Ohio State University
College of Social Work
Columbus, OH

Ohio University
Department of Social Work
Master's Degree Social Work Program
Athens, OH

University of Cincinnati
School of Social Work
Cincinnati, OH

*University of Toledo
Social Work Department
College of Health and Human Services
Toledo, OH

Oklahoma

University of Oklahoma
School of Social Work
Norman, OK

Oregon

Portland State University
Graduate School of Social Work
Portland, OR

Pennsylvania

Bryn Mawr College
Graduate School of Social Work and

Social Research
Bryn Mawr, PA

California University of Pennsylvania
Department of Social Work and
Gerontology
MSW Program
California, PA

*Edinboro University of Pennsylvania
Department of Social Work
Edinboro, PA

*Kutztown University
Social Work Program
Kutztown, PA

Marywood University
School of Social Work
Scranton, PA

Temple University
School of Social Administration
Philadelphia, PA

University of Pennsylvania
School of Social Work
Philadelphia, PA

University of Pittsburgh
School of Social Work
Pittsburgh, PA

West Chester University
Department of Graduate Social Work
West Chester, PA

Widener University
Center for Social Work Education
Chester, PA

Puerto Rico

Universidad Interamericana de Puerto
Rico, Recinto Metropolitano
School of Social Work
San Juan, PR

University of Puerto Rico, Rio Piedras
Campus
Beatriz La Salle Graduate School of
Social Work
San Juan, PR

Rhode Island

Rhode Island College
School of Social Work
Providence, RI

South Carolina

University of South Carolina
College of Social Work
Columbia, SC

Tennessee

*East Tennessee State University
Department of Social Work
Johnson City, TN

University of Tennessee
College of Social Work
Knoxville, TN

Texas

Baylor University
School of Social Work
Waco, TX

Our Lady of the Lake University
Worden School of Social Service
San Antonio, TX

Stephen F. Austin State University
Master of Social Work Program
School of Social Work
Nacogdoches, TX

*Texas A&M University—Commerce
Department of Social Work
Commerce, TX

Texas State University- San Marcos
School of Social Work
San Marcos, TX

University of Houston
Graduate School of Social Work
Houston, TX

University of Texas at Arlington
School of Social Work
Arlington, TX

University of Texas at Austin
School of Social Work
Austin, TX

University of Texas-Pan American
Department of Social Work
Edinburg, TX

Utah

Brigham Young University
School of Social Work
Provo, UT

University of Utah
College of Social Work
Salt Lake City, UT

Vermont

University of Vermont
Department of Social Work
Burlington, VT

Virginia

*George Mason University
Social Work Program
Arlington, VA

Norfolk State University
Ethelyn R. Strong School of Social
Work
Norfolk, VA

Radford University
School of Social Work
Radford, VA

Virginia Commonwealth University
School of Social Work
Richmond, VA

Washington

Eastern Washington University
School of Social Work and Human
Services
Cheney, WA

University of Washington
School of Social Work
Seattle, WA

Walla Walla College
Graduate School of Social Work
College Place, WA

West Virginia

West Virginia University
School of Applied Social Sciences
Division of Social Work
Morgantown, WV

Wisconsin

*University of Wisconsin-Green Bay and
Oshkosh
Social Work Professional Program
Green Bay, WI

University of Wisconsin-Madison
School of Social Work
Madison, WI

University of Wisconsin-Milwaukee
Helen Bader School of Social Welfare
Department of Social Work
Milwaukee, WI

Wyoming

University of Wyoming
Division of Social Work
Laramie, WY

* Program in candidacy for accreditation

The following is a list of graduate social work programs in Canada as of March 2005. The listed schools are accredited or in candidacy for accreditation by the Canadian Association of Schools of Social Work. The one in candidacy is indicated by an asterisk.

Carleton University
School of Social Work
Ottawa, ON

Dalhousie University
Maritime School of Social Work
Halifax, NS

King's University College
School of Social Work
University of Western Ontario
London, Ontario

Lakehead University
School of Social Work
Thunder Bay, Ontario

*Laurentian University/Universite
Laurentienne
School of Social Work/Ecole de Service
Social
Sudbury, Ontario

McGill University
School of Social Work
Montreal, Quebec

McMaster University
School of Social Work
Hamilton, Ontario

Memorial University of Newfoundland
School of Social Work
St. John's College
St. John's, Newfoundland

Ryerson University
School of Social Work
Toronto, Ontario

Universite Laval
Ecole de Service Social
Cité Universitaire
Québec, Québec

Universite de Moncton
Ecole de Travail Social
Moncton, Nouveau-Brunswick

Universite de Montreal
Ecole de Service Social
Montréal (Québec)

Universite d'Ottawa
Ecole de Service Social
Ottawa (Ontario)

Universite du Quebec a Montreal
Ecole de Travail Social
Montréal (Québec)

Universite du Quebec en Outaouais
Module de Travail Social
Hull (Québec)

University of British Columbia
School of Social Work
Vancouver, BC

University of Calgary
Faculty of Social Work
Calgary, Alberta

University of Manitoba
Faculty of Social Work
Winnipeg, Manitoba

The University of Northern British
Columbia
Faculty of Health and Human Sciences
Social Work Programme
Prince George, BC

University of Regina
Faculty of Social Work
Regina, Saskatchewan

University of Toronto
Faculty of Social Work
Toronto, Ontario

University of Victoria
School of Social Work
Victoria, B.C.

University of Windsor
School of Social Work
Windsor, Ontario

Wilfrid Laurier University
Faculty of Social Work
Waterloo, Ontario

York University
School of Social Work
Atkinson College
Downsview, Ontario

Appendix B

In Their Own Words:Responses to a Survey of Master of Social Work Programs in the United States

In an effort to provide the latest information from the schools themselves in this book, a survey was devised and distributed to all the social work graduate programs either accredited or in candidacy for accreditation by the Council on Social Work Education at the time of the survey. Seventy-three of the programs returned a completed survey.

The survey sought information in five major areas: contact information, descriptive information, unique aspects of each program, tips to applicants about unique factors the school looks for in applicants, and tips on common mistakes made by applicants. Most schools responded to every item, but a few chose not to respond to some items. Also, 34 schools' information from a previous, slightly different survey, is included (identified by an asterisk at the beginning of the listing).

Item I (contact information) of the survey had as its goal to provide applicants with as many current means of contacting and obtaining information from each school as possible. It asked the name of a contact person, mailing address, telephone and fax numbers, as well as e-mail and Web site addresses.

Item II (descriptive information) asked for specific factual information, including the school's accreditation status, number of students and faculty, percentage of applicants accepted, tuition costs, programs available (including advanced standing and distance education), and financial aid available. In cases in which the tuition information and accreditation status provided by the school have changed, the information listed here has been updated using information found on the schools' Web sites. Tuition costs refer to the 2004-2005 academic year, unless otherwise noted. Information that was not available is indicated with the "N.A." notation.

Item III (unique aspects of the program) sought to learn how each school views itself as compared to other programs. What does it offer (academically or otherwise) that is different from what is available at other schools? The responses are insightful not only in the information they provide about specific programs (such as rural or international social work options), but also because they reveal a great deal about each school's philosophy.

Item IV (tips for applicants) was intended to provide applicants with insight into each school's admission philosophy. It is interesting to note that each school seeks a match at two levels: (a) the general values of the profession of social work and (b) the program's specific values as reflected in its offerings.

Item V (common mistakes) sought to provide "words to the wise" about pitfalls to avoid in the application process. Some common themes emerged, and the reader would be wise to read the comments of all the schools, whether or not she intends to apply to a given school.

As much as the need for brevity allows, each school's responses are included in this Appendix essentially as the school itself wrote them. As might be expected, each school sought to "put its best foot forward" in its responses. Therefore, the responses also offer insight into what each school sees as its best qualities. In short, the responses are those of the schools, not of the publisher or the author, and do not imply any endorsement of any school or program on the part of the publisher or the author. Nevertheless, the responses are assumed to be accurate in that they were given in a responsible fashion by the schools. Applicants should obtain further information from the schools themselves, as the information provided at the time of the survey may have changed.

The responding schools are listed alphabetically. Additional schools accredited and in candidacy for accreditation by the Council on Social Work Education are listed in Appendix A.

Adelphi University School of Social Work, One South Avenue, Garden City, NY 11530. Admissions Contact: Ms. Marcia Edwards. Telephone: 516-877-4384. Fax: 516-877-4392. E-mail: edwards2@adelphi.edu Web site address: http://www. adelphi.edu/socialwork

Year accredited by CSWE: 1951
# of students: 992
# of full-time faculty: 23
# of part-time faculty: 76
% of applicants accepted: 65
Programs available: Master of Social Work (MSW) full-time, part-time, accelerated, advanced standing, one year residency. Advanced Certificate Programs in bilingual school social work, Addiction Specialist, and Human Resources Management. Doctorate of Social Welfare.
Advanced standing/advanced placement offered? yes
Distance education/online study offered? Selected video conferencing between campuses.
Tuition and/or typical assistance package: Full-time tuition & fees currently $19,550; part-time tuition currently $590 per credit. Approximately 80% of graduate social work students receive financial aid in some combination of loans, scholarships, graduate assistantships, fellowships, agency remission.
Unique aspects of the program: Our program features a concentration in clinical social work that prepares graduates for direct practice. We have flexible programming that allows students to complete degree requirements days, evenings, weekends, on a full-time or part-time basis.
Tips for applicants: Apply early, prepare application carefully, review all materials being submitted.
Common mistakes applicants make: Applicants often use the same essay for all school applications. They overlook making the changes needed for each individual application.

Andrews University, Social Work Department, Nethery Hall, Andrews University, Berrien Springs, MI 49104. Admissions Contact: Karen Stockton. Telephone: 269-471-6196. Fax: 269-471-3686. E-mail: stockton@andrews.edu Web site address: http://www.andrews.edu/SOWK

Year accredited by CSWE: 1996
# of students: 38
# of full-time faculty: 6
# of part-time faculty: 2
% of applicants accepted: 95
Programs available: MSW with concentration in Interpersonal Practice or Administration and Development.
Advanced standing/advanced placement offered? yes
Distance education/online study offered? no
Tuition and/or typical assistance package: About $545 per credit hour;

students may qualify for additional PELL grants, Michigan grants, and work-study (graduate assistantships).

Unique aspects of the program: Our mission statement emphasizes the importance of life-long learning and Christian compassion in action. It suggests that we will ever increase our store of knowledge to apply as we effectively empower others.

Tips for applicants: Designed for adult learners, our program encourages balance. All our required classes are held on Mondays, leaving the rest of the week for studying, electives, field placement settings, family life, and work, if necessary.

Common mistakes applicants make: Often we accept students pending their submitting GRE scores, with the contingency that they will turn them in by the end of their first semester. With the rigors of our program, however, they all too often do not take the exam before the deadline. They then have to petition to continue in the program.

*Arizona State University West, Department of Social Work, 4701 West Thunderbird Road, Glendale, AZ 85306-4908. Admissions Contact Person: Melissa Lavitt, Ph.D., Chair of Social Work Department, Associate Professor, and MSW Director. Telephone: 602-543-6602. Fax: 602-543-6612.
E-mail: melissa.lavitt@asu.edu
Web site address: http://www.west.asu.edu/chs/msw

Year accredited by CSWE: 2003
\# of students: 120
\# of full-time faculty: 11
\# of part-time faculty: 6
% of applicants accepted: 85

Tuition and/or typical assistance package: Tuition is $265 per credit hour for residents of Arizona and $565 per credit hour for non-residents. Title IV-E tuition waivers and stipends are available for current CPS employees, student workers. There are also scholarships for Spanish-speaking students willing to work in a Latino community agency.

Unique aspects of the program: The program prepares students to engage in culturally proficient and dynamic practice. Students are expected to develop expertise in an under-served or under-represented group. They will be able to identify "gaps" in service, theory, or research and complete an Applied Project to address these "gaps." Programs available are the MSW (Standard Program and Advanced Standing) and Title IV-E Child Welfare League Training Program. Some online courses are available.

Tips for applicants: The program looks for a commitment to social justice, as evidenced in the personal statement or work experience, as well as a commitment to and/or experience working with under-served populations.

Common mistakes applicants make: Submitting incomplete applications; not making application to both graduate studies and to the MSW program; submitting incomplete transcripts; and submitting a poorly or hastily written personal statement.

*Augsburg College, Social Work Department, 2211 Riverside Avenue South, Minneapolis, MN 55454. Admissions Contact Person: Janna Caywood. Telephone: 612-330-1233 (for application, 612-330-1763 (for questions). Fax: 612-330-1493. E-mail: swkinfo@augsburg.edu Web site address: http://www.augsburg.edu/msw

Year accredited by CSWE: 1994
#: of students: 75-100
# of full-time faculty: 17
# of part-time faculty: 5-7
% of applicants accepted: 60-70
Tuition and/or typical assistance package: Tuition is $1,600 per course (18 courses for entire curriculum, potentially as few as 13 for advanced standing). Fees include $25 per course Information Technology charge & $10 per trimester charge for parking. Ten social work scholarships are awarded to second-year students.
Unique aspects of the program: Major focus is on social justice and diversity. Courses are offered on a weekend intensive format on a trimester academic calendar (September-June). The curriculum is highly integrated and admissions operate on a cohort system. The setting is urban and class sizes are small. Field practica are offered in both urban and rural settings with a field seminar that is fully integrated with the curriculum. International electives are available, as are both micro and macro concentrations in social work practice. Concentrations include Family Practice, Program Development, and Policy and Administration. In addition, there is a dual degree program in Theology and Social Work. Online learning is not available.
Tips for applicants: Admission decisions are made on evidence of outstanding academics; solid foundation in liberal arts; ability to think clearly and communicate effectively; strong writing skills and command of English; healthy sense of self and concern for well-being of others; awareness of social issues; commitment to social justice; clear appreciation of the value base of the profession; leadership qualities; ability to work with diverse peoples and cultures.
Common mistakes applicants make: (1) No mention of limitations (important as they demonstrate self awareness and a willingness to learn). (2) When discussing personal trauma, disclosing names, or personal details that are not relevant to the topic at hand—your qualifications (if not handled professionally, this can suggest a lack of boundaries or unresolved personal issues). (3) Religious language that indicates intolerance for other religions, beliefs, or lifestyles (can suggest an inability to respect a client's values if different from yours). Augsburg is a Lutheran College, but is ecumenical in its outlook.

Aurora University, George Williams College of Health & Human Services, School of Social Work, 347 South Gladstone Avenue, Aurora, IL 60506. Admissions Contact: Ms. Jane Zimmerman, Director of University Graduate Admission. Telephone: 630-844-5292. E-mail: jzimmerm@aurora.edu Web site address: http://www.aurora.edu

Year accredited by CSWE: 1987
# of students: 300
# of full-time faculty: 12
# of part-time faculty: 9
% of applicants accepted: 80
Programs available: MSW; MSW Type 73 Illinois School Social Work; MSW cohort program at Lake Geneva, Wisconsin
Advanced standing/advanced placement offered? yes
Distance education/online study offered? no
Tuition and/or typical assistance package: Current tuition is $507.00 per semester hour. Assistance packages vary and include scholarships and loans
Unique aspects of the program: An educational philosophy that addresses social work practice with groups, understanding group affiliations as a base for human relationships, groups as sources of strength for individuals, families and the building of healthy communities as an ultimate goal of social work practice.
Tips for applicants: Desire students with GPA of 3.0 or better with strong backgrounds in human service work.
Common mistakes applicants make: Selection of recommendations that do not reflect applicant's capacity to do graduate level work.

*Barry University School of Social Work, 11300 N.E. 2nd Avenue, Miami Shores, FL 33161. Admissions Contact Person: Philip S. Mack, Director of Admissions. Telephone: 305-899-3900 or 800-756-6000, ext. 3900. Fax: 309-899-3934.
E-mail: pmack@mail.barry.edu.
Web site address: http://www.barry.edu/socialwork

Year accredited by CSWE: 1969
# of full-time faculty: 22
# of part-time faculty: 16
Programs available: BSW, MSW, Ph.D. in social work
Tuition and/or typical assistance package: $650/credit hour. More than 85% of MSW students receive scholarships or tuition discounts; more than $1.3 million is awarded each year.
Unique aspects of the program: The MSW program is known for its rich tradition of training graduates for clinical social work practice. Areas of specialization include: Children and Families and Health and Mental Health. Students may study full time or part time. Applicants who have a BSW degree received within the last five years may qualify for enrollment into the Advanced Standing program and graduate with the MSW degree in nine months.
Tips for applicants: The School looks for students who have a GPA of 3.0 or better in their last two years (60 credits) of college. Each individual application is reviewed and assessed based on the quality of each applicant's academic performance, work or volunteer experience, personal written statement, and references.
Common mistakes applicants make: Applicants often do not submit transcripts from each college attended, thereby delaying the review process.

Baylor University School of Social Work, One Bear Place, Box 97320, Waco, TX 76798. Admissions Contact: Dennis R. Myers. Telephone: 254-710-6400. Fax: 254-710-6455.
E-mail address: Dennis_Myers@baylor.edu
Web site address: http://www.baylor.edu/~Social_Work

Year accredited by CSWE: 2000
# of students: 50
# of full-time faculty: 12
# of part-time faculty: 4
% of applicants accepted: 80
Programs available: MSW-Full Program, MSW-Advanced Standing, Concentrations: (1) Physical and Mental Health and (2) Families; MDiv-MSW.
Advanced standing/advanced placement offered? yes
Distance education/online study offered? no
Tuition and/or typical assistance package: $8,950/semester; at least 50% of tuition cost may be funded
Unique aspects of the program: Students have the opportunity to integrate professional interests/social concerns within context of a flexible curriculum. Faculty are deeply committed to investment in the careers of all students. Evidence-based practice, the strengths perspective, and the ethical integration of faith and practice receive emphasis.
Tips for applicants: We seek students who are motivated by the possibility of contributing to wellness and justice for persons and communities.
Common mistakes applicants make: Not making sure references are sent and not getting the GRE completed on a timely basis.

Boise State University School of Social Work, 1910 University Drive, Boise, ID 83725-1940. Admissions Contact: William H. Simpson Whitaker. Telephone: 208-426-2579. Fax: 208-426-4291.
E-mail address: wwhitak@boisestate.edu
Web site address: http://http://www.boisestate.edu/socwork/msw/index.html

Year accredited by CSWE: 1992
# of students: N.A.
# of full-time faculty: 10
# of part-time faculty: 4
% of applicants accepted: N.A.
Programs available: One concentration: Advanced social work practice with families and individuals; school social work certificate; gerontology certificate; child welfare education through Title IV-E; International study and placement opportunities; legislative placements available (20-minute walk to state capitol). Strong macro and policy practice infusion in curriculum. Strong micro practice emphasis.
Advanced standing/advanced placement offered? yes
Distance education/online study offered? no

Tuition and/or typical assistance package: Fees for state residents (2004) $4,668/year. Fees for non-residents (2004) $11,388/year. Graduate assistantships, child welfare stipends, some grants, work study, loans, some agency stipends are available.

Unique aspects of the program: Boise State offers a first-class program with solid grounding in both micro and macro practice. Our location in Idaho's state capital is conducive to policy practice. We offer small classes, close interaction with faculty, and bonding with a small cohort of excellent students. We have a strong interest in social justice, global issues, and environmental context. We have easy access to Idaho's mountains, streams, and desert. Our students engage in a full range of outdoor recreational activities in one of the best locations in the United States.

Tips for applicants: We seek highly motivated students with a passion for social work and social justice. Experience as a member of or work with and commitment to practice with culturally diverse populations is desirable. Spanish language ability is an asset for social work practice in our region.

Common mistakes applicants make: Our application includes two important essays. These should reflect an applicant's very best critical thinking and very best writing. Applications for financial aid and graduate assistantships should reflect thoughtful, serious work. We begin reviewing applications in early February and use rolling admissions. It is to an applicant's advantage to submit a complete application by mid-January.

Boston University School of Social Work, 264 Bay State Road, Boston, MA 02215. Admissions Contact: Ed Greene. Telephone: 617-353-3765. Fax: 617-353-5612.
E-mail: busswad@bu.edu
Web site address: http://www.bu.edu/ssw

Year accredited by CSWE: 1939
# of students: 350
# of full-time faculty: 21
# of part-time faculty: 15
% of applicants accepted: 80
Programs available: Certificates in Human Service Management, Family Therapy, social work and behavioral medicine, and gerontology. MSW, MSW/JD, MSW/MED, MSW/EdD, MSW/MPH, MSW/STH, MSW/MDiv., MSW/DMin., Ph.D in Sociology and Social Work.
Advanced standing/advanced placement offered? yes
Distance education/online study offered? no
Tuition and/or typical assistance package: Tuition is $20,972 per year. $655/credit on campus, and $450/per credit off campus. Tuition assistance packets range from full tuition to half tuition, $5,000 awards and/or loans. Work study is available to those who qualify.
Unique aspects of the program: Boston University has an urban mission and is located in an urban area. We have major methods of Clinical and Macro Social Work. We offer a clinical major with a macro sub-specialization. We have leading faculty members, and students will get to know their professors. While

Boston University is large, the School of Social Work is small. Class sizes are 16-20 students.
Tips for applicants: We seek mature and committed students for our program. We look for students who know who they are, even if they do not know exactly in what segment of social work they will eventually work. Good students who have practical knowledge are desirable.
Common mistakes applicants make: Spelling mistakes in the personal statement. Also, poorly written statements that do not flow logically. Bad references. Get people who can speak to your ability to do graduate social work, and not friends of the family. One reference should be practical or from a work setting, and at least one should be from an academic setting.

Bridgewater State College, Graduate and Continuing Education, Maxwell Library, L 6, Bridgewater, MA 02325. Admissions Contact: Dr. James Decker. Telephone: 508-531-1300. Fax: 508-531-6162. E-mail: gradschool@bridgew.edu
Web site address: http://www.bridgew.edu/SocialWork/grad.cfm

Accredited by CSWE: no
In candidacy for accreditation: yes
# of students: 95
# of full-time faculty: 7
% of applicants accepted: 70
Programs available: Full-time program, Part-time program, Advanced Standing program, Part-time Advanced Standing program.
Advanced standing/advanced placement offered? yes
Distance education/online study offered? no
Tuition and/or typical assistance package: A graduate three-credit course in the evening (after 4 p.m.) including tuition and fees for Spring and Summer 2004 is $681.51. There is no additional charge for an out-of-state resident taking a graduate evening course.
Unique aspects of the program: Bridgewater State College is the only public higher education institution located in the Southeastern region of Massachusetts. We provide a quality program at an affordable price. Our faculty have outstanding reputations in this field and offer exceptional guidance for those students in the MSW program or thinking of joining.
Tips for applicants: Bridgewater State College is looking for those students dedicated to contributing their experiences, expertise, and commitment in a community setting. Students interested in applying should have a strong desire to strengthen community relationships and to have a positive working relationship with individuals, families, and groups.
Common mistakes applicants make: The most common mistakes we see from applicants are having a recommendation completed by a friend or relative and not having provided all application requirements by the required deadline. Applicants for the MSW program should attempt to obtain recommendations from supervisors in a relative field or associates in a volunteer organization. In addition, careful thought and consideration must be given to the essay. Any applicant who is concerned about the admissions criteria should not hesitate to

phone our office to make an appointment or to speak with the graduate coordinator.

Brigham Young University, School of Social Work, 221 Knight Mangum Building, Provo UT 84602. Admissions Contact: Lisa Willey. Telephone: 801-422-3282. Fax: 801-422-0624.
E-mail: socialwork@byu.edu
Web site address: http://www.socialwork.byu.edu

Year accredited by CSWE: 1981
# of students: 80
# of full-time faculty: 12
# of part-time faculty: 10
% of applicants accepted: 30
Programs available: MSW degree, emphasis in direct clinical practice with focus on family and children.
Advanced standing/advanced placement offered? no
Distance education/online study offered? no
Tuition and/or typical assistance package: Tuition per semester (5 semesters total) for members of The Church of Jesus Christ of Latter-Day Saints is $2,070. Tuition for members of other faiths is $3,105 per semester. We have three tuition-only scholarships, as well as graduate assistantships (work for pay), paid fieldwork placements, and applicants can apply for Stafford Loans (formerly Guaranteed Student Loans) and BYU Short-Term Loans. For more information, please refer to: http://fhss.byu.edu/socwork/mswfinancialaid.html
Unique aspects of the program: BYU is a private, religious-based university. The concentration of our curriculum is on direct clinical practice, with focus on family and children.
Tips for applicants: Please make sure you include your volunteer experience in your application. The applicants for our program are so numerous that those who have their prerequisites completed (as opposed to being currently enrolled, or "I'll take those after I'm accepted...") have quite the advantage.
Common mistakes applicants make: Please write the SOCIAL WORK statement of intent, as opposed to the generic BYU standard statement of intent. Please make sure you list all your prerequisites, and note those that are complete and those in which you are currently enrolled.

*Bryn Mawr College Graduate School of Social Work and Social Research, 300 Airdale Road, Bryn Mawr, PA 19010-1697. Admissions Contact Person: Nancy J. Kirby, Director of Admissions. Telephone: 610-520-2601. Fax: 610-520-2655.
E-mail: swadmiss@brynmawr.edu
Web site address: http://www.brynmawr.edu/socialwork/

Year accredited by CSWE: 1919
# of students: approximately 175
# of full-time faculty: 14
# of part-time faculty: 9

% of applicants accepted: 70

Tuition and/or typical assistance package: Tuition for 2003-2004 was $2,640 per course for the master's programs and $3,370 per doctoral course. Eighteen courses are required for the MSS degree, eight for the MLSP, and 14 for the Ph.D. The School offers generous financial aid. In 2003-2004, 74% of students were awarded financial aid by the institution, with the average award being $7,000 for part-time students and $11,500 for full-time students.

Unique aspects of the program: The Graduate School of Social Work and Social Research is a coeducational program located in suburban Philadelphia. A small, supportive learning environment with an interdisciplinary faculty, the School has been preparing social workers for practice and academia for over 85 years. Full-time and part-time courses of study are available, with classes held during day, afternoon, and evening hours. There are also two evening summer sessions. There are more than 160 agencies in the greater Philadelphia region used as field placement sites. It is possible for some students to use their employment as a field placement site. A comprehensive career development and job placement program is available to students and graduates. Bryn Mawr offers a unique joint degree program in social work and law and social policy. Bryn Mawr offers three degree programs: the Master of Social Service (MSS), the Master of Law and Social Policy (MLSP), and the Doctor of Philosophy (Ph.D.). Students in the MSS program can select from three concentrations: clinical social work, social service management, and planning and program development. Full-time students complete the degree in two years, while the part-time program is three years. The MLSP degree focuses on the use of legal skills and principles in the human services and is usually completed in 12 months, including one summer session. The MSS and the MLSP degrees may be pursued simultaneously. The Ph.D. program emphasizes policy analysis, program development, and clinical theory and research.

Distance education/online study offered? no

Advance standing/advanced placement offered? no

Tips for applicants: Admissions decisions are made by a committee composed of faculty members and current students. Accepted applicants have academic records that indicate the ability to handle a demanding graduate program, human services experience through employment, volunteer work, or internships, strong oral and written communication skills, maturity, and self-awareness.

Common mistakes applicants make: The most common mistake is not taking the time to present a thoughtful, clearly written and edited essay.

*California State University, Department of Social Work, 9001 Stockdale Highway, Bakersfield, CA 93311. Admissions Contact Person: Dr. Thomas Madhavappallil. Telephone: 661-664-2470. Fax: 661-665-6928.
E-mail: pcadena@csub.edu
Web site address: http://www.csub.edu/socialwork

Year accredited by CSWE: 2003
# of students: 85
# of full-time faculty: 10

# of part-time faculty: 2
% of applicants accepted: 70-80%
Tuition and/or typical assistance package: Current tuition for residents is approximately $940 per quarter for full-time study. Non-residents pay an additional $226/credit. There are about 40 scholarships of about $18,500 for full-time study. Other scholarships are available.
Unique aspects of the program: Two concentrations are offered: (1) Families and Children Services and (2) Health and Mental Health Services. The curriculum emphasizes research and technology. The program has a very experienced faculty.
Tips for applicants: We look for intellectual ability and leadership potential. Have a good GRE score and write the personal statement well.
Common mistakes applicants make: Poorly written personal statement.

California State University, Chico, School of Social Work, Chico, CA 95929-0550. Admissions Contact: Lesley Curry. Telephone: 530-898-4226. Fax: 530-898-5574.
E-mail: lcurry1@csuchico.edu
Web site address: http://www.csuchico.edu/swrk

Year accredited by CSWE: accredited, year not known
# of students: 73
# of full-time faculty: 7
# of part-time faculty: 10
% of applicants accepted: 45
Programs available: MSW—Advanced Generalist Practice with focus areas in Mental Health Services, and in Families, Children, and Youth Services.
Advanced standing/advanced placement offered? yes
Distance education/online study offered? no
Tuition and typical assistance package: Tuition prior to new state budget: full-time graduate student is $1,503 per semester plus books; non-residents pay an additional $282 for each semester unit taken. Title IV-E stipends are available for students in the 2-year program. Student loans are available.
Unique aspects of the program: Advanced standing available for eligible applicants. The MSW program emphasizes close student-faculty guidance and mentoring relationships resulting in high graduation and postgraduate employment rates. There are interesting practice electives that support the advanced generalist concentration focus areas. The program prepares all students for advanced practice that includes the ability to move into supervisory and program development and management roles.
Tips for applicants: The program seeks students who are dedicated to working with diverse populations to help meet the need for professional social work services in social service agencies, and who have a desire to improve the quality of human/social services.
Common mistakes applicants make: Not realizing that the program is full-time, and working and going to graduate school is very difficult. The personal statement is not well presented, thoughtful, clearly written, or edited.

California State University, San Bernardino, 5500 University Parkway, San Bernardino CA 92407-2397. Admissions Contact: Dr. Nancy L. Mary. Telephone: 909-880-5560. Fax: 909-880-7029. E-mail: nmary@csusb.edu Web site address: http://www.socialwork.csusb.edu.

Year accredited by CSWE: 2004
# of students: 150
# of full-time faculty: 12
# of part-time faculty: 3
% of applicants accepted: N.A.
Programs available: Master of Social Work
Advanced standing/advanced placement offered? no
Distance education/online study offered? no
Tuition and/or typical assistance package: $752.00 per quarter (3 quarters). Nonresident tuition is $188 per unit (Master's Program is 90 units). Department does not have scholarships. University offers some student scholarships and loans.
Unique aspects of the program: Our curriculum offers both micro and macro practice in both the foundation and advanced year of the program. We have done this in response to the employers who have told us that MSWs need to be able to practice at all levels in today's marketplace. The emphasis in the advanced year is on interdisciplinary and interagency change making and leadership. Students are not "tracked" into a limited number of specializations, but rather choose their own social problem, population, or field of practice as their specialization and then apply their advanced year research and classroom assignments to this topic.
Tips for applicants: We are looking for applicants who want to make change in both family systems and larger social systems.
Common mistakes applicants make: They do not consider how the demands of the program will affect the ability to work full time.

*California State University Stanislaus, Department of Social Work, 801 West Monte Vista, Turlock, CA 95382. Admissions Contact Person: Barbara Dimberg. Telephone: 209-667-3091. Fax: 209-667-3869. E-mail: bdimberg@stan.csustan.edu Web site address: http://www.csustan.edu/Social_Work/index.htm

Year accredited by CSWE: 1998
# of students: 120
# of full-time faculty: 12
# of part-time faculty: 3
% of applicants accepted: 50
Tuition and/or typical assistance package: For full-time students who are California residents, the tuition rate is $247 for Winter and $911 for Spring. Nonresidents pay an additional $339/credit. Child Welfare and Mental Health stipends are available as are more conventional financial aid packages.

Unique aspects of the program: The School offers the MSW degree. The School focuses on integrative practice, an empowerment approach, rural and urban practice, and preparation for practice in a multicultural environment. Advanced placement and distance education or online study are not available.

Tips for applicants: Applicants should demonstrate a desire to practice in agency settings with diverse populations through past experiences in multicultural settings.

Common mistakes applicants make: Inadequate autobiographical statement lacking in knowledge of the profession.

California University of Pennsylvania, MSW Program, Box 90, 250 University Drive, California, PA 15419-1394. Admissions Contact: Wilburn Hayden, Jr.. Telephone: 412-431-4022. Fax: 412-431-1651. E-mail: hayden@cup.edu
Web site address: http://www.cup.edu/graduate/msw/

Year accredited by CSWE: 2004
# of students: 45
# of full-time faculty: 6
% of applicants accepted: 95
Programs available: MSW—Advanced Generalist in Rural Social Work Practice
Advanced standing/advanced placement offered? yes
Distance education/online study offered? no
Tuition and/or typical assistance package: Tuition for 2004-2005 (subject to change). Additional fees are required. Pennsylvania Residents: Full-time Graduate (per semester), $2,886.00 for 9 to 15 credits Part-time Graduate (per semester), $321.00 per credit. Non-Pennsylvania Residents, Full-time Graduate (per semester), $4,618.00 for 9 to 15 credits Part-time Graduate (per semester), $513.00 per credit
Unique aspects of the program: Our MSW program, as supported by our Feasibility Study, is a response to the need for advanced generalist, professionally educated social workers with a concentration in small towns and rural social work practice. Our program integrates social work knowledge, skills, research, and values into a curriculum that prepares competent, effective social workers committed to providing services to a variety of persons living in diverse small towns and rural communities. At the center of our purpose is a commitment to people who are poor, oppressed, and at-risk as well as working to alleviate poverty, oppression, exploitation, discrimination, and other social toxins. Our students are prepared to work in all aspects of social work practice. This could be case management, therapy, group work, management, policy, community, or research, for example. One way to think of it is a GP in medicine, as opposed to a specialist physician. The difference is that an advanced generalist trained social worker can specialize without additional specialized course work. The degree enables them to use continuing education and work experience to develop the specialization, if they want to do so.
Tips for applicants: A desire to work, live, and play in small towns and rural environments is an important aspect.

Common mistakes applicants make: The two major mistakes students make in applying to our program are: waiting too late to submit the application materials and not scheduling the GRE in time. We have a July deadline for Fall and December deadline for Spring admissions. Applicants tend to wait and miss the deadlines.

Case Western Reserve University, The Mandel School, 10900 Euclid Avenue, Cleveland, OH 44106-7164. Admissions Contact: Joan Horinka. Telephone: 216-368-2280 or 1-800-863-6772. Fax: 216-368-5065. E-mail: msassadmit@po.cwru.edu Web site address: http://msass.cwru.edu

Year accredited by CSWE: 1919
# of students: 330
# of full-time faculty: 33
% of applicants accepted: N.A.
Programs available: Master of Science in Social Administration (M.S.S.A.); dual degrees with MBA, and Law and Management of Non-Profits. We also offer a Ph.D. in Social Welfare.
Advanced standing/advanced placement offered? yes
Distance education/online study offered? no
Tuition and/or typical assistance package: Tuition is $25,100. We offer full-time students a *paid field placement!*

*Clark Atlanta University School of Social Work, 223 James P. Brawley Drive, S.W., Atlanta, GA 30314-4391. Admissions Contact Person: Mary C. Ashong. Telephone: 404-880-8861. Fax: 404-880-6434. Web site address: http://www.cau.edu/

Year accredited by CSWE: accredited, year not known
Tuition and/or typical assistance package: $539/credit hour
Unique aspects of the program: The School has a clinical concentration. There are two areas of specialization: Health/Mental Health and Child and Family. The Child and Family has a sub-specialization in School Social Work.
Tips for applicants: (1) A baccalaureate degree that reflects a broad liberal arts base, (2) openness, (3) maturity, (4) capacity for empathy, (5) psychologically minded, (6) interest in working with people in a professional helping role.
Common mistakes applicants make: Some autobiographical statements are too short and do not reflect the applicants' experience and reasons for choosing social work as a profession.

College of St. Catherine/University of St. Thomas (joint program), School of Social Work, Mail #LOR 406, 2115 Summit Avenue, St. Paul, MN 55105. Admissions Contact: Jon Ruzek, MSW Program Manager. Telephone: 651-962-5810. Fax: 651-962-5819. E-mail: msw@stthomas.edu http://www.stthomas.edu/socialwork

Year accredited by CSWE: 1992
# of students: 250
# of full-time faculty: 10
# of part-time faculty: 9
% of applicants accepted: 70
Programs available: Dual degrees: MA Theology/MSW, Master of Divinity/ MSW, JD/MSW
Advanced standing/advanced placement offered? yes
Distance education/online study offered? Advanced standing, out-of-state weekend cohort comes to St. Paul one weekend a month, online assignments/ papers in between.
Tuition and/or typical assistance package: Tuition: $493.50 per credit (for 2004-2005 academic year). Types of financial aid: federal student loans, private/commercial student loans, university scholarships, department scholarships, research assistantships
Unique aspects of the program: Our clinical social work program is unique in the upper Midwest area, and only one of a few in the entire country. If you want to work as a clinician with individuals, small groups and families, you will leave our program well prepared! As a joint program, we have the strengths and resources of two institutions. Our faculty teach all our classes (no TAs). The faculty is nationally recognized and approachable. Our field placements are varied and we give personalized student service. You are never just a number in our program.
Tips for applicants: We look for students who have social work experience, or involvement with human services/volunteer activities. We want people who are willing to learn and listen to others' perspectives and have an interest in social justice and the welfare of others.
Common mistakes applicants make: Writing too little on the personal statement—one page will not do. Write something thoughtful, yet not too lengthy (4-6 pages). If you have no social work/human service/volunteering experience, you need to demonstrate in your activities why you are interested in pursuing the MSW degree.

Colorado State University, School of Social Work, 127 Education, Fort Collins, CO 80523-1586. Admissions Contact: Dawn Carlson. Telephone: 970-491-2536. Fax: 970-491-7280.
E-mail: dcarlson@cahs.colostate.edu
Web site address: http://www.cahs.colostate.edu/sw/ MSWProgram200203.htm

Year accredited by CSWE: 1987
# of students: 141
# of full-time faculty: 10
# of part-time faculty: 2
% of applicants accepted: 25
Programs available: Advanced Generalist
Advanced standing/advanced placement offered? yes

Distance education/online study offered? We have a current 3-year cohort on the western slope of Colorado. Not available for new students
Tuition and/or typical assistance package: $4,206 for residents, $14,929 for non-residents per year.
Unique aspects of the program: We are the only state university in Colorado offering the MSW. Our first-year students come to campus two days per week for the first year's curriculum. The concentration year has two options for coming to campus, while serving internships. They can either come one week per month, four times per semester, or two nights per week all semester.
Tips for applicants: We are looking for applicants with some experience in the human service field who can write well and have an understanding of the advanced generalist approach.
Common mistakes applicants make: Applicants need to follow the directions in the packet very carefully. We have a non-negotiable deadline of January 31. Some do not sufficiently answer the questions asked for their essays.

Dominican University Graduate School of Social Work, Priory Campus, 7200 W. Division Street, River Forest, IL 60305. Admissions Contact: Kate Hamilton, Director of Admissions. Telephone: 708-366-3463. Fax: 708-366-3446.
E-mail: msw@dom.edu
Web site address: http://www.socialwork.dom.edu

Year accredited by CSWE: 2004
# of students: 225
# of full-time faculty: 6
% of applicants accepted: N.A.
Programs available: Clinical Family Centered
Advanced standing/advanced placement offered? yes
Distance education/online study offered? no
Tuition and/or typical assistance package: $570/credit hour—every class is 3 credits, tuition assistance varies every semester. Students are encouraged to apply for the Dean's scholarship—based on individual need per semester.
Unique aspects of the program: The Graduate School of Social Work at Dominican University has a clinical family-centered, strength-based focus. Our program was the first family-centered MSW program in Illinois. The Graduate School of Social Work is conveniently located just 10 miles west of Chicago's loop. Our beautiful, wooded campus and ivy-covered Gothic architecture provides a unique and inviting atmosphere and an aesthetically pleasing learning environment. Students are trained to work with different age groups throughout the life cycle, and diverse populations, in a variety of settings. We offer a small, supportive atmosphere encouraging the pursuit of knowledge. Class sizes are purposefully kept small and intimate to provide for meaningful class discussions and group projects. The collaborative environment among students, and the low faculty-student ratio, ensure maximum learning. We offer four different programs: 2-year full-time program, 3-year part-time program, 1-year full-time advanced standing and 2-year part-time advanced standing. All part-time classes are available in the evenings, allowing for students to maintain employment while pursu-

ing their Master's degree. Our faculty and staff ensure flexibility with each individual student's academic and community interests. We offer a full-time Field Work Director to collaborate with students to form links with community agencies and sites. In the pursuit of social work research, the Graduate School of Social Work offers a research center to advance and strengthen student and faculty research interests. A student association provides further links between the School of Social Work and the community it serves. We are an actively growing program, accepting applications on a rolling basis. Students are welcome to start during the Fall, Spring, or Summer semesters.

Fayetteville State University, Department of Social Work, 1200 Murchison Road, Fayetteville, NC 28301-4298. Admissions Contact: Dr. Terri Moore Brown. Telephone: 910-672-1210. Fax: 910-672-1755.
E-mail: socialwork.dept@uncfsu.edu
Web site address: http://www.uncfsu.edu/sw/

Accredited by CSWE: no
In candidacy for accreditation: yes, accreditation expected 2006
# of students: 15
# of full-time faculty: 6
% of applicants accepted: 85
Programs available: Master of Social Work Program. Degree Awarded: MSW. Concentrations Areas: Children and Family Services, Mental Health and Substance Abuse.
Advanced standing/advanced placement offered? yes
Distance education/online study offered? no
Tuition and/or typical assistance package: In-state tuition is $2,309 per year and out-of-state tuition is $11,824 per year. Tuition assistance package includes loans, graduate assistantships, and other financial aid resources. Tuition and fees are subject to change.
Unique aspects of the program: The MSW program is designed to prepare students for advanced professional practice and leadership with a focus on children and families, and mental health and substance abuse. Students are also prepared to serve as leaders and advocates for socioeconomic justice in a multicultural society and in the global community. Additionally, students are prepared to engage in prevention, intervention, clinical practice, and administration activities that promote human well being in urban and rural areas. The program seeks to further students' knowledge in alleviating oppression, poverty, and discrimination. Fayetteville State University is located near the Fort Bragg and Pope Air Force Base military installations, which enables the program to give special emphasis on the effects of military life on individuals, families, groups, organizations, and communities.
Tips for applicants: Applicants should be able to advocate for at-risk populations and work effectively with diverse populations with passion, commitment, and resiliency. Applicants should demonstrate willingness to become leaders and change agents by generating and implementing innovative ideas for advanced social work practice.

Common mistakes applicants make: Common mistakes applicants make are: 1) not taking the GRE and submitting scores before the application admission deadline; and 2) not submitting all required documents (i.e., transcripts, recommendation letters, personal statement) needed to complete the student application package.

*Florida Atlantic University, School of Social Work, 777 Glades Road, Social Science Building, Boca Raton, FL 33431. Admissions Contact Person: Elwood R. Hamlin II, DSW. Telephone: 561-297-3234. Fax: 561-297-2866. E-mail: ehamin@fau.edu Web site address: http://www.fau.edu/divdept/caupa/

Year accredited by CSWE: 2002
# of students: 57
# of full-time faculty: 6
# of part-time faculty: 2
% of applicants accepted: 85
Tuition and/or typical assistance package: Graduate tuition is $191.04 per semester credit for Florida residents and $798.07 per semester for non-Florida residents.
Unique aspects of the program: Florida Atlantic University's School of Social Work is committed to offering quality experiences in clinical-community social work practice. The program is geared to meet the needs of the diverse populations in south Florida. There is a strong linkage between field education and the academic classroom. The program offers two concentrations in the advanced curriculum: children and families, and health and aging. Both are reflective of the current and future needs of south Florida. A child welfare certificate is also available. Advanced placement is offered; however, distance or online study is not.
Tips for applicants: The program looks for motivation and commitment to the social work profession as demonstrated by academic grades, life experiences, work history, and personal qualities such as a commitment to social and economic justice.
Common mistakes applicants make: The GRE is a state requirement, and some applicants fear the examination. The School advises applicants to take the GRE as soon as possible and submit the application at their earliest convenience and not later than April.

Florida Gulf Coast University, Division of Social Work, 10501 FGCU Boulevard South, Fort Myers, FL 33965-6565. Admissions Contact: Daysi Mejia, D.S.W.. Telephone: 239-590-7825. Fax: 239-590-7758. E-mail: graduate@fgcu.edu Web site address: cps.fgcu.edu/sw/index.html

Year accredited by CSWE: 2004
# of students: 35
# of full-time faculty: 8

# of part-time faculty: 5
% of applicants accepted: 50
Programs available: The Master of Social Work degree has its basis under the clinical community practice method. Specialization offered: Administrative Social Work
Advanced standing/advanced placement offered? yes
Distance education/online study offered? Several academic graduate courses are offered online.
Tuition and/or typical assistance package: $198.51/credit for in-state resident, $733.04/credit for out-of-state non-resident. Tuition assistance opportunities include: Federal Stafford Loan (low interest loans available for independent and dependent students), Graduate Assistantships (the number of tuition waivers available are allocated by individual colleges), and the Federal Work Study Program (Federally-funded program in which students can earn their financial aid award).
Unique aspects of the program: The Master of Social Work degree at Florida Gulf Coast University offers a program that prepares students with a solid foundation to become professional, autonomous, and pro-active social workers. In accordance with the university mission statement on diversity, the Master of Social Work program not only has a very diverse staff, but also offers comparative international exchanges in South America and Europe. When in their academic sessions, students learn how to integrate clinical practice in a community setting, as well as the integration of the Capstone project with their Research methods courses. Students are constantly challenged in the classroom to effectively intervene with individuals, groups, and communities.
Tips for applicants: The small classroom sizes provide grounds for students to integrate, question, and acquire the necessary information to be competent leaders in the social work field. The close-knit faculty and staff also provide ground for students to be at constant interaction in which they can acquire the utmost knowledge to develop into professional social workers.
Common mistakes applicants make: Not completing their supplemental package information.

**Florida State University, School of Social Work, 2500 University Center C, Tallahassee, FL 32306-2570. Admissions Contact: Craig Stanley. Telephone: 800-378-9550. Fax: 850-644-9750.
E-mail: grad@ssw.fsu.edu
Web site address: http://ssw.fsu.edu**

Year accredited by CSWE: 1950
# of students: 297
# of full-time faculty: 33
# of part-time faculty: 10
% of applicants accepted: 75
Programs available: Clinical Social Work Concentration, Social Policy and Administrative Social Work Concentration, MSW/Juris Doctorate Dual Degree Program, MSW/Master's in Public Administration Dual Degree Program, MSW/Ph.D.

Advanced standing/advanced placement offered? *yes*
Distance education/online study offered? We have the only CSWE-accredited, fully Web-based, advanced-standing MSW program in the nation.
Tuition and/or typical assistance package: Current In-State Tuition: $196.27/credit hour. Current Out-of-State Tuition: $730.80/credit hour. The School offers a variety of scholarships. The deadline for application is March 1 of each year. To view scholarships, visit: *http://ssw.fsu.edu/current-scholarships.html.* Graduate assistantships may be applied for when completing an application for any semester. Typically, assistantships entail tuition waiver money, as well as a stipend. For more information on these, visit: *http://ssw.fsu.edu/adm-financial-aid.html*
Unique aspects of the program: The FSU School of Social Work is the only school that is ranked by *U.S. News & World Report* in the State of Florida. FSU is a Florida Research I institution; faculty are engaged in a number of projects and studies that help to enhance student learning. The faculty are very available to students and enjoy engaging with students in and out of the classroom. Our Field Office is a very strong part of our formula for success. We have worked hard to foster field placements, throughout the State of Florida as well as internationally, to ensure that students have quality practica that are pertinent to the students' areas of interest. We are one of a few schools in the nation that offer a Social Policy and Administrative (SPA) concentration. We are located in the state capital of Florida, which makes this curriculum very hands-on for students who are interested in policy. We are the first School of Social Work that offers a totally Web-based MSW for advanced-standing students. This program is offered on a part-time basis only and is fully accredited by CSWE. It is currently only available to students residing in Florida and Southern Alabama.
Tips for applicants: We look for students who are well rounded as evidenced by a solid academic record, work/volunteer experience in human services, and strong personal character that exhibits social work values. We expect students to be able to articulate how they plan to utilize their education once they have completed our program.
Common mistakes applicants make: It is important to answer all of the questions that are asked in the guidelines for our personal statement. Prospective students often use a general statement that they have submitted to other schools, and this costs them on the application.

*Fordham University Graduate School of Social Service, 113 W. 60th Street, Lincoln Center Campus, New York, NY 10023-7479. Admissions Contact Person: Elaine Gerald, Assistant Dean and Director of Admissions. Telephone: 212-636-6600. Fax: 212-636-6613. E-mail: gerald@fordham.edu. Web site address: http://www.fordham.edu

Year accredited by CSWE: accredited, year not known
# of students: 950
# of full-time faculty: 42
# of part-time faculty: 85+
% of applicants accepted: approximately 60

Tuition and/or typical assistance package: Tuition is $605/credit hour. The program offers loan, scholarship, and work study opportunities. Financial aid packages are individualized, and financial aid at Fordham is a process, not an event. **Unique aspects of the program:** Fordham offers the degrees of BSW, MSW, and Ph.D. The MSW program has an advanced placement option and specializations in Children and Families, Substance Abuse, and Managed Care. Joint degrees include MSW/JD and MSW/MDiv. Fordham does not have distance or online study at this time. **Tips for applicants:** A mature, empathic applicant is a desirable candidate. Good writing skills are very important and are assessed by the quality of the statement. **Common mistakes applicants make:** Using a relative or therapist as a reference and not proofreading the statement.

Gallaudet University, 800 Florida Avenue N.E., Washington, DC 20002. Admissions Contact: Wednesday Luria-Appell. Telephone: 202-651-5000. E-mail: Wednesday.Luria-Appell@gallaudet.edu Web site address: http://gradschool.gallaudet.edu/gradschool/ index.html and http://depts.gallaudet.edu/social.work/

Year accredited by CSWE: 1994
# of students: 50
# of full-time faculty: 6
# of part-time faculty: 5
% of applicants accepted: N.A.
Programs available: MSW. School Social Work specialization is available. Dual degree option: MSW/MA Supervision and Administration.
Advanced standing/advanced placement offered? yes
Distance education/online study offered? Online courses are available during the last semester of the program to accommodate block internships.
Tuition and/or typical assistance package: $5,300 per semester. Stipends and ½-tuition scholarships are available to school social work students. Graduate assistantships, work study, and tuition scholarships are also available.
Unique aspects of the program: The MSW program at Gallaudet University is a unique accredited social work program that prepares students for advanced generalist social work practice concentrating on deaf and hard-of-hearing people, their families, communities, and organizations throughout the world. At Gallaudet, Deaf and hearing graduate students study together on a beautiful campus in our nation's capital. Students and faculty interact using American Sign Language. With support from the U.S. Department of Education, Gallaudet's MSW Program offers students the option of specializing in school social work with deaf and hard-of-hearing youth. The school social work specialization is accredited by NCATE. Students also have the option of a dual degree in social work (MSW) and Administration and Supervision. In addition, students have a variety of exciting internship options locally, nationally, and internationally in educational settings, clinical settings, mental health centers, family and child service agencies,

Congressional offices, hospitals, and many other community organizations. Graduates of our program find they are in high demand by employers who are seeking qualified social workers to provide services to deaf and hard-of-hearing people throughout the world.

Tips for applicants: Applicants should have an undergraduate GPA of 3.0 or higher, demonstrate a strong commitment to social justice, have an interest in working with people who are deaf and hard-of-hearing, and skills in American Sign Language.

Common mistakes applicants make: Applicants must understand that the goals of this program are to prepare graduates with the competence and commitment to work toward ensuring that deaf and hard of hearing people throughout the country and the world have the same opportunities and resources that are available to other groups. Applicants must demonstrate sufficient skills in conversational sign language to participate effectively in signed classroom interaction and internships with deaf and hard-of-hearing people.

*Indiana University, School of Social Work, 902 W. New York Street E/S4133, Indianapolis, IN 46202-5156. Admissions Contact Person: Sherry Gass, ACSW, LCSW. Telephone: 317-274-6705. Fax: 317-274-8630.
E-mail: stgass@iupui.edu
Web site address: http://socialwork.iu.edu

Year accredited by CSWE: 1923
# of students: 400
# of full-time faculty: 45
# of part-time faculty: varies
% of applicants accepted: N.A.

Tuition and/or typical assistance package: Tuition for Indiana residents is $201.85/credit hour and $582.55/credit hour for non-residents. Limited dollars are available for tuition assistance and work study positions.

Unique aspects of the program: The IU School of Social Work has an extensive network of statewide practicum opportunities. The School is in close proximity to the State Capitol, thereby allowing for direct access for impact on policy decisions. The School has an urban mission with a strong emphasis on social justice. IU offers concentrations in interpersonal practice and macro practice. Advanced placement is offered, and distance or online study is not.

Tips for applicants: IU looks for highly committed persons interested in advancing their knowledge base and practice skills and those persons who are committed to social justice—also, those interested in learning about social work practice in a variety of settings, including urban and rural areas.

Common mistakes applicants make: Displaying poor writing skills and submitting weak references.

Indiana University Northwest, 3400 Broadway, Gary, IN 46408. Admissions Contact: Cindy Abney. Telephone: 219-980-7111. Fax: 219-981-4264.

E-mail: cabney@iun.edu
Web site address: http://www.iun.edu/~socialwk

Year accredited by CSWE: 1996
# of students: 175
# of full-time faculty: 5
# of part-time faculty: 12
% of applicants accepted: 85
Programs available: Mental Health and Addiction concentration. Leadership concentration.
Advanced standing/advanced placement offered? yes
Distance education/online study offered? no
Tuition and/or typical assistance package: Currently the per credit hour fee is $184 for Indiana residents and $437.80 for non-residents. Additional course-related fees may apply. Loans and scholarships are available.
Unique aspects of the program: We offer a three-year part-time program with concentrations in Mental Health and Addictions, as well as Leadership. The program is designed for working professionals. Advanced standing is possible for graduates of CSWE-accredited BSW programs. We do not offer a full-time program.
Tips for applicants: We look for applicants who demonstrate a commitment to social and economic justice and are committed to the values of the social work profession.
Common mistakes applicants make: The most common mistake is emphasizing a narrow interest in a field of social work that does not reflect an appreciation for the values of the profession. Another common error is turning in a narrative that contains grammatical, spelling, or other major writing mistakes.

Jackson State University, School of Social Work, 3825 Ridgewood Road, Jackson, MS 39211. Admissions Contact: Dr. Desiree Stepteau-Watson. Telephone: 601-432-6819. Fax: 601-432-6827.
E-mail: mswprog@jsums.edu
Web site address: http://www.jsums.edu/socialwork/msw.htm

Year accredited by CSWE: 1998
Programs available: The Master of Social Work and Doctor of Philosophy in Social Work degrees are offered at Jackson State University. The focus of the MSW Program is clinical practice with children, youth, and families. The goal of the Ph.D. program is to develop social work scholars, researchers, and educators who will advance knowledge and skills about social work practice and social welfare policy, planning, and administration.
Advanced standing/advanced placement offered? yes
Distance education/online study offered? Some courses are available online.
Tuition and/or typical assistance package: Graduate scholarships, graduate assistantships, and graduate work-study are offered by the Jackson State University, Division of Graduate Studies. Scholarships provide either full or partial tuition waivers.
Unique aspects of the program: Jackson State University, School of Social

Work provides students with the knowledge, skills, and values and ethics of the profession. The School's goal is to produce graduates who will apply their knowledge and skills toward enhancing the quality of life in both urban and rural environments.

Tips for applicants: Desirable applicants include those who demonstrate the ability to conduct critical analysis of social issues and the unique position of the profession to respond to political, economic, and social problems.

Common mistakes applicants make: Common mistakes include failing to submit all required documents with the application and failing to submit a separate application to the Division of Graduate Studies. Another mistake is submitting a poorly written and constructed personal statement.

Kean University, 1000 Morris Union, NJ. Admissions Contact: Dorothy B. Rowe. Telephone: 908-737-4047. Fax: 908-7374064. E-mail: drowe@kean.edu Web site address: http://www.kean.edu

Year accredited by CSWE: 1996
# of students: 100
# of full-time faculty: 6
# of part-time faculty: 3
% of applicants accepted: 49
Programs available: MSW Advanced Generalist specialization
Advanced standing/advanced placement offered? yes
Distance education/online study offered? no
Tuition and/or typical assistance package: $4,651(tuition & fees). Graduate assistantships, financial aid, student loans, and work study are available.
Unique aspects of the program: The Advanced Generalist specialization not only gives you clinical training, but also provides exposure to management and supervisory issues, as well as grant writing. We offer small class size and ready access to professors. Tuition is low for the full-time program.
Tips for applicants: Write your own personal statement! Graduate school is a sacrifice—it is not easy!
Common mistakes applicants make: They don't write their own statements. If they do write their own statements, they don't let someone else read it to make sure that it makes sense.

Kutztown University of Pennsylvania, Social Work Program, P.O. Box 730, Kutztown, PA 19530. Admissions Contact: Dr. John Vafeas, DSW, LSW. Telephone: 610-683-4235. Fax: 610-683-4383. E-mail: msw@kutztown.edu Web site address: http://www.kutztown.edu

Accredited by CSWE: no
In candidacy for accreditation: yes, accreditation expected 2005
# of students: 25
# of full-time faculty: 10
# of part-time faculty: 5

% of applicants accepted: N.A.
Programs available: Advanced Generalist MSW in Family-in-Environment
Advanced standing/advanced placement offered? yes
Distance education/online study offered? no
Tuition and/or typical assistance package: Full-time, in-state tuition plus fees (subject to change): $3,432. Graduate assistantships (full tuition plus stipend) available to some students, as well as work study for eligible students' internships; research assistantships and supported internships may also be available on a limited basis
Unique aspects of the program: The program itself is a living example of family-centered policy practice: concepts of advanced generalist social work practice from the Family-in-Environment perspective are developed, taught, and carried out. The learning environment is designed to be one of accessible, affordable, academic excellence in which students are challenged to explore and define "family" in non-traditional ways. Students, faculty, and human service providers collaborate to provide services to families at risk, intervene with families in crisis, and change the social environment to support the families of today and tomorrow. Students develop specialization in counseling, administration, program evaluation, and other individualized areas through field experiences and six, one-credit elective courses.
Tips for applicants: Do not hesitate to take the GRE. It is one criterion of many considered in the application process.
Common mistakes applicants make: Do not include outdated research in the essay portion of the application.

*Loyola University Chicago, School of Social Work, 820 N. Michigan Avenue, Chicago, IL 60611. Admissions Contact Person: Jude Gonzales, Director of Admissions. Telephone: 312-915-7005. Fax: 312-915-7645.
E-mail: socialwork@luc.edu
Web site address: http://www.luc.edu/schools/socialwork

Year accredited by CSWE: accredited, year not known
# of students: 350
# of full-time faculty: 26
# of part-time faculty: 26
% of applicants accepted: N.A.
Tuition and/or typical assistance package: Tuition is $522 per credit hour. The MSW takes 55 credit hours to complete. Loyola's School of Social Work offers scholarships and graduate assistantships. There are both need- and merit-based awards.
Unique aspects of the program: Loyola University's Graduate School of Social Work is a single specialization school, concentrating on training students at the clinical level. This prepares students to practice in areas in which knowledge and skill in direct service are essential. These include mental health, school social work, medical social work, child welfare, elderly services, substance abuse, employee assistance, and counseling of individuals, families, and small groups. Loyola offers the MSW on a part-time or full-time basis. Dual degrees offered

include; MSW/JD, MSW/M.Div, MSW/MJ in Child and Family Law, and MSW/ MS in Child Development. The MSW can be taken at the Water Tower Campus (downtown Chicago) or at Carthage College (in Wisconsin). Advanced placement is offered.

Tips for applicants: Loyola looks favorably on a well rounded undergraduate preparation, preferably in the liberal arts. Some experience in the field of social services (paid or volunteer) is also recommended. Letters of recommendation should come from different sources, with at least one being a social service setting.

Common mistakes applicants make: Sending an incomplete application. Send it only when all the information required has been collected.

Marywood University School of Social Work, 2300 Adams Ave, Scranton, PA 18509. Telephone: 866-279-9663. Fax: 570-961-4742. E-mail: grad_adm@marywood.edu http://www.marywood.edu/ssw/main.stm

Year accredited by CSWE: 1969
# of students: 350
# of full-time faculty: 16
# of part-time faculty: 14
% of applicants accepted: 80
Programs available: MSW, MSW/MPA (Master's of Public Administration), MSW/MPA (Master's of Public Administration with concentration in Criminal Justice), MSW/MHSA (Master's of Health Services Administration), MSW/AT (Certificate of Advanced Graduate Studies in Art Therapy), MSW/MDiv or MSW/ MPC (Master's of Divinity or Pastoral Counseling. This is a joint program with Moravian Seminary)
Advanced standing/advanced placement offered? yes
Distance education/online study offered? Portions of some courses
Tuition and/or typical assistance package: $627/credit. Scholarship assistance for new students is need-based; additional scholarships related to field placement, (e.g., work study funds for field experience hours), Social Justice Incentive scholarships for field experience in social justice-focused agencies. Most students apply for federal student loan funds.
Unique aspects of the program: First, Marywood SSW's curriculum stresses breadth of preparation. Students select electives and field placements to add depth in areas of their choosing. Knowledge and skills are intended for practice in under-resourced communities, which include small cities and towns and rural America, as well as economically and socially disadvantaged groups. Second, the program develops strongly cohesive cohorts of students, whose learning benefits from the opportunity to gain from each others' experience.
Tips for applicants: The graduates we are proudest of are those who demonstrate commitment, resourcefulness, and energy in their careers, so that's what we hope to see in applicants.
Common mistakes applicants make: A common mistake is failing to develop goals for oneself— "what do I want to gain from this degree program"— which will be the basis for all the choices a student has to make in the course of Marywood's MSW program.

Michigan State University, School of Social Work, 254 Baker Hall, East Lansing, MI 48824. Admissions Contact: Joan Ilardo Deller, MSW for program questions or Nancy Gray for process questions. Telephone: 517-353-8632. Fax: 517-353-3038. E-mail: socialwork@ssc.msu.edu http://www.ssc.msu.edu/~sw

Year accredited by CSWE: 1952
# of students: 300
# of full-time faculty: 15
# of part-time faculty: 15
% of applicants accepted: 80
Programs available: Master's in Clinical Social Work, Master's in Organizational and Community Practice Social Work, Certificate programs in: Clinical Social Work with Families, Child and Family Advocacy/Law and Social Work Program, School Social Work, Social Work with Older Adults, Organizational and Community Practice in the Urban Arena, Infant Studies
Advanced standing/advanced placement offered? yes
Distance education/online study offered? We have a branch campus in Flint, Michigan and offer the MSW program in other areas of the state.
Tuition and/or typical assistance package: Current in-state tuition is $291 per credit hour. Out-of-state tuition is $589.25.
Unique aspects of the program: Through our teaching, research, and outreach, we are committed to a leadership role promoting positive social change. We are committed to social justice and encourage thoughtful and effective activism. We foster and encourage accessibility with regard to our educational programs. We are committed to work in collaborative relationships with other professionals, professions, disciplines, and organizations. Our educational offerings and programs encourage critical thinking, personal respect and freedom of thought and expression. We promote diversity with regard to characteristics, qualities, and viewpoints as a necessary and valued foundation for the achievement of our mission. Our programs encourage creativity, reflect the best strength-based practices in the field, connect field education and community-based experiences to classroom instruction, and support high standards of professional achievement by our graduates.
Tips for applicants: We use a holistic admissions process that assesses applicants' professional and academic characteristics as evidenced by their GPA, work and volunteer experiences, references, and applicant essay.
Common mistakes applicants make: Not reading and following the directions for completing the application materials.

*Monmouth University, Department of Social Work, 400 Cedar Avenue, West Long Branch, NJ 07764. Admissions Contact Person: Dr. Mark Rodgers. Telephone: 732-571-3606. Fax: 732-263-5217. E-mail: rodgers@monmouth.edu. Web site address: http://www.monmouth.edu/socialwork/

Year accredited by CSWE: accredited, year not known
# of students: 180
# of full-time faculty: 12
# of part-time faculty: 6
% of applicants accepted: 60
Tuition and/or typical assistance package: Tuition is $605/credit hour. Loans are available through the Financial Aid Office. Graduate assistantships are available on a limited basis campus-wide.

Unique aspects of the program: The program developed the first American MSW concentration in International Community Development. Students in this concentration can elect to complete their field internship overseas in approved sites. Concentrations available include (1) Practice with Families and Children (PFC) and (2) International Community Development (ICD). Advanced placement is offered, as is distance or online study. Many courses are Web enhanced and some courses (i.e., supervision) are conducted entirely online.

**New Mexico Highlands University, P.O. Box 9000, Las Vegas, NM 87701. Admissions Contact: Evelyn Estrada, Interim Admissions. Telephone: 505-454-3310. Fax: 505-454-3290.
E-mail: maragon@nmhu.edu
Web site address: http://www.nmhu.edu/socialwork**

Year accredited by CSWE: 1978
# of students: 150
# of full-time faculty: 15
# of part-time faculty: 20
% of applicants accepted: N.A.
Programs available: Master of Social Work. Concentrations are Direct Practice, Clinical Practice, Community Practice.
Advanced standing/advanced placement offered? yes
Distance education/online study offered? Interactive television courses
Tuition and/or typical assistance package: Approximately $1,100 in-state, approximately $4,500 out-of-state.
Unique aspects of the program: Our program is designed to develop culturally aware and sensitive social workers to serve the populations in the southwest United States—Hispanic and American Indian clientele. We are recognized as an "Academic School of Excellence."
Tips for applicants: Demonstrate an interest in working with diverse populations. Have an interest in working with populations in the southwest. Have human service work experience.
Common mistakes applicants make: Failure to submit a professionally written career objective statement with application. Failure to submit official transcripts from all institutions of higher learning.

New Mexico State University, School of Social Work, P.O. Box 30001, MSC 3446, Las Cruces, NM 88003. Admissions Contact: Carol L. MacAllister, MSW. Telephone: 505-646-3529 or 505-646-3227. Fax: 505-646-6166.

E-mail: cmacalli@nmsu.edu
Web site address: http://www.nmsu.edu/~socwork/

Year accredited by CSWE: 1991
# of students: 200
# of full-time faculty: 12
# of part-time faculty: 8
% of applicants accepted: 50
Programs available: Master's with two minors: gerontology, and alcohol and drug counseling
Advanced standing/advanced placement offered? yes
Distance education/online study offered? MSW is offered on a part-time basis in Albuquerque in compressed format. In this off campus site, as well as on the main campus, some courses are offered on WebCT, but the entire program is not available online.
Tuition and/or typical assistance package: Graduate tuition is currently $1,800 per semester for NM residents and $5,800 for non-residents per semester. Title IV-E stipends, work study, and graduate assistantships are available. Other financial aid information can be found on the NMSU Web site, the Graduate School page, and Financial Aid page: http://www.nmsu.edu
Unique aspects of the program: Our graduate specialization in family centered practice in multi-cultural settings. The school is located in a border community with Mexico.
Tips for applicants: Strong liberal arts background and willingness to explore new cultures.
Common mistakes applicants make: 1. Not realizing that the application requires two parallel steps—application to the NMSU Graduate School AND application to the School of Social Work. 2. Insufficient attention to the specifics requested in the applicant's personal statement. 3. Failure to observe the application deadline date.

*New York University, Ehrenkranz School of Social Work, 1 Washington Square North, New York, NY 10003. Admissions Contact Person: Director of Admissions and Financial Aid. Telephone: 212-998-5910. Fax: 212-995-4171.
E-mail: essw.admissions@nyu.edu
Web site address: http://www.socialwork.nyu.edu

Year accredited by CSWE: 1955
# of students: 1,200
# of full-time faculty: 45
# of part-time faculty: 120
% of applicants accepted: 40
Tuition and/or typical assistance package: Tuition is $620.00 per credit with a $45.00 services fee. Our typical aid package includes the full array of student loans and the availability of scholarships that can total anywhere from 25% to 60% of tuition. Any applicant interested must complete the FAFSA. Approximately 75% of our full-time students get scholarship assistance.

Unique aspects of the program: The New York University Shirley M. Ehrenkranz School of Social Work is widely known for professional education in clinical work with individuals, families, and groups. Study in all programs is organized around small classes, articulation of hands-on field placement and academic work, experienced faculty members who practice what they teach, and a uniquely supportive advisement system. Students in all programs are trained in two or more of the 350 field instruction sites at which the school has arranged experienced on-site supervision. NYU is an integral part of the metropolitan community of New York City, an international capital of art, culture, business, and finance and home of the United Nations. Located in historic Washington Square in the heart of Greenwich Village, NYU allows students to have the city's extraordinary resources at their doorstep. Programs available include BSW, MSW, and Ph.D. in Clinical Social Work. The MSW can be completed full-time in the two-year, 16-month continuous study, or in one year through advanced standing programs. The MSW can be done part-time in the one-year residence or Matriculating Individualized Plan. The two-year program begins only in September, as does the advanced standing program. The 16-month continuous study begins only in January. The part-time programs can start in September, January, or May. Programs are offered at four sites, Washington Square (the main campus), Rockland County, Staten Island, and Westchester County. There is a joint MSW/MS with the School of Public Service with majors in Health Care Administration or Health Care Policy, as well as Public Administration or Public Policy. There is also a joint MSW/JD with the law school. Distance or online study is not offered.
Tips for applicants: The school looks for applicants who are committed to social justice and care about people and their well being.

*Newman University, Graduate School of Social Work, 3100 McCormick Avenue, Wichita, KS 67213. Admissions Contact Person: Mike Smith, Dean. Telephone: 316-942-4291, ext. 324. Fax: 316-942-4483.
E-mail: smithm@newmanu.edu
Web site address: http://www.newmanu.edu

Year accredited by CSWE: accredited, year not known
Tuition and/or typical assistance package: $346/credit hour. The MSW scholarship is available to employees of Catholic organizations who demonstrate financial need. ($500/semester).
Unique aspects of the program: MSW graduate program with a family-centered concentration. We offer full-time and part-time programs, as well as an advanced standing program. We feature small classes with individualized attention and a nurturing learning environment with highly qualified faculty.

Ohio State University College of Social Work, 1947 College Road, Columbus, OH 43210. Admissions Contact: Sharon Schweitzer. Telephone: 614-292-2972. Fax: 614-292-6940.
E-mail: schweitzer.2@osu.edu
Web site address: http://www.csw.ohio-state.edu

Year accredited by CSWE: 1919
# of students: 390
# of full-time faculty: 28
# of part-time faculty: 10
% of applicants accepted: 50
Tuition and/or typical assistance package: $8,250 for Ohio residents, $20,133 for non-residents.
Programs available: Joint degrees in public policy and management and city and regional planning. Interdisciplinary specialization in aging. Joint MSW/Ph.D. program.
Advanced standing/advanced placement offered? yes
Distance education/online study offered? no
Unique aspects of the program: We prepare excellent practitioners. Our practice faculty have considerable practice experience, and we place a high emphasis in the second MSW year on practical application. Our faculty are highly prolific writers. You will learn from faculty who wrote the books and articles, and who have practiced what they teach.
Tips for applicants: We seek a diverse student body that is committed to their own personal and educational growth, and committed to the values of the social work profession.

Ohio University Department of Social Work, 416 Morton Hall, Athens, OH 45701. Admissions Contact: Dr. Susan Sarnoff. Telephone: 740-593-1292. Fax: 740-593-0247.
E-mail: sarnoff@ohio.edu
Web site address: http://www.socialwork.ohiou.edu/

Year accredited by CSWE: 2002
# of students: 65
# of full-time faculty: 12
# of part-time faculty: 2
% of applicants accepted: N.A.
Programs available: BASW, MSW with a specialization in Rural Social Work and a choice of Concentrations in Clinical or Administrative Social Work.
Advanced standing/advanced placement offered? yes
Distance education/online study offered? Some online electives, cohort program rotationally delivered to regional campuses.
Tuition and/or typical assistance package: Graduate tuition per quarter (9-18 credits) is $2,651 for residents, $5,095 for non-residents. Federal grants and loans are available, as well as scholarships based upon merit. Graduate research and teaching assistantships are available based upon merit and ability to perform research/teach.
Unique aspects of the program: Our small, rural-focused program offers frequent faculty contact and close interaction among students and faculty. We also focus on providing the tools for self-learning and continuing education—development of library search skills, writing skills, and the ability to communicate with clients, colleagues, funders, and advocacy targets via oral presentations, text, graphics, and technology.

Tips for applicants: We seek applicants with a commitment to serving rural families and communities and learning best practices through research and continued, self-directed education.

Common mistakes applicants make: Not following instructions, especially not following up with referees or in regard to transcripts, not meeting deadlines, especially for stipends, focusing on interest in the profession rather than the ability to contribute to it.

Portland State University Graduate School of Social Work, P.O. Box 751, Portland, OR 97207. Admissions Contact: Janet Putnam. Telephone: 1-800-547-8887 ext 4712. Fax: 503-725-5545. E-mail: putnamj@pdx.edu Web site address: http://www.ssw.pdx.edu

Year accredited by CSWE: 1964

# of students: 387

# of full-time faculty: 33

# of part-time faculty: 12

% of applicants accepted: 33

Programs available: Master in Social Work with concentrations in Direct Human Services, Community Based Practice, and Social Service Administration and Management; Ph.D. in Social Work and Social Work Research.

Advanced standing/advanced placement offered? yes

Distance education/online study offered? 3-year cohorts in Oregon, currently centered in Salem and Ashland

Tuition and/or typical assistance package: Resident $195 per credit hour; non-resident $364 per credit hour; Federally guaranteed student loans up to federal maximum; work study if qualified.

Unique aspects of the program: Two-, three-, and four-year options; classes meet once a week with concurrent field placements two days a week. Eighteen credit hours of elective options in children and families, aging studies, mental health, health, policy-practice, and at-risk populations.

Tips for applicants: Demonstrated academic success, experience related to social work, references who can speak to performance and promise in the social work field, and a personal statement that reflects an understanding of social work values and commitment to service to vulnerable populations.

Common mistakes applicants make: 1. Not answering the guiding questions in the personal statement. 2. Applying without having gained experience in the social work field.

Radford University, Radford University School of Social Work, Radford University, P.O. Box 6958, Radford, VA 24142. Admissions Contact: Anne Dornberg. Telephone: 540-831-7684. Fax: 540-831-7670. E-mail: adornber@radford.edu Web site address: http://www.radford.edu/~sowk-web

Year accredited by CSWE: 1996

# of full-time faculty: 8

# of part-time faculty: 5
% of applicants accepted: N.A.
Programs available: MSW (Community-based family practice focus)
Advanced standing/advanced placement offered? yes
Distance education/online study offered? We have another campus in Abingdon, Virginia, but do not have online study.
Tuition and/or typical assistance package: Current tuition is $215.00/ credit hour for in-state students and $397.00 per credit hour for out-of-state students. Most students who want them are able to get an assistantship ($3,100-$5,214) and many of our students are awarded child welfare stipends ($8,000/ yr). Students also receive loans and Veteran's administration stipends.
Unique aspects of the program: We excel in teaching social work practice in rural communities, and we also do a great job of teaching students to work with diverse client populations. We also offer a part-time advanced standing program, while many other schools do not.
Tips for applicants: We look for applicants who have a passion for social work, have strong interpersonal skills, write well, are compassionate, and who are critical thinkers. There is something very refreshing about an applicant who knows how s/he wants to utilize the MSW—someone who has a vision of how s/he will put the program into practice when they graduate.
Common mistakes applicants make: (1) Writing a personal essay that lacks real insight, and/or has grammatical errors. (2) Not having the application in on time.

Roberts Wesleyan College, 2301 Westside Drive, Rochester, NY 14624. Admissions Contact: Jim Sheets. Telephone: 585-594-6011. Fax: 585-594-6480.
E-mail: mswadmissions@roberts.edu
Web site address: http://www.roberts.edu/msw

Year accredited by CSWE: 1996
# of students: 138
# of full-time faculty: 9
# of part-time faculty: 8
% of applicants accepted: 65
Programs available: Child & Family Services, Church Social Work, Community Practice, Child & Family Services, Physical & Mental Health Services, Physical & Mental Health Services, Collaborative MSW/MDiv.
Advanced standing/advanced placement offered? yes
Distance education/online study offered? no
Tuition and/or typical assistance package: $449 per credit hour, Fellowship Grant, Stafford Loan.
Unique aspects of the program: Only program that offers Church Social Work. One of three Christian MSW programs in the country. 96% pass licensure exam (the national average is 78%). First accredited social work program in Rochester, NY.
Tips for applicants: We look to see if the applicant has the ability to write at a graduate level through the autobiographical statement they turn in. List every-

thing you can think of that might even remotely fall into the social work category.

Common mistakes applicants make: (1) Not listing all the colleges/universities where they have taken college credit. (2) They do not use the recommendation forms that we provide. All recommendation forms must be filled out using one of our forms.

Salem State College School of Social Work, 352 Lafayette Street, Salem, MA 019790. Admissions Contact: Donna Besecker. Telephone: 978-542-6340. Fax: 978-542-7215. E-mail: donna.besecker@salemstate.edu Web site address: http://www.salemstate.edu

Year accredited by CSWE: 1989
# of students: 250
# of full-time faculty: 15
# of part-time faculty: 25
% of applicants accepted: N.A.
Programs available: Advanced Standing Program: MSW; MSW Program
Advanced standing/advanced placement offered? yes
Distance education/online study offered? First online course offered in the Fall of 2004. The course will combine periodic on-campus meetings with the majority of the course available online.
Tuition and/or typical assistance package: Advanced Standing tuition and fees: $9,900. Regular MSW Program: $13,950. Because our tuition is so affordable, financial assistance is primarily in the form of Federal Low Interest Education Loans. We also offer a number of graduate assistantship positions for which students receive full tuition remission and a monthly stipend. Commonwealth of Massachusetts employees are eligible for a 50% tuition remission.
Unique aspects of the program: With an Advanced Generalist orientation, students receive a combination of clinical theory and training, along with macro theory and training throughout the curriculum. We offer small seminar style classes taught by faculty who are accessible and actively engaged in the social work community, locally and nationally. Students select an area of concentration among the following: Child & Family Services, Health & Mental Health Services, and Older Adult/End of Life Care Services. Field placements are plentiful and designed to accommodate students' learning needs in a convenient geography. Field placements are accompanied by integrated field seminars conducted by faculty. Each year, there is an international seminar involving travel (7-21 days) and study in another country (El Salvador, Barbados, India, China, to name a few).
Tips for applicants: We seek a diverse, mature student body, ideally with paid work experience in the human services. We also look for applicants committed to work with oppressed and vulnerable populations in the public sector or publicly funded agencies.
Common mistakes applicants make: Less than careful editing and proofreading of personal statement.

San Diego State University, School of Social Work, College of Health and Human Services, San Diego State University, 5500 Campanile Drive, San Diego CA 92182-4119. Admissions Contact: Student Affairs Coordinator. Telephone: 619-594-6865. Fax: 619-594-5991. E-mail: socwork@mail.sdsu.edu
Web site address: http://www.sdsu.edu (go to social work in directory of departments)

Year accredited by CSWE: 1966
# of students: 400
# of full-time faculty: 15-20
# of part-time faculty: 5-10
% of applicants accepted: 33
Programs available: Master of Social Work; MSW/MPH Master of Social Work/Public Health, MSW/JD Master of Social Work/Juris Doctorate Law; Pupil Personnel Services Credential (School Social Work); Child Welfare Training Program.
Advanced standing/advanced placement offered? no
Distance education/online study offered? About every three years, we offer a distance education program in the Imperial Valley for residents of the Valley area.
Tuition and/or typical assistance package: For California residents, fees are approximately $1,300 per semester for students taking 6.1 units or more. Non-residents pay the same rate plus an additional fee of about $280 per unit. Sixty percent of social work students receive financial aid. Must submit the FAFSA application through the Financial Aid Office on campus. Work study is available for undergraduate students.
Unique aspects of the program: We have an excellent faculty who strive to make the students' educational experience a good one. Our academic program is rigorous, exhilarating, and absorbing. Students will have many opportunities to examine, probe, and challenge their ideas and capabilities. The School takes very seriously its responsibility for the education of new social workers who will ultimately initiate, provide direction for, and implement the changes that will be necessary in their communities. We look forward to engaging those challenges and involving students in working toward the development of solutions to society's needs.
Tips for applicants: Applicant should understand and express a commitment to the profession of social work, values related to the profession of social work, and be prepared to the level of commitment required to obtain a degree in social work including internship/field requirements.
Common mistakes applicants make: Having limited knowledge or narrow view of the social work profession as expressed in the personal statement, low Bachelor's GPA without an explanation of how applicant will handle graduate level work (i.e., maintain a 3.0 GPA).

Smith College School for Social Work, Office of Admission, Lilly Hall, Northampton, Massachusetts 01063. Admissions Contact: Pat Graham. Telephone: 413-585-7960. Fax: 413-585-7990.

E-mail: sswadmis@email.smith.edu
Web site address: http://www.smith.edu/ssw

Year accredited by CSWE: 1923
# of students: 351
# of full-time faculty: 14
# of part-time faculty: 110
% of applicants accepted: N.A.
Programs available: Master of Social Work, Ph.D. in Clinical Social Work.
Advanced standing/advanced placement offered? yes
Distance education/online study offered? no
Tuition and/or typical assistance package: MSW full 27-month tuition is $34,610.
Unique aspects of the program: The Smith College School for Social Work offers clinical training toward an MSW or Ph.D. in Social Work, including field internships around the country. Classes are held during a 10-week on-campus instruction period. Field placements take place between September and April in agencies across the country.
Tips for applicants: Candidates for admission must be graduates of accredited colleges and universities, though no specific undergraduate major is required. We normally require 20 semester hours in social, biological, or psychological sciences and prefer candidates with at least one year of paid or volunteer experience in human services.
Common mistakes applicants make: It is important to be at least familiar with the structure of the program, because it is a unique block plan.

Southern Illinois University Carbondale School of Social Work, 875 S. Normal Avenue, Quigley Hall, Carbondale, IL 62901-4329. Admissions Contact: Judy Wright. Telephone: 618-453-2243. Fax: 618-453-4291.
E-mail: mmmjw@siu.edu
Web site address: http://www.siu.edu/~socwork

Year accredited by CSWE: 1988
# of students: 72
# of full-time faculty: 6
# of part-time faculty: 3
% of applicants accepted: 50
Programs available: The School offers the MSW degree with emphasis on community-based social services. Concentrations in (1) Children, Youth, and Families and (2) Health/Mental Health are offered. Also, students in the Children, Youth, and Families concentration can qualify to take the School Social Work Certificate exam by taking additional courses. The School offers a concurrent degree program with law (J.D./MSW).
Advanced standing/advanced placement offered? yes
Distance education/online study offered? no
Tuition and/or typical assistance package: Current tuition is $179.00 per semester hour for Illinois residents and $358.00 for non-residents, plus student

fees. There are graduate assistantships, fellowships, and loans available.
Unique aspects of the program: Our School provides training that will emphasize an advanced area of concentration for practice with individuals, families, groups, organizations, and communities. The curriculum is designed for practice in small towns and rural communities but is applicable to communities and neighborhoods in urban and suburban areas and international settings, as well. Our diverse faculty has a breadth and depth of talents as educators, scholars, and social workers in a variety of specialty areas. Our School provides numerous opportunities for your professional development through course work and projects, practica and association with our child welfare and community-based social development initiatives.

Tips for applicants: We look for a clear commitment to human services, particularly to disadvantaged populations. Preference is given to those with paid or volunteer experience in the human services field.

Common mistakes applicants make: Poorly written personal statements, failure to send official transcripts from all colleges/universities attended.

*Southern Illinois University Edwardsville Department of Social Work, Box 1450, Edwardsville, IL 62026. Admissions Contact Person: Dr. Donald Scandell. Telephone: 618-650-5758. Fax: 618-650-3509. Web site address: http://www.siue.edu/social/

Year accredited by CSWE: 2004
Tuition and/or typical assistance package: Tuition for 2005-2006 is $190/ credit for Illinois residents, $380 for out-of-state residents.
Unique aspects of the program: Academic offerings include generalist practice in Children and Family Services and in Health, Mental Health, and Disabilities Services. Predominantly evening class schedule to accommodate nontraditional students.
Tips for applicants: We look for applicants with commitment to practice with vulnerable at-risk populations.

*Southern University at New Orleans, School of Social Work, 6200 Press Drive, New Orleans, LA 70119. Admissions Contact Person: James Donald Smith, ACSW, Associate Professor and Director of Student Affairs. Telephone: 504-286-5376. Fax: 504-286-5387.

Year accredited by CSWE: 1985
# of students: 256
# of full-time faculty: 21
# of part-time faculty: 15
% of applicants accepted: 88
Unique aspects of the program: The School attracts a diversity of students from a variety of economic, social, and ethnic backgrounds. The classroom experiences are exciting (and challenging) as students struggle to understand and share the "richness of differences" that shape modern society. Within the context of a diversified learning environment, traditional views are challenged and students are encouraged to eliminate personal and institutionalized barriers that

limit the growth potential within themselves and individuals in society. The School offers concentrations in Health/Mental Health; Children, Youth, and Families; and Gerontology. Advanced placement is available, and the School is exploring options for distance and online study.

Tips for applicants: Past academic performance, work experience, references, and a personal statement are all considered.

Common mistakes applicants make: The School requires a liberal arts core of courses, and some applicants don't realize that they must take these courses to be eligible to apply for admission.

*Southwest Missouri State University, School of Social Work, 901 South National Avenue, Springfield, MO 65804-0095. Admissions Contact Person: Mary Ann Jennings, MSW, Ph.D., MSW Program Chair. Telephone: 417-836-5069 or 417-836-5787. Fax: 417-836-7688. E-mail: maj398f@smsu.edu Web site address: http://www.smsu.edu/swk/index.html

Year accredited by CSWE: 1998
# of students: 100
# of full-time faculty: 12
# of part-time faculty: 8
% of applicants accepted: 65

Tuition and/or typical assistance package: Tuition for Missouri residents is $177 per credit hour. Tuition for non-residents is $354 per credit hour. Fees are $254 for seven or more hours. Students from surrounding states attending the program offered in Joplin, Missouri do not pay out-of-state tuition or fees. The program currently offers one scholarship in the amount of $600 to $750. There are typically four graduate assistantships in the department, which cover tuition and fees and provide a $6,000 per year stipend. There are numerous graduate assistantships in other departments on campus. Student loans are available, and there are limited paid practica.

Unique aspects of the program: The program offers the only Family Health concentration in the country. The focus is on promoting and maintaining wellness of families as the primary unit of socialization and support in our society. Students can concentrate their efforts on families at various stages of the family development cycle. The MSW program is offered primarily in the afternoon, late afternoon, and evening to accommodate working students. The MSW part-time program is offered in Joplin, Missouri, approximately 70 miles southwest of Springfield. Students from Oklahoma, Arkansas, Kansas, and Missouri attend the Joplin campus. The program is offered only in the evening to accommodate working students. Advanced placement is offered. The program typically offers at least one class per year through distance learning. As of yet, there are no courses offered online.

Tips for applicants: (1) Apply on time. (2) Be sure the application package is complete. (3) Be sure to understand the mission of the School of Social Work and what the profession of social work entails.

Common mistakes applicants make: (1) Thinking you can apply any time and be admitted. (2) Thinking the program will prepare you to be a psychotherapist upon graduation.

Spalding University School of Social Work, 851 S. Fourth Street, Louisville, KY 40203. Admissions Contact: Susan Grace. Telephone: 502-585-9911 ext. 2183. Fax: 502-992-2413.
E-mail: socialwork@spalding.edu
Web site address: http://www.spalding.edu/socialwork

Year accredited by CSWE: 1999
# of students: 50
# of full-time faculty: 7
# of part-time faculty: 9
% of applicants accepted: 85
Programs available: MSW
Advanced standing/advanced placement offered? yes
Distance education/online study offered? no
Tuition and/or typical assistance package: Tuition is $460/hr plus course-related fees of approximately $200/semester. Our financial aid office works with the student to secure all eligible financial aid. There is a graduate assistantship that is controlled by the university, plus one scholarship in research worth approximately $1,200. Scholarships are available in child welfare. Employees of the Kentucky Cabinet on Children and Families receive a 25% discount.
Unique aspects of the program: The Spalding University School of Social Work is designed for the non-traditional student interested in social justice, critical thinking, and integrative practice at the micro, mezzo, and macro levels. The small enrollment allows for a high-touch faculty. All courses are offered on the weekend. Students take two courses at a time and meet every other weekend for six sessions, then move on to the next set of courses. It is regarded as a full-time program and students do complete the MSW in two years (Advanced Standing is available). The weekend program allows students to enroll from a large geographic region. 80% of our students do not reside in the Louisville area, but commute in for the weekend classes.
Tips for applicants: Applicants with experience and an idea of where they are going in practice are helpful. All applicants are interviewed as part of the application process, allowing us to reflect on the applicant as a whole person, not just a set of scores.
Common mistakes applicants make: Potential applicants often assume that a "low" GPA rules you out. This is not so, as we look at the whole person. Applicants sometimes wait until they have all their materials to send in. Don't wait; we start processing your application with whatever we receive. Earlier is better, but we do rolling admission until two weeks before the start of classes.

*Springfield College School of Social Work, 263 Alden Street, Springfield, MA 01109-3797. Admissions Contact Person: Mae Chillson, Admissions Coordinator. Telephone: 413-748-3060 or 413-748-3225. Fax: 413-748-3069.
E-mail: Mae_Chillson@spfldcol.edu
Web site address: http://www.springfieldcollege.edu

Year accredited by CSWE: 1993
# of students: 200
# of full-time faculty: 8
# of part-time faculty: 6
% of applicants accepted: N.A.
Tuition and/or typical assistance package: Tuition is currently $611/credit hour for 2005-2006.
Unique aspects of the program: Students may complete the MSW in a weekend program of study consisting of eight semesters. There is the MSW/JD combined degree program with Western New England College School of Law and an advanced standing program for qualified graduates of BSW programs accredited by CSWE. One online elective course is available.
Tips for applicants: The School looks closely at a personal statement describing (1) professional goals and reasons for pursuing an MSW degree at Springfield College; and (2) the education, professional/work experience, and personal characteristics that make the applicant a good candidate for an advanced generalist MSW program.
Common mistakes applicants make: Limited or no experience, lack of knowledge concerning advanced generalist practice, and inability to commit to field practicum during regular business hours.

St. Ambrose University, 518 W. Locust Street, Davenport, IA 52803. Admissions Contact: Toni Wamsley. Telephone: 563-333-6379. Fax: 563-333-6097.
E-mail: msw@sau.edu
Web site address: http://www.sau.edu/msw

Year accredited by CSWE: 1999
# of students: 67
# of full-time faculty: 7
# of part-time faculty: 10
% of applicants accepted: N.A.
Programs available: Master of Social Work, Certification in School Social Work
Advanced standing/advanced placement offered? yes
Distance education/online study offered? no
Tuition and/or typical assistance package: $547 per credit hour; some small scholarships available; 6 graduate assistantships.
Unique aspects of the program: St. Ambrose University's Master of Social Work Program offers a full-time, part-time, and advanced standing curriculum with a concentration in Advanced Empowerment Social Work Practice. Advanced empowerment social workers develop an unwavering commitment to social justice. This highly acclaimed practice method prepares social work graduates for confronting social issues and needs, equipping them with the ability to help clients attain their full potential through conscious and informed knowledge. The Admissions Committee meets monthly to review applications until class limits are reached. Students are advised to apply early in the year preceding enroll-

ment. Class sizes are small, with the opportunity for collaborative projects in the social service community.

Tips for applicants: Applicants should have strong academic preparation in the social sciences and liberal arts, and must have an undergraduate GPA of 3.0 or better. Experience in social services is preferred.

Common mistakes applicants make: Personal statement should reflect a commitment to social justice. Personal statement should be grammatically correct. References should include professional and academic (no personal references).

St. Louis University School of Social Service, 3550 Lindell Boulevard, St. Louis, MO 63103-1024. Admissions Contact: Jane M. Sprankel. Telephone: 314-977-2722. Fax: 314-977-2731. E-mail: socserv@slu.edu Web site address: http://www.slu.edu/colleges/SOCSVC/

Year accredited by CSWE: 1930
Programs available: BSSW; MSW; Concentration areas of study in Community, Family, and Health; School Social Work Specialization. Dual degrees in MSW/MPH (Master in Public Health) and MSW/MAPS (Master of Arts and Pastoral Studies)
Advanced standing/advanced placement offered? yes
Distance education/online study offered? no
Tuition and/or typical assistance package: Current tuition is $650 per credit hour. Students may apply for scholarships, loans, work study, and practicum stipends through the Center for Social Justice.
Unique aspects of the program: Practice focused curriculum in community, health, and family. Center for Social Justice provides practice and research opportunities for students, locally, nationally, and internationally. We have over 400 practicum sites, with a structured self selection process for choosing practicum sites. We offer flexible scheduling with day, evening, and Saturday classes; small class size; and faculty excellence in teaching, scholarship, community service, and student mentoring. We offer a solid Jesuit education with required Values and Ethics course and social work values integrated throughout the curriculum. There is a dual degree Master's program with Public Health and Pastoral Studies. Student organizations include the MSWSA and the BSSWSA, plus other university organizations to enhance student life.
Tips for applicants: Well-developed writing skills and the ability to think and speak in a critical analytic manner are highly valued, as is a mature work experience that demonstrates responsibility and leadership.
Common mistakes applicants make: Poorly written professional statement; not completing the application process as directed.

Stephen F. Austin State University School of Social Work, Box 6104-SFA Station, Nacogdoches, TX 75962-6104. Admissions Contact: Janet Mather, Recruitment Assistant. Telephone: 936-468-5105. Fax: 936-468-7201. E-mail: matherj@sfasu.edu Web site address: http://www.sfasu.edu/aas/socwk

Year accredited by CSWE: 2001
# of students: 80
# of full-time faculty: 6
# of part-time faculty: 5
% of applicants accepted: 90
Programs available: Master of Social Work, with concentration of Advanced Generalist in a Rural Context
Advanced standing/advanced placement offered? yes
Distance education/online study offered? We offer courses on other campuses. Currently we have classes at Kilgore College.
Tuition and/or typical assistance package: Texas resident graduate tuition is $132 per credit plus fees. SFA provides graduate students traditional financial assistance in the form of state grants, work-study programs, and student loans. Graduate assistantships and scholarships are also available.
Unique aspects of the program: Small class sizes, all classes taught by faculty (no T.A.s), a culturally diverse faculty and student body. A beautiful campus among the pines of East Texas, a close community in the oldest town in the state of Texas. Our own School of Social Work is located in a beautiful old restored church close to the main campus. The MSW program offers an advanced generalist concentration within a rural context. This concentration is appropriate for working with people who have rural lifestyles and with rural communities.
Tips for applicants: Applicants should be committed to the advancement of human well-being and to alleviating problems related to poverty, oppression, and discrimination.

Stony Brook University, School of Social Welfare, Health Sciences Center, L2093, Stony Brook, NY 11794-8230. Admissions Contact: Kathleen A. Albin. Telephone: 631-444-3141. Fax: 631-444-7565. E-mail: kalbin@notes.cc.sunysb.edu Web site address: http://www.uhmc.sunysb.edu/socwelf

Year accredited by CSWE: 1973
# of students: 350
# of full-time faculty: 20
# of part-time faculty: 8
% of applicants accepted: 35
Programs available: MSW; Specializations in Health and a sub-specialization in Alcohol and Substance Abuse and Student-Community Development; Dual Degree MSW/JD with Touro Law Center; Ph.D.
Advanced standing/advanced placement offered? yes
Distance education/online study offered? no
Tuition and/or typical assistance package: $288 per credit; $3,450 per semester full-time—in-state; $438 per credit; $5,250 per semester full-time—out-of-state.
Unique aspects of the program: We offer a specialization in Health and Substance Abuse and are the only school in the United States that offers a specialization in Student Community Development.
Tips for applicants: Demonstrate a commitment to social and economic justice for every human being.

Common mistakes applicants make: (1) Not reading and answering the essay appropriately. (2) Not providing references of people who can evaluate their readiness for graduate education. Letters of reference should be written by previous supervisors in social work agencies.

Syracuse University, Office of Enrollment Management, 340 Sims Hall, Syracuse, NY 13244-1230. Admissions Contact: David Mancini. Telephone: 315-443-5555. Fax: 315-443-4806. E-mail address: inquire@hshp.syr.edu Web site address: http://socialwork.syr.edu

Year accredited by CSWE: 1958
# of students: 200
# of full-time faculty: 13
% of applicants accepted: 80
Tuition and/or typical assistance package: $14,508, based on 18 credit hours at $806/credit hour, plus fees of $1,366.
Programs available: The School offers two concentrations at the graduate level: Advanced Practice in Community Organization, Policy, Planning and Administration (COPPA); and Advanced Practice with Individuals, Families, and Groups (IFG). The COPPA curriculum includes a selection of advanced social work practice courses addressing practice theory, methods, and skills in community organization and development; policy planning and advocacy; and administration applied to practice settings such as health, mental health, gerontological, and child welfare. The IF&G curriculum offers advanced clinical social work practice theory, methods, and skills in a series of courses applied to social work with individuals, families, and groups in various practice settings such as health, mental health, gerontological, and child welfare and with modalities that include long- and short-term interventions, groups, and treatment for substance abuse problems.
Advanced standing/advanced placement offered? yes
Distance education/online study offered? no
Tuition and/or typical assistance package: Graduate students construct a package of support through a combination of need-based tuition scholarships, graduate assistantships that include tuition and stipend, tuition support from federal or state grant projects, named scholarships, and federal student loans. Some field placement sites offer some support or stipend. Students who also are agency employees of field placement agencies may be supported with remitted tuition.
Unique aspects of the program: The majority of our classes are taught by full-time faculty who are nationally recognized for their scholarship and professional leadership. No courses are taught by graduate assistants. Faculty are accessible and supportive of students. Opportunities exist for students to work with faculty as research assistants or to participate with faculty on joint projects or scholarship. The greater Syracuse area is rich in human services that permit the School to offer an extensive array of field placement possibilities, including placements in a wide geographic area of Central New York. Students have the opportunity to interview with several potential field settings before accepting a place-

ment. The School and the university have special strength in aging and child welfare in terms of faculty expertise, courses, and student opportunities. Certificates of Advanced Study can be earned concurrently with MSW enrollment in Women's Studies, Gerontology, or Health Services Management (the latter two through the Maxwell School). Students can pursue joint degrees for MSW/MPA and MSW/JD through collaborative plans worked out with other degree programs.

Tips for applicants: Syracuse University's School of Social Work places heavy emphasis on three criteria: (1) Demonstrated capacity to perform academically at a very high level. (2) Appropriateness for the field as demonstrated by prior work or volunteer experience, a thoughtful self-assessment of strengths, and suitability and academic capacity and suitability for the profession. (3) The capacity to think critically about human diversity and current issues confronting the profession as demonstrated by a well-written personal essay.

Common mistakes applicants make: (1) Submitting an essay that contains poor grammar, punctuation errors, and misspelled words. (2) Submitting an essay that fails to meet the requirements spelled out in the application. (3) Soliciting references from people who are not qualified to address the candidate's fit with the profession or academic capacity.

University of Alabama School of Social Work, Box 870314, Tuscaloosa, AL 35487-0314. Admissions Contact: Mary A. Sella, MSW. Telephone: 205-348-8557. Fax: 205-348-9419.
E-mail: msella@sw.ua.edu
Web site address: http://www.socialwork.ua.edu

Year accredited by CSWE: 1969
# of students: 217
# of full-time faculty: 19
# of part-time faculty: 15
% of applicants accepted: 74
Programs available: MSW with concentrations in Health; Mental Health; Children, Youth, and Families; Social Work Practice with Older Persons; and Program and Agency Administration. MSW/MPH Dual-degree program. Ph.D.
Advanced standing/advanced placement offered? yes
Distance education/online study offered? We offer off-campus programs in Mobile and Montgomery, AL.
Tuition and/or typical assistance package: $2,067 per semester for full-time in-state graduate students (2003-2004 rate); $5,647 per semester for full-time out-of-state graduate students (2003-2004 rate). Assistance packages vary.
Unique aspects of the program: The University of Alabama is the only comprehensive School of Social Work in Alabama, offering the BSW, MSW, and Ph.D. degrees. The MSW program is offered in Mobile and Montgomery, as well as in Tuscaloosa. MSW students have the opportunity to complete a dual-degree-MSW/MPH. The MPH courses are taught at the University of Alabama at Birmingham (UAB). The Washington, D.C. Internship Program is available to students in their concentration year of study. The University of Alabama is also

home to the oldest international MSW Program in the nation, offering the MSW in conjunction with Shue Yan College in Hong Kong.
Common mistakes applicants make: Applicants often rush through their statement of purpose, which is a critical piece of the application and should be proofread carefully.

University of Alaska Anchorage School of Social Work, 3211 Providence Drive, Anchorage AK 99508. Admissions Contact: Mary Parker. Telephone: 907-786-6900. Fax: 907-786-6911.
E-mail: mary@uaa.alaska.edu
Web site address: http://socwork.uaa.alaska.edu/

Year accredited by CSWE: 1999
# of students: 65
# of full-time faculty: 9
# of part-time faculty: 3
% of applicants accepted: 50
Programs available: Master of Social Work
Advanced standing/advanced placement offered? yes
Distance education/online study offered? One Alaskan distance cohort is currently in place in the part-time program.
Tuition and/or typical assistance package: Resident graduate tuition for Fall 2004 was $222 per credit hour; non-resident rate $453 per credit hour; both rates subject to additional $111 per credit hour Professional Fee (super tuition). Scholarship assistance is limited. Office of Student Financial Aid (http://www.uaa.alaska.edu/financialaid/index.cfm) can provide further details.
Unique aspects of the program: The UAA Master of Social Work Program has as its mission education for the development of knowledge, skills, and values essential to assume multiple professional social work roles and the preparation of practitioners sensitive to diverse populations. Emphasis is placed upon the development, implementation, and evaluation of policies and programs within the framework of advanced generalist social work practice. Alaska's unique and rich multicultural populations, geographic remoteness, and frontier status allow the real potential for skilled social work professionals to make a profound impact on social and economic injustice in our state. This is the only MSW program offered in the state of Alaska.
Tips for applicants: The well prepared applicant has completed a liberal arts undergraduate degree with a grade point average above 3.0; has developed and can exhibit excellent writing skills; and can relate previous experience and future professional interest to at least one field of social work.
Common mistakes applicants make: Failure to submit a timely, complete application is the most common error.

University of California, Berkeley, School of Social Welfare, 120 Haviland Hall #7400, University of California, Berkeley, Berkeley, CA 94720-7400. Admissions Contact: Admissions Office. Telephone: 510-642-9042. Fax: 510-643-6126.
E-mail: socwelf@berkeley.edu
Web site address: socialwelfare.berkeley.edu

Year accredited by CSWE: 1944
# of students: 194
# of full-time faculty: 25
# of part-time faculty: 10
% of applicants accepted: 23
Programs available: Master in Social Welfare (MSW) with specializations in: Children and Family Services, Community Mental Health, Health, Gerontology, Management and Planning. Special programs in: MSW/MPH (Public Health), MSW/IAS (International Area Studies), MSW/JD (Law), MSW with PPSC (Pupil Personnel Services Credential for school social work), MSW with Title IV-E (Child Welfare Training Program), MSW/Ph.D. (Combined Master's and Doctorate), Doctorate (Ph.D.).
Advanced standing/advanced placement offered? no
Distance education/online study offered? no
Tuition and/or typical assistance package: For 2003-2004, the tuition for California residents was $6,168.90 per year and for non-residents $18,659.90. The maximum financial aid package for most students is $8,500 in subsidized loans, $10,000 in unsubsidized loans, and $10,000 in work study. There are also fellowships in the amount of $500-$7,500 and Graduate Opportunity funds for fees plus $10,000.
Unique aspects of the program: We have very high caliber graduate students and faculty, as well as exposure to cutting edge research and an excellent internship program. Also, the Bay Area has an exciting and diverse cultural milieu to enhance your educational experience.
Tips for applicants: We look for applicants who have a strong (1-2 full-time years) background in human services that would provide a solid foundation for their studies. Additionally, we desire an academically promising applicant who can successfully complete our rigorous program.
Common mistakes applicants make: Please apply early and keep in touch! Many students do not complete their files in a timely manner and may miss the first round of reviews. Again, significant experience in human services and strong academic performance helps.

*University of Central Florida School of Social Work, P.O. Box 163358, Orlando, FL 32816-3358. Admissions Contact Person: R. Paul Maiden, Ph.D. Telephone: 407-823-6167. Fax: 407-823-5697.

Year accredited by CSWE: 1996
# of students: 216
# of full-time faculty: 15
# of part-time faculty: 19
% of applicants accepted: 85
Tuition and/or typical assistance package: Current in-state tuition and fees are $207 per credit hour and out-of-state tuition and fees are $776.27 per credit hour. Tuition assistance includes fellowships, grants, teaching and research assistantships, and positions with faculty grants.
Unique aspects of the program: The MSW program has a community-based clinical practice orientation. It also offers certificates in addictions, gerontology, and children's services. The addictions certificate courses are offered online.

Additional online courses are in development. Certificates can be earned along with the MSW. Advanced placement is offered.

Tips for applicants: The School looks for well-written personal statements, narrative comments in personal recommendations, and exceptional or unusual life experiences.

Common mistakes applicants make: Inappropriate self-disclosure in application materials. Not adhering to timelines in the submission of application materials.

University of Chicago School of Social Service Administration (SSA/ Chicago), 969 E. 60th Street, Chicago, IL 60637. Admissions Contact: Madeleine Metzler. Telephone: 773-702-1492. Fax: 773-834-4751.
E-mail: admissions@ssa.uchicago.edu
Web site address: http://www.ssa.uchicago.edu

Year accredited by CSWE: 1919
# of students: 400
# of full-time faculty: 29
# of part-time faculty: 44
% of applicants accepted: N.A.

Programs available: SSA offers a master's degree in social work, with concentrations in either Clinical Practice or Social Administration and Policy. Specialization areas in the master's program include: Services to Children, Adolescents, and Families; Older Adult Studies; Community Schools; School Social Work; Physical Health/Mental Health; Community Organizing, Planning and Development; Program Evaluation and Policy Analysis; Health Administration Studies; Non-Profit Management; and Family Support. Joint master's degrees are available with the Harris School of Public Policy, the Graduate School of Business, and the Divinity School. Combined degrees are available with the Chicago Cluster of Theological Seminaries. SSA also offers a doctoral degree and a combined master's and doctoral degree program.

Advanced standing/advanced placement offered? no
Distance education/online study offered? no
Tuition and/or typical assistance package: The tuition for the 2003-2004 academic year was $26,000 for full-time study and $18,590 for part-time study. SSA offers extensive financial aid—over 90% of our students receive scholarship aid. Additionally, students are eligible for work study and student loans through the federally-funded financial aid programs.

Unique aspects of the program: SSA excels at balancing direct service with administrative skills. It is a challenging program that teaches you both the theory and practice of social work. It provides the skills and training to have an immediate impact on the communities you serve, to have a successful and rewarding career, and to continue to develop your social work skills long after you leave graduate school. SSA has had a profound impact in shaping the field of social work and continues to develop new leaders for the field.

Tips for applicants: SSA values students who think critically—that is, students who can assess and analyze questions from a variety of perspectives. Be sure to consider not only what you wish to get out of a graduate program, but also what you would contribute to the school. **Common mistakes applicants make:** Schools' policies and application procedures vary quite a bit. Be sure that you are following each school's application processes and requirements. If you are uncertain about a regulation or requirement, contact the school. When researching funding opportunities, both internal and external, be sure to start early.

University of Connecticut, School of Social Work, 1798 Asylum Avenue, West Hartford, CT 06117. Admissions Contact: Tilitha Conyers. Telephone: 860-570-9118. Fax: 860-570-9419. E-mail: swadmit1@uconnvm.uconn.edu Web site address: http://www.ssw.uconn.edu

Year accredited by CSWE: 1946
# of students: 380
# of full-time faculty: 33
% of applicants accepted: 40
Programs available: Major Methods—Casework, Group Work, Community Organization, Administration & Policy Practice. Substantive Areas—Black Studies for Social Work Practice, International Issues in Social Work, Mental Health and Substance Abuse in Social Work Practice, Puerto Rican/Latino/a Studies in Social Work, Social Work Practice with Older Adults, Social Work with Women and Children in Families, and Urban Issues in Social Work. Joint/Dual Degrees—Yale Divinity School/UConn School of Law, Business Administration and Public Health. Institutes/Center—Institute for Violence Reduction (IVR), Institute for the Advancement of Political Social Work Practice (IAPSWP), and Center for International Social Work Studies.
Advanced standing/advanced placement offered? yes
Distance education/online study offered? no
Tuition and/or typical assistance package: Tuition In-State is $6,854.00. and $17,206 for out-of-state. Regional tuition is $10,094. Tuition assistance package includes grant/scholarships, Federal Work Study, interest subsidized educational loans, and unsubsidized educational loans.
Unique aspects of the program: The University of Connecticut School of Social Work offers the opportunity to pursue a methods-based specialization in social work practice (concentration areas are Casework, Group Work, Community Organization, Administration, & Policy Practice).
Tips for applicants: Applicants should have a solid background in Liberal Arts courses (18 credits), cumulative GPA of 3.0 or better, and knowledge of the field (prior learning or work experience).
Common mistakes applicants make: (1) Not addressing all questions asked in the personal statement, (2) not choosing appropriate references that address academic and/or professional work history, (3) failure to indicate a method choice.

University of Denver Graduate School of Social Work, 2148 South High Street, Denver, CO 80208. Admissions Contact: Pat Sheller. Telephone: 303-871-2841. Fax: 303-871-2845. E-mail: gssw-admission@du.edu Web site address: http://www.du.edu/gssw

Year accredited by CSWE: 1933
# of students: 340
# of full-time faculty: 25
# of part-time faculty: 40
% of applicants accepted: N.A.

Programs available: The University of Denver Graduate School of Social Work (GSSW) offers courses of study leading to a master's degree (MSW), a doctoral degree (Ph.D.), and certificates in social work with Latinos, trauma response and recovery, and animal-assisted social work. A certificate in couples and family therapy is offered in cooperation with the Denver Family Institute. Dual-degree programs are offered in international studies, law, human communication, and theology. Students also may propose a dual degree that fits their goals.

Advanced standing/advanced placement offered? yes

Distance education/online study offered? One distance education site in Durango, Colorado only. An online degree is not offered.

Tuition and/or typical assistance package: For 2004-2005, tuition for full-time study (12 to 18 quarter-hour credits) is $25,956 per year, or $8,652 per quarter. Part-time students pay $721 per credit hour. Health insurance and other fees are also required. Financial aid for MSW students includes federal loans, GSSW scholarships, the Federal Work-Study Program, and Colorado Graduate Grants. Graduate teaching assistantships, graduate research assistantships, and Colorado fellowships are forms of financial aid available for doctoral students. Filing the Free Application for Federal Student Aid (FAFSA) online is required.

Unique aspects of the program: The University of Denver Graduate School of Social Work (ranked nationally in the top quarter) offers several unique certificate programs for MSW students, including Social Work With Latinos/as, Trauma Response and Recovery, and Animal-Assisted Social Work. A certificate in Couples and Family Therapy is offered in partnership with the Denver Family Institute, allowing MSW students to begin work toward certification prior to graduation. GSSW offers the opportunity to specialize in child welfare, families, high-risk youth, adults, or leadership for community and organizational practice. We offer 400 approved field placement sites and flexible scheduling. The curriculum emphasizes cultural competency, ethics, and values. There are small classes, highly accessible faculty, and many opportunities to develop strong mentoring relationships.

Tips for applicants: In addition to a baccalaureate degree from a regionally accredited college or university, GSSW seeks students who desire to grow intellectually, evidence emotional maturity and self-awareness, demonstrate the values and ethics of the profession, respect the value of multiculturalism, and are committed to service. We seek students who communicate well orally and in writing, and who think critically and reflectively.

Common mistakes applicants make: Late applicants who miss key deadlines limit their opportunities for top merit scholarships and other types of departmental financial aid.

*University of Georgia School of Social Work, Tucker Hall, Athens, GA 30602-7016. Admissions Contact Person: Ray H. MacNair, Director of

**MSW Admissions. Telephone: 706-542-5421. Fax: 877-535-6590.
E-mail: mswadm@arches.uga.edu
Web site address: http://www.ssw.uga.edu**

Year accredited by CSWE: accredited, year not known
Unique aspects of the program: We have two concentrations: Family Centered Social Work Practice (Clinical) and Community Empowerment and Program Development.
Tips for applicants: Our admissions criteria include emphasis on work history in the human services, experiences in cultural diversity, addressing social problems on multiple levels, and clarity and specificity of career objectives.
Common mistakes applicants make: Applicants should follow the "Checklist" in "Application Procedures" on our Web site.

**University of Houston Graduate School of Social Work, MSW Admissions Office, 237 Social Work Building, Houston, TX 77204-4013. Admissions Contact: Amber M. Mollhagen. Telephone: 713-743-8078. Fax: 713-743-7426.
E-mail: mswinfo@sw.uh.edu
Web site address: http://www.sw.uh.edu**

Year accredited by CSWE: 1970
# of students: 350
# of full-time faculty: 24
# of part-time faculty: 15
% of applicants accepted: 50
Programs available: The school has MSW and Ph.D. programs. We offer advanced standing for those who hold a BSW degree. There are full-time and part-time programs with several advanced concentrations that include nationally recognized programs in gerontology, children & families, mental health and health care, and political social work (the only political social work concentration in the nation). Dual degree programs are available in conjunction with Master of Public Health, Master of Business Administration, Juris Doctor, and Doctor of Philosophy.
Advanced standing/advanced placement offered? yes
Distance education/online study offered? A number of foundation year and elective courses are offered through distance education. The school also sponsors off-site MSW programs (please contact MSW Admissions Office for more information).
Tuition and/or typical assistance package: Approximate cost is $3,500 per semester for tuition and fees. The Graduate School of Social Work offers a variety of student financial assistance, including 15 named scholarships, Child Welfare Training stipends, gerontology stipends, and graduate and teaching assistantships. Scholarships range from $500 per semester to $20,000 per year.
Unique aspects of the program: Houston, the fourth largest city in the United States with a vast array of opportunities, is an international city with great diversity. The GSSW has incredible proactive faculty dedicated to advancing social justice, small classes with practice classes limited to 20 students, more than 400

field internship sites in the Houston area and in Washington, D.C., a number of courses available via distance education, international coursework in United Kingdom and Asia, and sponsors numerous off-campus service and research programs. Graduates of the School average around 88% (state average is 70%) on the Texas state social work licensing examination. Recently, we were very proud to add to our faculty Jody Williams, 1997 Nobel Laureate for Peace.

Tips for applicants: Rolling admissions review begins in the fall. The School values individuals committed to making a difference in their communities and dedicated to promoting social and economic justice. The school's motto, "social work for education for change," speaks for itself.

Common mistakes applicants make: Incomplete applications—some packets are missing letters of recommendations, transcripts, or scores. We don't review packets until they have every item requested on our application checklist.

University of Illinois at Chicago, Jane Addams College of Social Work, 1040 W. Harrison (M/C 309), Chicago, IL 60607-7134. Admissions Contact: Henrika McCoy. Telephone: 312-996-3218. Fax: 312- 996-2770.
E-mail: jacswadm@uic.edu
Web site address: http://www.uic.edu/jaddams/college

Year accredited by CSWE: 1946
# of students: 550
# of full-time faculty: 35
# of part-time faculty: 20
% of applicants accepted: N.A.
Programs available: Concentrations: School Social Work, Child and Family Health, Mental Health, Community Administrative Practice.
Advanced standing/advanced placement offered? yes
Distance education/online study offered? no
Tuition and/or typical assistance package: The 2004-2005 tuition and fees for a resident full-time student are $8,070 a year. Most students are eligible for loans, work study, and/or scholarships. College scholarships range from $500 a year to full tuition plus a stipend. In addition, some students accept research assistantships, which may cover full tuition and/or a stipend.
Unique aspects of the program: Because Jane Addams is located in the heart of Chicago, we are able to prepare students fully to work in urban environments with disenfranchised and at-risk populations. In addition to the concentrations that students are able to choose from, our faculty have expertise in the areas of HIV/AIDS, domestic violence, substance abuse, the criminal justice system, kinship care, and minority health care. Finally, UIC is one of the most diverse universities in the country, and Jane Addams easily reflects that diversity. Having these experiences allows students to enter the profession as well rounded social workers.
Tips for applicants: Applicants should carefully weigh whether or not they are committed to working with the most vulnerable, at-risk, and disenfranchised populations. This is the College's commitment and is what we seek in applicants, as well.

Common mistakes applicants make: Applicants often fail to apply early, which can result in a longer wait time for an admission decision. In addition, applicants fail to read the application instructions carefully and omit required information, or they do not pay close attention to the personal statement instructions.

University of Kansas School of Social Welfare, Twente Hall, 1545 Lilac Lane, Lawrence, KS 66044-3184. Admissions Contact: Becky Hofer, Director of Admissions. Telephone: 785-864-4720. Fax: 785-864-5277.
E-mail: admissionsmsw@ku.edu
http://www.socwel.ku.edu

Year accredited by CSWE: 1948
# of students: 320
# of full-time faculty: 26
# of part-time faculty: 20
% of applicants accepted: N.A.
Programs available: MSW, specializations in Clinical Practice and Social Administration. MSW/JD joint degree program. Ph.D. in Social Work.
Advanced standing/advanced placement offered? yes
Distance education/online study offered? no
Tuition and/or typical assistance package: Tuition and fees are assessed by the Office of the University Registrar. A full description of tuition and fees is available each semester at: http://www.registrar.ku.edu/timetable. Rates are set by the Kansas Board of Regents and are subject to change. See http://www.ku.edu/tuition for current information. For more information on scholarship opportunities available from the School of Social Welfare, go to: http://www.socwel.ku.edu/academics.
Unique aspects of the program: The mission of the KU School of Social Welfare is to educate students, conduct scholarly research, and perform community service in order to promote an approach to social work practice that advances the empowerment and well-being of individuals and communities. KU is recognized internationally as a leader in the development of the strengths model of social work practice. The KU School of Social Welfare was recently ranked 8th among public institutions and 11th overall.
Tips for applicants: Make sure you fill in all the boxes, and sign and date areas that require this.
Common mistakes applicants make: (1) Missing start and stop dates for work and volunteer experiences. (2) Not believing that we really do require a transcript from each and every college attended, EVEN if the information is presented on another university's transcript. (3) Not providing a transcript for "college credits" that were earned while in high school.

*University of Kentucky College of Social Work, 615 Patterson Office Tower, Lexington, KY 40506. Admissions Contact Person: Kathleen Bailey. Telephone: 859-257-6652. Fax: 859-323-1030.
E-mail: kbbail2@uky.edu
Web site address: http://www.uky.edu/SocialWork

Year accredited by CSWE: 1972

# of students: 300
# of full-time faculty: 24
# of part-time faculty: 25
% of applicants accepted: N.A.

Tuition and/or typical assistance package: In-state full-time tuition is $2,826.25 per semester; part-time is $298.55 per credit hour. Out-of-state full-time tuition is $6546.25 per semester; part-time is $711.55 per credit hour. Residence hall advisors and research assistants have out-of-state tuition waived. Persons of color who are Kentucky residents qualify for the Commonwealth Incentive Award, which underwrites tuition and textbooks.

Unique aspects of the program: The College offers two concentrations: mental health and family/community. The mental health curriculum is innovative and includes problem-based learning and such courses as adult assessment and treatment, substance misuse & violence, and child/adolescent assessment and treatment. The family/community concentration provides courses on family assessment, community development, and administration/supervision. Students may attend either full-time (day classes) or part-time (evening classes). Off-campus locations are available in the Cincinnati area, as well as Morehead and Hazard, KY. The MSW offers mental health or family/community concentrations. The Ph.D. is intended to prepare social work educators and researchers. If accepted into the Ph.D. program, students may take classes at either the University of Louisville or the University of Kentucky. Advanced placement is offered. A few classes are offered by interactive TV. Faculty members are discussing some innovative designs that would combine Web, television, and intensive course sessions. Students may take classes in Lexington or other off-campus locations.

Tips for applicants: Take the time to proofread and revise your written statements so that everything has a professional appearance. Prepare for the GRE—don't walk in and take it cold.

Common mistakes applicants make: (1) Not taking undergraduate studies seriously enough and earning a low GPA. (2) Waiting too late to take the GRE. (3) Not taking statistics as an undergraduate.

University of Louisville, Kent School of Social Work. Admissions Contact: Maureen Slaton, MSSW, CSW. Telephone: 502-852-0414. Fax: 502-852-0422.
E-mail address: maureen.slaton@louisville.edu
http://www.louisville.edu/kent

Year accredited by CSWE: 1937

# of students: 350
# of full-time faculty: 26
# of part-time faculty: 52
% of applicants accepted: N.A.

Programs available: MSSW Master of Science in Social Work; MSSW—Marriage and Family Therapy Specialization; MSSW-School Social Work; MSSW - Preparation toward Certified Alcohol and Drug Counselor credential; MSSW/JD with Brandeis School of Law at University of Louisville; MSSW/MDiv with

Louisville Presbyterian Seminary; MSSW/PAS with Pan African Studies at University of Louisville (approval pending).
Advanced standing/advanced placement offered? yes
Distance education/online study offered? Satellite campus in Owensboro, KY and availability of weekend classes
Tuition and/or typical assistance package: Resident tuition $304 per credit hour. Non-resident tuition $838 per credit hour. Some scholarship money available from Kent School. University of Louisville Student Financial Aid office works with students to arrange loans and Federal Work Study.
Unique aspects of the program: Kent School has a proud history of awarding MSSW degrees since 1937. We have the only Marriage and Family Therapy program in the country that is within a school of social work. Our Weekend Program (part-time and full-time) allows students to meet for classes on the weekend and to complete their practicum in their home area, making Kent School an option for students from a wide radius.
Tips for applicants: We select students with proven academic success who also express the desire to work creatively to improve the lives of oppressed members of society.
Common mistakes applicants make: One significant mistake that some students make is to wait until the last minute before the deadline to apply.

*University of Maryland Baltimore School of Social Work, 525 W. Redwood St., Baltimore, MD 21201. Admissions Contact Person: Assistant Dean Marianne Wood. Telephone: 410-706-3025. Fax: 410-706-6046.
E-mail: mwood@ssw.umaryland.edu
Web site address: http://ssw.umaryland.edu

Year accredited by CSWE: 1962
# of students: 880
# of full-time faculty: 45
# of part-time faculty: 50
% of applicants accepted: 80
Tuition and/or typical assistance package: Full-time non-residents are charged $7,243 per semester plus fees. Maryland residents pay $3,649 per semester. Merit awards for outstanding applicants are awarded, as are diversity grants.
Unique aspects of the program: The School has the following dual degree programs with Johns Hopkins University: MSW/JD, MSW/MBA, MSW/MA (Jewish Communal Service), and MSW/MPH. Advanced year concentrations include clinical, management, and community organization along with seven specializations: aging, employee assistance programs, families and children, health, mental health, social action and community development, and substance abuse. Faculty are highly published. There are off-campus programs throughout the state and online courses in the foundation and advanced year. The School has the premier social work community outreach service in the country, whereby clients are served in neighboring communities through a community-based program at the School of Social Work. In this way, the School is

directly involved in service to the residents of Maryland and particularly those in Baltimore. Advanced placement is offered as is distance or online study. Specifically, a foundation research course, an advanced psychopathology course, and an advanced child welfare research course are offered online.

Tips for applicants: The School looks for students with an interest in working with underserved populations. Because of its clinical and community-based emphasis, the School looks for students with a demonstrated interest in these areas. The program is especially interested in VISTA, AmeriCorps, and Peace Corps volunteers.

Common mistakes applicants make: Students must write clearly in the statements they are required to submit to the School. They must have references from professional people, rather than family members.

*University of Michigan School of Social Work, 1080 S. University Avenue, Room 1748. Ann Arbor, MI 48109-1106. Admissions Contact Person: Tim Colenback, Assistant Dean. Telephone: 734-764-3309. Fax: 734-936-1961.
E-mail: ssw.msw.info@umich.edu
Web site address: http://www.ssw.umich.edu

Year accredited by CSWE: accredited, year not known
Tuition and/or typical assistance package: $7,569 in-state for nine or more credit hours, $13,204 out-of-state. Part time: $1,128 for the first credit hour, $806 for additional hours in-state; $1,754 first hour, $1,432 for additional hours out-of-state.
Unique aspects of the program: Concentrations are available across a number of practice areas and methods. Practice areas include Aging in Families and Society, Children and Youth in Families in Society, Community and Social Systems, Health, and Mental Health. Practice methods include Interpersonal Practice, Community Organization, Management of Human Services, and Social Policy and Evaluation. Specialization and Certificate options include Specialist in Aging Certificate, Certificate in Jewish Communal Service and Judaic Studies (Drachler Program), Social Work in the Public Schools, and Social Work in the Workplace. Doctoral programs in social work and social science are also offered. Curriculum schedules include Advanced Standing (12-month schedule), 16-month schedule, 20-month schedule, Fifth Term Option, and the Extended Degree (partial part-time) Program. Dual degree options include Social Work and Business Administration, Social Work and Information, Social Work and Law, Social Work and Public Health, Social Work and Public Policy, and Social Work and Urban Planning. Students may also set up Student Initiated Dual Degree programs with other departments and schools within the University of Michigan. Student organizations include Social Work Student Union; Association of Black Social Work Students (ABSWS); Rainbow Network; Coalition of Asian Social Work Students; Women's Action Coalition; Sigma Phi Omega Honor Society (Gerontological Honor Society); Adventure Based Counseling; Social Welfare Action Alliance; School Social Work Club; Doctoral Student Organization; Social Work International; Christians in Social Work Association; Student Organization of Latina/o Social Workers (SOLASW).

Tips for applicants: Admissions decisions are based primarily on an evaluation of previous undergraduate and graduate work, recommendations, experience in the human services (paid, volunteer, research, and internship), and the applicant's written supplementary statement.

Common mistakes applicants make: Waiting until the priority deadline to apply; delaying completion of financial aid application; failing to address all of the questions in the supplementary statement.

University of Minnesota Duluth, 1207 Ordean Court, 220 Bohannon Hall, Duluth, MN 55812. Admissions Contact: Sandy Maturi. Telephone: 218-726-8497. Fax: 218-726-7185.
E-mail: smaturi@d.umn.edu
Web site address: http://www.d.umn.edu/sw

Year accredited by CSWE: 1989
# of students: 80
# of full-time faculty: 5
# of part-time faculty: 4
% of applicants accepted: 85
Programs available: Master of Social Work
Advanced standing/advanced placement offered? yes
Distance education/online study offered? (Sites) Bemidji State University and Hibbing, Minnesota,
Tuition and/or typical assistance package: $681.17/semester credit for residents, $1,272.84 for non-residents. Full-time: $4,087 residents, $7,637 non-residents.
Unique aspects of the program: The School features an Advanced Generalist program as well as a Child Welfare Scholar program. The MSW is offered on a conventional basis or on an advanced placement basis. Currently, distance education courses are offered at Bemidji State University in Bemidji, Minnesota and at Arrowhead College Region in Hibbing, Minnesota.
Tips for applicants: The Student Affairs Committee looks at the undergraduate GPA and for applicants who have some volunteer experience and/or work experience in the social work field.
Common mistakes applicants make: Not sending official transcripts prior to application deadline. Not getting recommendation forms prior to application deadline.

University of Missouri-Columbia School of Social Work, 725 Clark Hall, Columbia, MO 65211. Admissions Contact: Tammy Freelin. Telephone: 573-882-6206. Fax: 573-882-8926.
E-mail: ssw@missouri.edu
Web site address: http://ssw.missouri.edu

Year accredited by CSWE: 1919
# of students: 144
# of full-time faculty: 12
# of part-time faculty: 5

% of applicants accepted: N.A.

Programs available: MSW. Concentrations offered: Clinical Practice or Policy Planning & Administration. Clinical Specializations offered: Family & Children Services, Mental Health Services, Physical Health Services. 37-hour Advanced Standing program, Ph.D.

Advanced standing/advanced placement offered? yes

Distance education/online study offered? Off-campus sites in several locations of the state utilize a combination of interactive television (ITV), Web-based, and live course delivery.

Tuition and/or typical assistance package: Tuition is currently approximately $254.30 per credit hour for residents and $402.40 for non-residents. Most students utilize student loans. Scholarship awards range from $700-$5,300 per academic year. Assistantships waive tuition and provide a stipend of approximately $2,000 per semester. Fellowships for highly qualified, underrepresented minority students waive tuition and provide a stipend of approximately $5,000 per year.

Unique aspects of the program: We are in an elite group of public, land-grant, AAU, Doctoral/Research Extensive institutions with a School of Social Work—one of just seven institutions nationally. Although we are in a fairly large university, the School of Social Work is relatively small. Students get personal attention and won't get "lost in the crowd." We consistently hear from field agencies and employers that we produce graduates who are excellent practitioners. A number of our faculty members regularly conduct international research and incorporate those experiences in the classroom. We are situated in the middle of the state, between St. Louis and Kansas City, and just 30 minutes from the state capital. Our location allows us to easily place students in their desired practicum location, ranging from urban to rural, and local to state government.

Tips for applicants: We look for a commitment to social work. While many applicants demonstrate this through work experience, volunteerism is also quite acceptable. Applicants without much work experience can often be very desirable in terms of their volunteerism and community involvement.

Common mistakes applicants make: A common mistake for applicants is not taking the personal statement seriously. Since we don't interview individual applicants, the personal statement becomes very important in assessing an applicant's readiness for graduate education.

*University of Missouri-Kansas City, Graduate Social Work, 4825 Troost, Suite 106, Kansas City, MO 64110. Admissions Contact Person: Heidi Updike. Telephone: 816-235-1025. Fax: 816-235-6573. E-mail: updikeh@umkc.edu

Year accredited by CSWE: accredited, year not known

# of students: 100

# of full-time faculty: 6

# of part-time faculty: 3

% of applicants accepted: 75

Tuition and/or typical assistance package: Tuition for Winter term 2005 is $254.30/credit for residents, $656.70 for non-residents. UMKC offers schol-

arships, grants, long-term loans, short-term loans, and Federal work-study positions.
Unique aspects of the program: An urban mid-western environment characterizes the program. Approximately 30% of students are minority population and most are currently working. The three fields of practice offered are Children and Families, Mental Health and Substance Abuse, and Aging. Advanced placement is available, while distance or online study is not.
Tips for applicants: The program looks for evidence of a commitment to urban social work and social justice.
Common mistakes applicants make: Failure to submit all transcripts and letters of reference.

University of Missouri-St. Louis, School of Social Welfare, 590 Lucas Hall, One University Blvd., St. Louis MO 63121. Admissions Contact: Kathy Burney. Telephone: 314-516-5632. Fax: 314-516-5816. E-mail: socialwork@umsl.edu Web site address: http://www.umsl.edu/%7Esocialwk/

Year accredited by CSWE: 2002
# of students: 120
# of full-time faculty: 8
# of part-time faculty: 6
% of applicants accepted: 50
Programs available: Concentrations in (1) family practice and (2) organization and community development.
Advanced standing/advanced placement offered? yes
Distance education/online study offered? We are just beginning to develop distance courses for the MSW program.
Tuition and/or typical assistance package: Educational fees for state residents are $254.30 per credit hour and $402.40 per credit hour for non-residents. Additional fees are charged for student activities and computers. Students taking 12 hours can expect to pay $3,325. Non-resident students will pay approximately $8,150 for 12 hours.
Unique aspects of the program: The MSW program at the University of Missouri at St. Louis is committed to training social workers to work in the public metropolitan sector and particularly aims to meet the needs of non-traditional students. Students come from a range of backgrounds, including business, psychology, and art.
Tips for applicants: The program looks for applicants with a good GPA (preferably above 3.0 on a 4.0 scale) and strong letters of recommendation. The essay is highly weighted, a little less on content, as socialization into the profession is not expected at this stage, but heavy emphasis is on writing style, clarity, organization, grammar, and spelling.
Common mistakes applicants make: Putting little effort into writing the essay. Using friends as references.

*University of New England School of Social Work, 716 Stevens Avenue, Portland, ME 04103. Admissions Contact Person: Joanne

Thompson. **Telephone: 207-283-0171. Fax: 207-878-4719. E-mail: jthompson@mailbox.une.edu. Web site address: http://www.une.edu/chp/socialwork/index.html**

Year accredited by CSWE: accredited, year not known
Tuition and/or typical assistance package: Tuition is $33,000, plus a $420 general service fee.
Unique aspects of the program: Students have an opportunity to specialize in clinical or integrated practice. Both concentrations emphasize a strengths perspective and students acquiring skills in implementing change across all systems levels. The School is also developing opportunities to explore social work through the arts and international exchanges.
Tips for applicants: Applications are reviewed for life experiences, applicant's understanding and support of the School's Mission Statement, a commitment to social justice, and the alleviation of all forms of oppression. The applicant's personal statement is very important.
Common mistakes applicants make: Insufficient attention to the School's Mission Statement; inadequate completion of personal statement.

*University of New Hampshire Department of Social Work, Murkland Hall 25, 15 Library Way, Durham, NH 03824. Admissions Contact Person: Elizabeth Forshay, Admissions Coordinator. Telephone: 603-862-0076. Fax: 603-862-4374. E-mail: eforshay@hopper.unh.edu Web site address: http://www.unh.edu/social-work/index.html

Year accredited by CSWE: accredited, year not known
Tuition and/or typical assistance package: Full-time: $3,755 per semester for residents, $4,131 per semester for non-residents; $417/credit for residents, $459/credit for non-residents.
Unique aspects of the program: We are a new and growing program recently accredited by CSWE. Faculty research and interests range from child welfare to gerontology to evaluation of welfare reform. We are the first MSW program in New Hampshire.
Tips for applicants: The admissions committee looks at transcripts, references, work experience, and personal statements. Personal statements are very important—they are the one chance for the admissions committee to get to know the applicant.
Common mistakes applicants make: The most common mistake is not including all relevant social services and work experience. We would like to know about volunteer and work experience—it is often helpful to include a résumé.

University of North Carolina-Chapel Hill School of Social Work, 301 Pittsboro Street, CB 3550, Chapel Hill, NC 27599-3550. Admissions Contact: Linda T. Wilson. Telephone: 919-962-6442. Fax: 919-843-8562. E-mail: ltw2517@email.unc.edu Web site address: http://www.ssw.unc.edu

Year accredited by CSWE: 1920
\# of students: 326
\# of full-time faculty: 32
\# of part-time faculty: 38
% of applicants accepted: 49
Programs available: MSW, Ph.D. Dual programs: MSW/MPA, MSW/MSPH, MSW/JD, MSW/MDiv
Advanced standing/advanced placement offered? yes
Distance education/online study offered? Students can begin part-time MSW study at one of 3 different off-campus sites—Durham, Asheville, or Fayetteville.
Tuition and/or typical assistance package: For in-state full-time annually: $4,868.54 for tuition and fees. For out-of-state full-time annually: $17,099.58 for tuition and fees. Most students have loans; some get scholarships or work study.
Unique aspects of the program: Our school has almost 85 years of making a difference in families and communities, and is ranked in the top ten schools in the nation. Our faculty and staff care about our students and do everything possible to give them a good experience and education while here at UNC. Our students have many choices for their field placements and get to learn firsthand what to expect in the "real" world. The Jordan Institute for Families is the "research arm" of our school, which not only is involved with social work research, but also distributing that information to families and communities through trainings and workshops throughout North Carolina. There are also opportunities to participate in international social work.
Tips for applicants: We're looking for applicants who have a good sense of what social work is. They need to have a commitment to the profession, which is usually demonstrated through their social work volunteer/paid experience. We seek a diverse applicant pool with different life experiences, different ages, gender, and race, different socioeconomic levels, sexual orientations, religious backgrounds, and different experiences working with specific populations.
Common mistakes applicants make: (1) They get their family members or pastor to write recommendations, or ask people who write only two to three sentences that are not substantive. (2) They make many grammatical errors in their narrative. (3) They take the GRE "cold turkey" without studying. This is a big mistake.

University of North Carolina at Charlotte, Department of Social Work, 9201 University City Boulevard, Charlotte, NC 28223-0001. Admissions Contact: Gay Jordan, MSW, LCSW. Telephone: 704-687-4076. Fax: 704-687-2343.
E-mail: gjordan@email.uncc.edu
Web site address: http://www.//health/uncc.edu

Year accredited by CSWE: accredited, year not known
\# of students: 60
\# of full-time faculty: 10

# of part-time faculty: 5
% of applicants accepted: 30
Programs available: MSW with a concentration in interpersonal practice with individuals, families, and small groups.
Advanced standing/advanced placement offered? no
Distance education/online study offered? no
Tuition and/or typical assistance package: For full-time study (nine or more credits), tuition is typically $1,776 per semester for in-state students and $6879.50 for out-of-state students. Tuition assistance generally includes Research Assistantships, but they are limited and competitive.
Unique aspects of the program: We offer a faculty with both practice and academic experience in the areas of practice with individuals, families, and small groups. Likewise, we have a small cadre of faculty who engage in policy practice. Many faculty have established research agendas as well, but all faculty engage in student advising and mentoring. Our program is still small enough to provide lots of individual attention to students.
Tips for applicants: We especially desire applicants who have a passion for practice with individuals, families, and small groups. We also desire students who invest in understanding a wholistic picture of human functioning and social contexts.
Common mistakes applicants make: Common mistakes include inappropriate references and poorly written and organized essays.

University of North Dakota, Department of Social Work, P.O. Box 7135, Grand Forks, ND 58202-7135. Admissions Contact: Pat Conway. Telephone: 701-777-3768. Fax: E-mail: pat.conway@mail.und.nodak.edu Web site address: http://www.und.edu/

Year accredited by CSWE: 1993
# of students: 50
# of full-time faculty: 6
% of applicants accepted: N.A.
Programs available: Advanced Generalist Concentration
Advanced standing/advanced placement offered? yes
Distance education/online study offered? A cohort, approximately every four years, part-time, through compressed video, on campus in the summer, and the Web.
Tuition and/or typical assistance package: See information on the UND Web site.
Unique aspects of the program: The graduate social work program at UND provides a personalized education for persons interested in advanced generalist social work and social work in rural settings.
Tips for applicants: Applicants who are able to think critically, with a commitment to social work values and an appreciation for diversity, are most likely to be admitted.
Common mistakes applicants make: Not contacting us for more detailed information.

*University of Pittsburgh School of Social Work, 2103 Cathedral of Learning, 5th and Bigelow, Pittsburgh, PA 15260. Admissions Contact Person: Elaine McCollough. Telephone: 412-624-6302. Fax: 412-624-6323. E-mail: elainssw@pitt.edu Web site address: http://www.pitt.edu/~pittssw/index2.html

Year accredited by CSWE: accredited, year not known
Unique aspects of the program: The Center for Mental Health Services Research (CMHSR) at the University is one of seven national social work research development centers funded by the National Institute of Mental Health. An interdisciplinary initiative, the CMHSR capitalizes on the School of Social Work's extensive knowledge of the community and the Department of Psychiatry's clinical research expertise. Emphasis is on the identification and study of variables that facilitate or hinder the effective use of mental health treatment services, including access to care and adherence to treatment. The School is the recent recipient of a $20.5 million Child Welfare Grant. Student organizations include Student Executive Council (SEC), Black Action Society (BAS), Community Organization Group (COG), Bachelor of Arts in Social Work Club (BASW)
Tips for applicants: We look for students who are mature, have earned an excellent academic record, have good interpersonal skills, a good work ethic, commitment to the social work profession, and a positive attitude.
Common mistakes applicants make: A common mistake is waiting until the last day of the application period before submitting application materials.

*University of South Carolina College of Social Work, Columbia, SC 29208. Admissions Contact Person: Dr. John T. Gandy, Associate Dean. Telephone: 803-777-5273. Fax: 803-777-3498. Web site address: http://www.sc.edu/cosw

Year accredited by CSWE: 1969
# of students: 455
# of full-time faculty: 29
# of part-time faculty: 28
% of applicants accepted: 70
Tuition and/or typical assistance package: Tuition is $2,550 and graduate assistantships are offered.
Unique aspects of the program: The MSW is offered on a full- or part-time basis and Advanced Standing is available. A doctoral program is also available. The program has been offering distance education for thirty years, utilizing live TV instruction, study courses, and an organized Distance Education program.
Tips for applicants: Take time and do a very thorough job on the application. The School looks at four components of a file: GPA, autobiography, references, and work or volunteer experience. Be your own best advocate.
Common mistakes applicants make: Autobiographical statement is sometimes poorly done and reflects little thought. Another mistake is leaving items blank on the application form.

University of Southern California, School of Social Work, Admissions & Financial Aid, Social Work Center, Room 114, Los Angeles, CA 90089. Admissions Contact: Carrie Lew. Telephone: 213-740-2013. Fax: 213-821-1235.
E-mail: sswadm@usc.edu
Web site address: http://usc.edu/socialwork

Year accredited by CSWE: 1922
# of students: 500
# of full-time faculty: 33
# of part-time faculty: 32
% of applicants accepted: 57
Programs available: (1) MSW with five Concentrations: Health; Industrial; Mental Health; Families & Children; Community Organization, Planning, Administration. (2) One Specialized Option: Nurse Social Work Practitioner. (3) six Dual Degrees: Master's in Business Administration (MBA/MSW); Juris Doctorate (JD/MSW); Master's in Public Administration (MPA/MSW); Master's in Planning (MPl/MSW); Jewish Communal Service (MA/MSW); Master of Science in Gerontology (MSG/MSW). (4) Ph.D.
Advanced standing/advanced placement offered? no
Distance education/online study offered? no
Tuition and/or typical assistance package: Tuition: $1,010 (a unit); $14,994 flat rate once enrolled in 15 units or more. Typical package includes: Stafford Loan, Perkins Loan, Work Study, Scholarships.
Unique aspects of the program: The USC School of Social Work is the oldest program on the west coast. Our program is consistently ranked among the top 10 graduate social work programs, according to *U.S. News & World Report*. We have a 3-year part-time option; 4-year part-time option; as well as a full-time option. There are three campus locations to choose from: Los Angeles, Orange County, and West Los Angeles. We have a priority filing deadline of February 1 that guarantees applicants a decision by April 1, as well as our regular application deadline of April 1. We do not require the GRE nor do applicants have to complete a human biology course. Our campus is located in a large urban setting that allows students an opportunity to work with diverse populations from various socioeconomic backgrounds.
Tips for applicants: We strongly consider applicants who have a strong commitment to social work values, exhibit strong academic promise, and preferably have had experience providing service to people. We also look for applicants who have personal qualifications essential for professional competence for social work, such as maturity, emotional stability, sensitivity and responsiveness in relationships, capacity for self-awareness, concern for the needs of others, ability for abstract reasoning, conceptual thinking, and strong communication skills.
Common mistakes applicants make: (1) Many times, students submit autobiographical statements that are filled with grammatical errors, typos, or list another school name within the body of the statement. (2) Many students fail to follow instructions when completing our application. We urge applicants to thoroughly read all application instruction materials. For example our application deadline is a "received by" deadline, not a postmarked deadline.

*University of Southern Mississippi School of Social Work, Box 5114, Hattiesburg, MS 39406. Admissions Contact Person: Michael Forster. Telephone: 601-266-4163. Fax: 601-266-4165. E-mail: michael.forster@usm.edu Web site address: http://www-dept.usm.edu/~socwork/

Year accredited by CSWE: accredited, year not known
Tuition and/or typical assistance package: Tuition for 9-12 credits is $2,053 for residents and $2,585 for non-residents. Part-time tuition is $229/credit hour for residents and $576 for non-residents.
Unique aspects of the program: We are among a relatively small number of programs that offer the "advanced generalist" concentration. In contrast to concentrations in, for example, child welfare or administration, the advanced generalist curriculum prepares MSWs to address complex, multi-dimensional problems in a full range of contexts spanning the five systems of individual, family, group, organization, and community. We believe that the advanced generalist is an especially appropriate preparation for social workers who expect to practice in settings with limited professional resources. Advanced Standing may be available to qualified candidates.
Tips for applicants: Applicants should develop strong personal statements that reflect the applicant's motivation to pursue a professional social work career, a clear appreciation of the value base of the profession, and, ideally, life experiences that illustrate the applicant's commitment to addressing injustice, oppression, and other social problems.
Common mistakes applicants make: Our process calls for the applicant to submit most application materials, including reference letters, in one package to the School. A common mistake of applicants is to submit materials piecemeal. Another common mistake is to submit weak reference letters from family friends or others who cannot effectively speak to either the academic or professional promise of the applicant.

*University of Tennessee College of Social Work, 201 Henson Hall, Admissions Office, Knoxville, TN 37996-3333. Admissions Contact Person: Sylvia A. Nash, Administrative Services Assistant. Telephone: 423-974-6697. Fax: 423-974-4803. E-mail: snash@utk.edu Web site address: http://www.csw.utk.edu

Year accredited by CSWE: accredited, year not known
Unique aspects of the program: Full MSSW program available on three campuses: Knoxville, Nashville, and Memphis. Full-time, Extended Study, and Advanced Standing programs are available. Two concentrations are Clinical Social Work and Management and Community Practice. Field placements are available in the regions surrounding each campus. The College of Social Work has the Children's Mental Health Research Center.
Tips for applicants: Preference is given to applicants with a GPA of 3.0 or above in their undergraduate work, appropriate preparation in the social sciences, and work or volunteer experience directly related to the field of social work.

Common mistakes applicants make: Sending materials to the wrong address; assuming that requested transcripts and reference evaluation forms have actually been received by the College. You may call us to check what has been received.

University of Texas at Arlington School of Social Work, 211 South Cooper, Box 19129, Arlington, TX 76019. Admissions Contact: Darlene R. Santee. Telephone: 817-272-3181. Fax: 817-272-2046. E-mail: santeed@uta.edu
Web site address: http://www.uta.edu/ssw/mssw

Year accredited by CSWE: 1970
# of students: 590
# of full-time faculty: 34
% of applicants accepted: N.A.
Programs available: Master of Science in Social Work (MSSW). Five dual degree programs: MSSW and: Master of City and Regional Planning, Master of Public Administration, Master of Arts in Urban Affairs, Master of Arts in Criminology and Criminal Justice, and Master of Arts in Sociology.
Advanced standing/advanced placement offered? yes
Distance education/online study offered? We have a Cooperative Distance Education program with West Texas A & M University in Canyon, TX. We currently only offer a Social Welfare Policy course online.
Unique aspects of the program: Our concentrations and specialty areas set us apart from other Schools of Social Work. If one wants to prepare for a career in Direct Practice (DP), there are two specialty areas, (1) Children and Families or (2) Mental Health. Our Community and Administrative Practice (CAP) concentration prepares students for career opportunities in the macro practice of social work. A student selecting the CAP concentration can then specialize in either Community Practice, Administrative Practice, or both for a combined specialization.
Tips for applicants: Prior to applying to the School of Social Work, we would like for prospective students to have a reasonable knowledge of the field. It would also be helpful if the prospective student had experiences as a client, volunteer, or paid employee in social work or a related field.
Common mistakes applicants make: The most common mistakes relate to the preparation of the required narrative (essay). Students should be aware that this writing sample speaks volumes, and he/she needs to take time and give careful consideration to its development.

*The University of Texas at Austin School of Social Work, 1925 San Jacinto Boulevard, Austin, TX 78712. Admissions Contact Person: Office of Recruitment. Telephone: 512-471-9819 or 877-875-7352 Toll Free. Fax: 512-471-9600.
E-mail: sswinfo@utxvms.cc.utexas.edu
Web site address: http://www.utexas.edu/ssw

Year accredited by CSWE: 1952
\# of students: 280
\# of full-time faculty: 32
\# of part-time faculty: 35
% of applicants accepted: N.A.
Tuition and/or typical assistance package: See chart at: http://
www.utexas.edu/business/accounting/pubs/0405fee.pdf. For example, tuition
and fees for 12 credits are $3,042.52 for residents and $6,618.52 for non-
residents. The Graduate School of Social Work offers several Departmental Scholarships, Graduate Research Assistantships, and Graduate Teaching Assistantships. In addition, work study positions, loans, grants and federally funded stipends are available.
Distance education/online study offered? no
Unique aspects of the program: The nationally ranked School of Social
Work at the University of Texas at Austin offers masters' and doctoral degrees to
those interested in social work practice, policy, administration, research, and
teaching. The School has innovative research and training opportunities in child
welfare and substance abuse. It is a small learning community within a large
research university that fosters personal and professional growth and leadership.
The diverse members of the faculty have practice, teaching, and research experience in a broad range of social work areas. The School offers field opportunities with more than 400 agencies around the country and the world. Services for
students and alumni are offered through the Office of Career Services & Alumni
Relations, Office of Professional Development, and the Learning Resource Center. The School offers full-time, full-time extended, and part-time options for its
regular and advanced standing Master of Science in Social Work programs. There
are flexible course schedules and program start dates. Concentrations are offered in Clinical Social Work or Administration and Planning. Distance or online
study is not available.
Tips for applicants: The program seeks to admit applicants who demonstrate
a commitment to the values of the social work profession, including a commitment to social and economic justice; fit with the mission and goals of the School;
diversity through life experience, cultural background, or ethnicity; and show a
personal and professional readiness for graduate education.
Common mistakes applicants make: Common mistakes include not following written instructions, submitting incomplete applications, not taking the GRE
before the priority deadline date, and not completing applications to both the
School of Social Work and the UT-Austin Graduate School.

**University of Texas—Pan American, 1201 West University Drive,
Edinburg, Texas 78539-2999. Admissions Contact: Dr. Alonzo
Cavazos. Telephone: 956-381-3575. Fax: 956-381-3516.
E-mail: alonso@Panam.edu
Web site address: http://www.panam.edu**

Year accredited by CSWE: 2003
\# of students: 34
\# of full-time faculty: 6

# of part-time faculty: 2
% of applicants accepted: 88
Programs available: MSSW Degree (Hispanic Family Practice Focus)
Advanced standing/advanced placement offered? yes
Distance education/online study offered? no
Tuition and/or typical assistance package: The tuition cost for a full-time load (15 credit hours) is $4,929. Financial assistance is available from the Federal Work-Study Program (FWS) for graduate students with financial need. A Texas Public Educational Grant (TPEG) is also available. Loans are also available, including Federal Perkins Loans, and the Federal Family Educational Loan Program (FFELP). For additional information, please contact the Student Financial Services Office at 956-381-2958.
Unique aspects of the program: We are a small, new MSSW program. Our graduates are prepared to work with Hispanic client populations. The concentration curriculum focuses on clinical practice with the family as the unit of intervention.
Tips for applicants: Prospective applicants, who appreciate (value) cultural diversity and understand the dynamics associated with having minority status, are viewed as being highly desirable. Additionally, applicants who have experience advocating for rights of others are strongly encouraged to apply to our program.
Common mistakes applicants make: Some applicants do not follow through to ensure that their letters of references are actually sent; applications are submitted after the posted deadline, and insufficient thought is given to the preparation of the personal narrative.

University of Vermont, Department of Social Work, 443 Waterman Building, University of Vermont, Burlington, VT 05405. Admissions Contact: Lisa K. Lax, MSW, LICSW, MSW Admissions Coordinator. Telephone: 802-656-8800. Fax: 802-656-8565.
E-mail: lisa.lax@uvm.edu
Web site address: http://www.uvm.edu/~socwork/

Year accredited by CSWE: 1992
# of students: 60
# of full-time faculty: 9
# of part-time faculty: 3
% of applicants accepted: a high percentage are accepted; percentage varies from one academic year to another
Programs available: The MSW program offers three options for study within one program: Full Time Regular Track of 60 credits over four semesters, Full Time Advanced Standing of 42 credits typically over three academic semesters, and a part-time course of study of 60 credits over eight semesters.
Advanced standing/advanced placement offered? yes
Distance education/online study offered? At present, some courses are offered through interactive television to sites located within the state of Vermont.
Tuition and/or typical assistance package: In-state tuition is $362 per credit hour. Out-of-state tuition is $906 per credit hour. The Department has

several sources of financial support available to qualified graduate students, including Graduate College Fellowships, Graduate College Teaching Fellowships, and Research Assistantships. In addition, students can utilize Federal Work Study monies in conjunction with field education hours, and can inquire about stipends available through some agency field placements. The Department also has some funds available to support student research through faculty sponsored grants and special projects. In the past, these have included VT-AHEC (Vermont Agency Health and Education Consortium) Project monies, and CSWE Geriatric Enrichment Grant monies through the Hartford Foundation.

Unique aspects of the program: There are many unique characteristics to our MSW program, which include but are not limited to our program curriculum and philosophy, the opportunity for individual attention, and the advantages of our locale. The MSW curriculum at UVM emphasizes principles of human rights, social justice, social constructionist thought, and a strengths orientation to practice. Our students are exposed to "cutting edge" philosophy and a post modern orientation to social work practice. The curriculum prepares students to practice in a variety of roles and agency settings, from direct practice in mental health or family agencies to community based practice or to policy practice on the state or federal level. Our students are challenged to be social work scholars as well as practitioners. Students have the opportunity to interact regularly with their student and faculty colleagues in a small community atmosphere, given our program size, curriculum design, and the shared philosophy about teaching and practice. Class size tends to be under 30 for all MSW courses and 15 or under for practice courses. Further, through the final project requirement, concentration or second year students have the opportunity to work closely through independent study with a faculty mentor. Many of our faculty have a national or international reputation in such areas as Anti-Violence Work, Feminist Practice, Human Rights, Youth Justice, Mental Health Practice, Aging and Disabilities, and Social Work in the Global Context. At the heart of our MSW program is the Field Education Curriculum. Students are placed in a wide variety of community agencies throughout Vermont, allowing for exposure to practice in both small urban and rural environments, in large state agencies or in small private nonprofit organizations. A student's field education is supported by a faculty field liaison who visits agency field sites regularly to collaborate closely with the agency-based field instructor and student to help design an experience that best meets the student's learning needs. Finally, one unique aspect of our program, is our setting. Vermont offers beautiful scenery, a relaxed environment, and diverse recreational activities, in addition to a progressive tradition that is pleasing to many in our profession. Burlington is a small city of under 40,000, yet offers a rich array of cultural events, shops, restaurants and recreational activities for students to enjoy.

Tips for applicants: We are looking for students who are interested in our program philosophy and orientation, who can meet the challenge of scholarly inquiry combined with professional practice in social work, who thrive in small personalized educational settings, and who have some paid or volunteer practice experience in human services prior to application. We welcome students from diverse backgrounds.

Common mistakes applicants make: Faculty look carefully at an applicant's written expression, at the applicant's understanding of our particular program, and at the applicant's prior life, educational, and work experience leading to the decision to apply for graduate education in social work. Therefore, an especially important part of the application is the personal statement. In addition, it is important that an applicant provide recommendations from both an academic and human service source, if at all possible. Finally, because our program requires the GRE (looking at scores in relation to the whole application), it is important for an applicant to take the GRE well in advance of the application deadline if s/he wishes to apply for any financial supports.

*University of Wisconsin—Madison School of Social Work, 1350 University Avenue, Madison, WI 53706. Admissions Contact Person: Sue Thoele. Telephone: 608-263-3660. Fax: 608-263-3836. E-mail: sjthoele@facstaff.wisc.edu Web site address: http://polyglot.lss.wisc.edu/socwork/index.html

Year accredited by CSWE: accredited, year not known
# of students: 226
# of full-time faculty: 18
# of part-time faculty: N.A.
% of applicants accepted: 50-60
Tuition and/or typical assistance package: Wisconsin residents' tuition is $4,160 per full-time semester. Minnesota residents' tuition is $4,392 per full-time semester. Non-resident tuition is $11,795 per full-time semester. Part time tuition is $521/credit for residents, $551/credit for Minnesota residents, and $1,476/credit for non-residents.
Unique aspects of the program: The School offers five Advance Practice Concentrations: Aging; Children, Youth, & Families; Developmental Disabilities; Health; and Mental Health. It offers two subconcentrations: (1) Child Welfare and (2) Adults with Serious and Long-Term Mental Illnesses. It operates on a faculty-based field education model. The School is the "home" of the generalist model of social work. Advanced placement is offered, while distance or online study is not.
Tips for applicants: Applicants are evaluated on the basis of academic record, essay on reasons for seeking graduate study in social work, strength of letters of recommendation, and life and work experiences as they pertain to social work.
Common mistakes applicants make: Poorly or badly written essays and reference letters from friends or colleagues.

University of Wyoming, Division of Social Work, Dept. 3632, 1000 E. University Ave, Laramie, WY 82071. Admissions Contact: Gail Leedy or Ruth Nielsen. Telephone: 307-766-5422. Fax: 307-766-6839. E-mail: Socialwork@uwyo.edu Web site address: http://www.uwyo.edu/socialwork

Year accredited by CSWE: 2000
# of students: 50
# of full-time faculty: 9
# of part-time faculty: 4

% of applicants accepted: 70

Programs available: The University of Wyoming offers an advanced generalist concentration. Full- and part-time programs are available for both the advanced standing program and our 58-hour program. School social work certification is available.

Advanced standing/advanced placement offered? yes

Distance education/online study offered? Compressed format, compressed video within Wyoming

Tuition and/or typical assistance package: Full-time Wyoming residents pay $142/credit hour, non-residents pay $408.00/credit hour. Fees are $134 for less than 9 credit hours and $284.75 for more than nine credit hours. Scholarships, graduate assistantships, and loans are available to qualified and outstanding students.

Unique aspects of the program: The University of Wyoming offers an advanced generalist concentration in social work that focuses on rural/frontier practice with Native Americans living on reservations and isolated farm and ranch families. School social work certification is available.

Tips for applicants: The University of Wyoming MSW program seeks students committed to social and economic justice, especially as it applies to practice in a rural or frontier setting.

Common mistakes applicants make: At times, applications are incomplete or received after the admissions deadline dates (The deadline is February 15. Additional deadlines may be set for March 15 and April 15, if space is available. There may also be a July 15 deadline for applications to the 58 credit-hour program, if space is available). Another common mistake is applying for the graduate school and not also requesting the MSW packet from the Division of Social Work.

Valdosta State University, 1500 N. Patterson St., Valdosta, GA 31698-0128. Admissions Contact: Sherry Kurpis. Telephone: 229-249-4864. Fax: 229-249-4341.
E-mail: sbrugh@valdosta.edu
Web site address: http://www.valdosta.edu

Year accredited by CSWE: 1998

# of students: 72

# of full-time faculty: 8

# of part-time faculty: 5

% of applicants accepted: 65

Programs available: Advanced generalist degree

Advanced standing/advanced placement offered? yes

Distance education/online study offered? We offer Web-based programs, which require one weekend a month face-to-face class time.

Tuition and/or typical assistance package: For the Spring 2005 semester, tuition is $1,393 for state residents, $5,573 for out-of-state residents for 12 credits or more. Part-time: $117/credit for in-state, $465 for out-of-state. Various scholarships and loans offered through the Financial Aid Office. Graduate Assistantships, DFCS IV-E Grant.

Unique aspects of the program: Valdosta State University Division of Social Work offers students a supportive, enriching learning environment. We offer face-to-face traditional classes and Web-based classes. Our faculty is diverse and eager to work closely with students.

Tips for applicants: The VSU MSW program looks for applicants who are well prepared academically, very motivated, with a desire to learn and commitment to the field of social work.

Common mistakes applicants make: Applying after the March 15 deadline. Sending "non-professional" recommendations. Recommendations should come from professionals and educators.

Virginia Commonwealth University, School of Social Work, 1001 W. Franklin Street, P.O. Box 842027, Richmond, VA 23284-2027. Admissions Contact: Ann Nichols-Casebolt. Telephone: 804-828-0703. Fax: 804-828-0716.
E-mail: ssw-info@vcu.edu
http://www.vcu.edu/slwweb/admissions/msw.html

Year accredited by CSWE: 1919
# of students: 485
# of full-time faculty: 33
# of part-time faculty: 30
% of applicants accepted: 75
Programs available: We offer our MSW in both Richmond and an off-campus site in Alexandria, Virginia (near Washington, D.C.). The School of Social Work offers several options for study toward the MSW degree combined with other programs, certificates, or additional degrees. These options include the MSW and Certificate in Aging Studies, School Social Work Certification, Certificate in Early Infant Intervention, Dual Degree in Law and Social Work, the Cooperative Program with the Presbyterian School of Christian Education, the Dual Degree Program with Richmond Theological Consortium. and the Certificate in Nonprofit Management through George Mason University. These options are available generally only on the Richmond campus. The School Social Work Certification may be available off-campus if there is sufficient enrollment. For more detail on each of these options, please visit our Web site at http://www.vcu.edu/slwweb/academicprograms/programsofstudy/msw_specoptions.html
Advanced standing/advanced placement offered? yes
Distance education/online study offered? no
Tuition and/or typical assistance package: Tuition and fees for full-time students (9-15 credits), is approximately $3,700/year; tuition per credit for 1-8 credits is approximately $380/credit. These amounts are subject to change. For up-to-date tuition and fee information, please check the VCU Web site at: http://www.vcu.edu/enroll/sa/tuition/. The VCU School of Social Work tuition stipends are available in amounts of $500 and above based on demonstrated need and merit. Full-time MSW students in the first year or second year of study may apply. We also have a child welfare stipend program and scholarships available for those who want to specialize in the area of aging. For more information about our financial assistance, please go to our Web site at:

http://www.vcu.edu/slwweb/currentstudents/financial_support.html

Unique aspects of the program: We offer our MSW program in both the Virginia state capitol (Richmond) and near the Nation's Capitol in Alexandria, Virginia. In the latest *U.S. News and World Report* ranking we were 14th among 166 accredited MSW programs. Our faculty have written some of the most often used textbooks in social work education, and are well known nationally for their scholarly work. We have a faculty committed to excellence in teaching, and we offer a very strong field internship component. We also have a child welfare stipend program and a Hearst Foundation scholarship program for those interested in the field of aging.

Tips for applicants: We are looking for individuals who have a strong academic background, and work or volunteer experiences that demonstrate their commitment to the field of social work and the principles of social justice.

Common mistakes applicants make: When individuals apply to our program, they should be sure they have a complete application packet (including the submission of the supplementary forms). Applicants should also provide a well written and thoughtful personal statement that addresses their background as well as their motivation for the MSW, and their commitment and understanding of the values of the social work profession and the NASW *Code of Ethics.*

Walla Walla College School of Social Work, 204 S. College Avenue, College Place, WA 99324. Admissions Contact: Doreena Schwartz. Telephone: 800-854-8678. Fax: 509-527-2434.
E-mail: schwdo@wwc.edu
Web site address: http://social-work.wwc.edu

Year accredited by CSWE: 1992
# of students: 220
# of full-time faculty: 23
# of part-time faculty: 15
% of applicants accepted: 90
Programs available: Clinical Social Work, School Social Work Certification, Mental Health specialization, Children and Families specialization
Advanced standing/advanced placement offered? yes
Distance education/online study offered? Some online courses available, but not the whole program.
Tuition and/or typical assistance package: Options include the Federal Stafford Loan Program, Federal Work-Study Program, School of Social Work Merit Scholarship, MSW Grant, Diversity Scholarship.
Unique aspects of the program: The Walla Walla College School of Social Work program combines generalist practice with clinical practice to meet the varying needs of the rural areas of the Northwest. The school takes a direct practice/systems approach to social work education by integrating theory and practice experience. The curriculum includes the study of the use of spirituality in social work practice. The MSW program is offered in College Place, Washington; Missoula, Montana; and Billings, Montana. Emphasis can be in a number of areas, including Addictions, Aging, Children & Families, Child Welfare, Mental Health, and School Social Work.

Tips for applicants: The School looks for individuals who show compassion and commitment for the social condition and are dedicated to improving the quality of life; individuals who show they have the desire for lifelong learning. **Common mistakes applicants make:** Incomplete, partial applications that do not include all transcripts or are missing reference letters. Personal statements that do not address all areas required in the application.

Washburn University, Department of Social Work, 1700 S.W. College Avenue, 405 Benton Hall, Topeka, KS 66621-0001. Admissions Contact: Jay Memmott, Ph.D., LSCSW. Telephone: 785-231-1010, Ext. 1616. Fax: 785-231-1027.
E-mail: social-work@washburn.edu
Web site address: http://www.washburn.edu/sas/social-work

Year accredited by CSWE: 1996
# of students: 120
# of full-time faculty: 7
# of part-time faculty: 7
% of applicants accepted: 90
Programs available: MSW in Clinical Social Work
Advanced standing/advanced placement offered? yes
Distance education/online study offered? no
Tuition and/or typical assistance package: Resident graduate tuition is $185 per credit hour. Non-resident graduate tuition is $377 per credit hour. Scholarships (a limited number) are available through the School of Applied Studies, of which the social work department is part. We will, when educationally prudent, work with students to develop employment-based practica placements. Students may also work with the Financial Aid Office to develop a plan to fund their educational programs.
Unique aspects of the program: The MSW program at Washburn University is one of the few truly clinical social work programs in the country. All of our full-time and part-time faculty have recent and abundant clinical experience in a variety of practice settings with diverse client populations. While we help our students develop a strong professional identity as social workers, we also prepare them for the rigors and realities of clinical practice.
Tips for applicants: First and foremost, we are looking for applicants who are committed to the values and ethics of social work. We seek applicants who are critical thinkers, who have a strong work ethic, and who love to work with challenging people, human dilemmas, difficult and complex problems, and the riddles/puzzles of every day life. Finally, we seek applicants who will meet and work with people "where they are," seeking to understand and help clients and client systems through constructive helping relationships based on a clear sense of what is possible and how to get there.
Common mistakes applicants make: They do not read our program materials closely and they do not follow written instructions in the application packet. Also, some applicants do not understand that they are not merely earning a degree; rather, they are being socialized into a profession with a knowledge base, skill sets, and a clear code of ethics.

Washington University in St. Louis, George Warren Brown School of Social Work, Campus Box 1196, One Brookings Drive, St. Louis, MO 63130. Admissions Contact: Brian W. Legate, MSW, Director of Admissions. Telephone: 877-321-2426 (toll-free), 314-935-6676. Fax: 314-935-4859. E-mail: msw@gwbmail.wustl.edu Web site address: http://www.gwbweb.wustl.edu

Year accredited by CSWE: 1928
# of students: 400
# of full-time faculty: 32
# of part-time faculty: 51
% of applicants accepted: 80
Programs available: Concentrations: children, youth, and families; gerontology; health; mental health; social and economic development; and individually designed concentration. Specializations: family therapy, management, and research. MSW, Ph.D., MSW/MHA, MSW/JD, MSW/MBA, MSW/MAJCS, MSW/M.Arch.
Advanced standing/advanced placement offered? yes
Distance education/online study offered? no
Tuition and/or typical assistance package: Tuition is $795 per semester hour/credit. There are 204 merit-based scholarships, as well as a full range of student loans and tuition remission.
Unique aspects of the program: The School is ranked number 2 by U.S. News & World Report among the top schools of social work in the nation. The School has an outstanding faculty, talented and idealistic students from 44 states and 33 foreign countries, offers extensive financial aid, and offers a challenging curriculum combining theory, policy, practice methods, evaluation techniques, and skills training. There are six concentrations (children, youth, and families; gerontology; health; mental health; social and economic development; and individually designed concentration); three specializations (family therapy, management, and research); and dual degrees with law, business, architecture, and Jewish communal studies. There are possibilities of international field placements; specialized career planning and placement services; world-class facilities, including state-of-the-art technology and one of the best social work libraries in the country; excellent research opportunities through our research centers: Center for Mental Health Services Research; Comorbidity and Addictions Center; Center for American Indian Studies and the Center for Social Development.
Tips for applicants: Unique factors the School looks for in applicants include (1) demonstrated potential for future leadership in the social work profession, and (2) outstanding academic background.
Common mistakes applicants make: Not submitting all required information; misspelled words, typographical errors, or incorrect punctuation in essays; late applications; and lack of academic or professional references.

*Wayne State University School of Social Work, 4756 Cass Avenue, Detroit, MI 48202. Admissions Contact Person: Janet M. Clerk, Director of Admissions and Student Services. Telephone: 313-577-4409.**

Fax: 313-577-42.
E-mail: ac2027@wayne.edu
Web site address: http://www.socialwork.wayne.edu

Year accredited by CSWE: accredited, year not known
# of students: 550
# of full-time faculty: 19
# of part-time faculty: 43
% of applicants accepted: 75
Tuition and/or typical assistance package: Current tuition is $207.70 per credit hour plus $17.50 omnibus fee per credit hour. Private scholarships via the School of Social Work are available. Students may also apply for federal loans and university based grants.
Unique aspects of the program: Students may choose a macro practice or interpersonal practice concentration during the advanced year. Within the interpersonal practice concentration, students may choose from three theoretical frameworks to focus on in their practice/HBSE sequence: family systems, cognitive/behavioral, or psychodynamic. A Master of Social Work Graduate Certificate in Social Work Practice with Families and Couples is available. Advanced placement is offered. Designated courses are offered online completely or partially.
Tips for applicants: The School looks for a well-rounded application both academically and professionally and a personal interest statement that is well written and incorporating guidelines requested.
Common mistakes applicants make: Applying late and submitting a poorly written personal interest statement.

West Chester University, Graduate Social Work Department, Reynolds Hall, West Chester, PA 19383. Admissions Contact: Ann A. Abbott, Ph.D., LCSW. Telephone: 610-436-2664. Fax: 610-738-0375. E-mail address: mswprogram@wcupa.edu Web site address: http://wcupa.edu

Year accredited by CSWE: 1999
# of students: 60
# of full-time faculty: 6
# of part-time faculty: 4
% of applicants accepted: 75
Programs available: Direct Practice with Individuals, Families and Communities
Advanced standing/advanced placement offered? yes
Distance education/online study offered? no
Tuition and/or typical assistance package: Full-time tuition is $2,886/semester for Pennsylvania residents and $4,618 for non-residents. Part-time: $321/credit for residents and $513/credit for non-residents. The university does offer a limited number of graduate assistantships, work study opportunities, and loans. Field placement stipends are available on a limited basis. Eligible applicants can apply for the CWEL (Child Welfare Education for Leadership) program.

Unique aspects of the program: Small class size, opportunities to work with faculty on research projects, diverse student body, located in a growing suburban community approximately 30 miles from Philadelphia.

Tips for applicants: Pay close attention to the personal statement. In most cases it is used in lieu of a personal interview. Previous social work volunteer experience is helpful. Commitment to social justice is essential.

Common mistakes applicants make: References do not speak to the applicant's academic potential. Applicants do not proofread personal statements or share information about relevant volunteer or work experience.

West Virginia University Division of Social Work, P.O. Box 6830, Morgantown WV 26506-6830. Admissions Contact: Brenda Morgan-Patrick, MSW, LCSW. Telephone: 304-293-3501 ext. 3128. Fax: 304-293-5936.
E-mail: bmorgan@wvu.edu
Web site address: sw.as.wvu.edu

Year accredited by CSWE: 1942
# of students: 233
# of full-time faculty: 18
# of part-time faculty: 4
% of applicants accepted: N.A.

Programs available: Students have the opportunity to focus their practice interests by selecting one of two practice tracks— (1) Direct Practice or (2) Community Organization and Social Administration and one of three fields of practice— (1) Children and Families, (2) Aging and Health Care or (3) Community Mental Health. Regular and advanced standing MSW programs are available. Also available is a dual MSW/MPA (Social Work and Public Administration). The program currently supports part-time graduate study at the main campus in Morgantown and part-time graduate study at the off-campus site in the Southern Region's Charleston and Beckley area, in the Northern Region's Wheeling area and in the Eastern Region's Martinsburg area. The Division of Social Work also offers from time to time a SatNet course statewide that can be taken for graduate credit or for continuing education credit.

Advanced standing/advanced placement offered? yes

Distance education/online study offered? See the four off-campus locations mentioned above (Charleston, Beckley, Wheeling, and Martinsburg).

Tuition and/or typical assistance package: Tuition cost per semester for full-time West Virginia residents is $1,627 and for part-time the cost is $183 per credit hour. Tuition cost per semester for full-time non-residents is $5,682 and for part-time the cost is $633 per credit hour. Student fees each semester are $539 for full-time students and for part-time the fees are $61 per credit hour.

Unique aspects of the program: The Division of Social Work at West Virginia University, located in the only land grant institution in the state, has defined a special mission to prepare social workers who can practice effectively and sensitively in rural areas and small communities. We are nationally recognized in the area of rural social work practice and nonprofit management.

Tips for applicants: Preference is given to those applicants with volunteer or paid experience in social work, but particularly promising students who have limited formal experience may be admitted, as well. Preference is given to applicants who wish to practice social work in rural areas and small towns. If the applicant graduated in the last three years, at least one academic reference that addresses the applicant's potential for graduate study must be submitted. Also, at least one letter of reference concerning employment and/or volunteer experience in the human services must be included. References should be sealed and sent with the other required application materials as one complete application packet. The Graduate Record Examination (the General Test) is required before a final admission decision can be made.

Common mistakes applicants make: Applying late, not submitting the required references, not taking the GRE and submitting the scores in a timely way, and submitting a weak or poorly written personal statement.

Western Kentucky University, 1 Big Red Way, Department of Social Work, Bowling Green, KY 42101. Admissions Contact: Suzie T. Cashwell, Ph.D. Telephone: 270-745-2088. Fax: 270-745-6841. E-mail: swrk@wku.edu Web site address: http://www.wku.edu/Dept/Academic/chhs/socialwork/

Accredited by CSWE: no
In candidacy for accreditation: yes, accreditation expected 2006
# of students: 62
# of full-time faculty: 7
# of part-time faculty: 3
% of applicants accepted: 75
Programs available: Concentration: Advance Direct Practice in Rural Settings
Advanced standing/advanced placement offered? yes
Distance education/online study offered? Many of our classes are Web-based. In addition, some are ITV to assist with travel.
Tuition and/or typical assistance package: Current tuition is $2,199 per semester for full-time students or $222 per hour for part-time students. We have some scholarships ranging from $50 to $800. There are limited graduate assistantships ($7,400).
Unique aspects of the program: WKU's MSW program focuses on rural social work practice. This program was designed with the needs of rural communities and individuals in mind. Many of our students work full time and attend school full time. This program aims to allow individuals in the social service field to continue their education by using a variety of delivery methods and non-traditional class hours.
Tips for applicants: The personal statement is key. The committee examines grammar, syntax, and fit to the profession through this statement.
Common mistakes applicants make: Applicants fail to edit their personal statements. Applicants fail to turn in materials in a timely manner.

Western Michigan University, School of Social Work, 1903 W. Michigan Ave., Mail Stop 5354, Kalamazoo, MI 49008-5354. Admissions

Contact: Nancy McFadden, MSW/CSW. Telephone: 269-387-3200. Fax: 269-387-3183.
E-mail: nancy.mcfadden@wmich.edu
Web site address: http://www.wmich.edu

Year accredited by CSWE: 1969
\# of students: 242
\# of full-time faculty: 19
% of applicants accepted: 78
Programs available: All degree programs are MSW programs. These include: Advanced-standing program (for BSW graduates only, 12-month program, 39 credit hours); full-time program (20-month program, 60 credit hours); extended-study program (three-year, part-time, evening program); Concentrations in Interpersonal Practice (advanced clinical) and Policy, Planning, and Administration. Specializations in School Social Work, Alcohol and Drug Abuse, Gerontology, Holistic Health, Health Care Administration, and Nonprofit Leadership. No joint degree programs are offered at this time.
Advanced standing/advanced placement offered? yes
Distance education/online study offered? We have one course taught as an independent study and one course that combines classroom and Web CT.
Tuition and/or typical assistance package: Tuition for graduate courses: Resident—Kalamazoo Campus: $233.53/credit hour, Resident—Extended University Programs: $293.53/credit hour (Grand Rapids and Benton Harbor campuses), Non-Resident—Kalamazoo Campus: $569.00/credit hour, Non-Resident—Extended University Programs: $293.53/credit hour (no out-of-state tuition for Benton Harbor and Grand Rapids campuses).
Unique aspects of the program: We are a small program and offer small class sizes. We do not utilize graduate assistants for teaching. All courses are taught by full-time faculty and adjunct professionals from the community.
Tips for applicants: The Admissions Committee has high regard for the above average undergraduate GPA and professional social work experience when evaluating applications. Students who plan to continue working a full-time job while in school should apply to the extended-study program rather than the full-time or advanced-standing programs. These same students should prepare to flex their work hours around their need to attend a field placement two days/week from 8-5 during the work week for two academic years.
Common mistakes applicants make: The most common mistakes: (1) Applicants who complete the online application to the University do not realize that they must also call the School of Social Work to request the graduate social work application packet, and complete it by the given deadline. (2) Applicants often send us an incomplete application that is then not completed before the application deadline. The most common materials lacking in the application are official transcripts from all universities/colleges attended prior to graduate application, one of the three required references, and the School of Social Work one-page application form. (3) The most frustrating mistake that applicants can make is to contact the admissions office and conduct themselves in an unprofessional manner. Applicants must remember that the application process includes their conduct/professional presentation throughout the application process, particularly when addressing admissions staff, in person and by phone or e-mail.

*Widener University Center for Social Work Education, One University Place, Bruce Hall, Chester, PA 19013. Admissions Contact Person: Ms. Maureen Sullivan. Telephone: 610-499-1153. Fax: 610-499-4617.
E-mail: social.work@widener.edu
Web site address: http://www.widener.edu

Year accredited by CSWE: 1995
# of students: 225
# of full-time faculty: 14
# of part-time faculty: 8
% of applicants accepted: 75
Tuition and/or typical assistance package: Tuition for Spring 2005 is $760/credit for day classes and $385/credit for evening classes. A typical assistance package includes loans and work study. Grants and scholarships are also available.
Unique aspects of the program: The program prepares graduates for effective clinical social work practice with individuals, families, and groups in agency-based settings. The program features small, interactive classes and caters to working students who have multiple responsibilities. The field instruction program takes great care to include students in the field selection process. Full-time and part-time enrollment options are available. There is a single concentration in clinical social work practice. A regular (62 credit hours) program and an advanced standing (38 credit hours) program for students who have earned a BSW from a CSWE-accredited undergraduate social work program are offered. Joint programs include MSW/PA Home and School Visitor Certification, MSW/Certificate in Health Service Management Administration, and MSW/Ed.D. in Human Sexuality.
Tips for applicants: The School looks for evidence that the applicant has a good rationale for choosing social work training as a career direction.
Common mistakes applicants make: Poorly written (both grammatically and substantively) personal statement and lack of specificity with regard to reasons for career choice.

Yeshiva University—Wurzweiler School of Social Work, 2495 Amsterdam Avenue New York, NY 10033. Admissions Contact: Ruth Bigman,MSW. Telephone: 212-960-0800. Fax: 212-960-0821.
E-mail: wsswadmissions@yu.edu
Web site address: http://www.yu.edu/wurzweiler

Year accredited by CSWE: 1959
# of students: 400
# of full-time faculty: 20
# of part-time faculty: 32
% of applicants accepted: N.A.
Programs available: MSW , MSW+ Certificate in Jewish Communal Service, Ph.D.
Advanced standing/advanced placement offered? yes

Distance education/online study offered? no
Tuition and/or typical assistance package: $10,630 per semester, full-time. Scholarships are available that are both merit- and need-based. Loans are also available.
Unique aspects of the program: Advanced concentrations in casework, social group work and community organization. Advisor centered school with practice teacher serving as both field liaison and academic advisor. Summer intensive eight-week block program. Certificate in Jewish Communal Service. Highly diverse student body. Major emphasis on values and ethics.
Tips for applicants: Demonstrate a high level of maturity, previous volunteer service, and the ability to articulate knowledge and interests.
Common mistakes applicants make: Underestimating both the cost and time commitment required for graduate social work degree. Asking for life experience credit.

Appendix C

Social Work Licensing Boards

Knowing the licensing requirements in the state or province where you plan to practice social work will help you make informed decisions and plan ahead. The material in this Appendix is reprinted with permission of the Association of Social Work Boards (ASWB) and is current as of February 2005. For more information, contact ASWB, 400 South Ridge Parkway, Suite B, Culpeper, Virginia 22701. Telephone (800) 225-6880 or (540) 829-6880, Fax (540) 829-0142. E-Mail: info@aswb.org. Web: http://www.aswb.org.

United States Licensing Boards

ALABAMA   **State Board of Social Work Examiners**
RAS Union Building
100 North Union Street, Suite 736
Montgomery, AL 36130-1620
334-242-5860
http://www.abswe.state.al.us

Title	Education	Experience	ASWB Exam
Private Independent Practice (PIP)	DSW / MSW	2 yrs POST	Not required (Board Review)
Licensed Certified Social Worker (LCSW)	DSW / MSW	2 yrs POST	Clinical/Adv. Gen.
Licensed Graduate Social Worker (LGSW)	MSW	None	Masters
Licensed Bachelor Social Worker (LBSW)	BSW	None	Bachelors

ALASKA   **Board of Social Work Examiners**
Division of Occupational Licensing
P. O. Box 110806
Juneau, AK 99811-0806

907-465-2551
http://www.dced.state.ak.us/occ/pcsw.htm

Title	Education	Experience	ASWB Exam
Licensed Clinical Social Worker (LCSW)	DSW/MSW	2 yrs POST	Clinical
Licensed Master Social Worker (LMSW)	DSW/MSW	None	Masters
Licensed Baccalaureate Social Worker (LBSW)	BSW	None	Bachelors

ARIZONA

Board of Behavioral Health Examiners
1400 West Washington, #350
Phoenix, AZ 85007
602-542-1882
http://www.bbhe.state.az.us/

Title	Education	Experience	ASWB Exam
Licensed Clinical Social Worker (LCSW)	DSW/MSW	2 yrs POST	Clinical/Adv. Gen.
Licensed Master Social Worker (LMSW)	DSW/MSW	None	Masters
Licensed Bachelor Social Worker (LBSW)	BSW	None	Bachelors

ARKANSAS

Social Work Licensing Board
2020 West Third Street, Suite 503
P. O. Box 250381
Little Rock, AR 72225
501-372-5071
http://www.state.ar.us/swlb

Title	Education	Experience	ASWB Exam
Licensed Certified Social Worker (LCSW)	MSW	2 yrs POST	Clinical/Adv. Gen.
Licensed Master Social Worker (LMSW)	MSW	None	Masters
Licensed Social Worker (LSW)	BSW	None	Bachelors

CALIFORNIA

Board of Behavioral Science Examiners
400 R Street, Suite 3150
Sacramento, CA 95814-6240

916-445-4933
http://www.bbs.ca.gov

Title	Education	Experience	ASWB Exam
Licensed Clinical Social Worker (LCSW)	MSW	2 yrs POST	State specific exam*
Associate Clinical Social Worker (ASW)	MSW	None	Not required

*oral exam also required. ASWB exam not accepted in California.

COLORADO **Board of Social Work Examiners**
1560 Broadway, Suite 880
Denver, CO 80202
303-894-7766
http://www.dora.state.co.us/mental-health

Title	Education	Experience	ASWB Exam
Licensed Clinical Social Worker (LCSW)	DSW or MSW	1 yr POST 2 yrs POST	Clinical/Adv. Gen. Clinical/Adv. Gen.
Licensed Independent Social Worker (LISW)	DSW or MSW	1 yr POST 2 yrs POST	Clinical/Adv. Gen. Clinical/Adv. Gen.
Licensed Social Worker (LSW)	MSW	None	Masters
Registered Social Worker (RSW)	BSW	None	Bachelors

CONNECTICUT **Department of Public Health**
Social Work Licensure
410 Capitol Avenue, MS #12APP
P.O. Box 340308
Hartford, CT 06314-0308
860-509-7603
http://www.dph.state.ct.us

Title	Education	Experience	ASWB Exam
Licensed Clinical Social Worker (LCSW)	DSW /MSW	3000 hrs POST plus 100 hrs supervision	Clinical

DELAWARE **Board of Clinical Social Work Examiners**
Cannon Bldg. Suite 203
861 Silverlake Boulevard

Dover, DE 19904-2467
302-744-4500
http://www.professionallicensing.state.de.us/boards/
socialworkers/index.shtml

Title	Education	Experience	ASWB Exam
Licensed Clinical Social Worker (LCSW)	DSW /MSW	2 yrs POST	Clinical

DISTRICT OF COLUMBIA

Board of Social Work
D.C. Department of Health
825 N. Capitol Street, NE, Second Floor
Washington, DC 20001
202-442-9200
http://dchealth.dc.gov

Title	Education	Experience	ASWB Exam
Licensed Independent Clinical Social Worker (LICSW)	MSW	3000 hrs POST	Clinical
Licensed Independent Social Worker (LISW)	MSW	3000 hrs POST	Adv. Gen.
Licensed Graduate Social Worker (LGSW)	MSW	None	Masters
Licensed Social Work Associate (LSWA)	BSW	None	Bachelors

FLORIDA

Board of Clinical Social Work, Marriage and Family Therapy, and Mental Health Counseling
4052 Bald Cypress Way, Bin #C0
Tallahassee, FL 32399-3258
850-245-4474
http://www.doh.state.fl.us/mqa/491/soc_home.html

Title	Education	Experience	ASWB Exam
Licensed Clinical Social Worker (LCSW)	DSW/MSW	2 yrs POST	Clinical
Certified Master Social Worker (CMSW)	MSW	2 yrs POST	Masters

GEORGIA

Composite Board of Professional Counselors, Social Workers, and Marriage & Family Therapists

237 Coliseum Drive
Macon, GA 31217-3855
478-207-1670
http://www.sos.state.ga.us/plb/counselors

Title	Education	Experience	ASWB Exam
Licensed Clinical Social Worker (LCSW)	MSW	3 yrs POST	Clinical/Adv. Gen.
Licensed Master Social Worker (LMSW)	MSW	None	Masters

HAWAII

Department of Commerce and Consumer Affairs
Social Work Program
P.O. Box 3469
Honolulu, HI 96801
808-586-3000
http://www.state.hi.us/dcca/

Title	Education	Experience	ASWB Exam
Licensed Clinical Social Worker (LCSW)	DSW/MSW	3000 hrs POST	Clinical
Licensed Social Worker (LSW)	DSW/MSW	None	Masters
Licensed Bachelor Social Worker (LBSW)	BSW	None	Bachelors

IDAHO

State Board of Social Work Examiners
Bureau of Occupational Licensing
Owyhee Plaza-1109 Main Street, Suite 220
Boise, ID 83702
208-334-3233
http://www2.state.id.us/ibol/swo.htm

Title	Education	Experience	ASWB Exam
Independent Practice (LCSW)	DSW/MSW	2 yrs POST	Clinical
Certified Social Worker (LMSW)	DSW/MSW	None	Masters
Social Worker (LSW)	BSW	None	Bachelors

ILLINOIS

Social Work Examining and Disciplinary Board
Department of Professional Regulation
320 West Washington Street, 3rd Floor
Springfield, IL 62786
217-785-0800
http://www.dpr.state.il.us

Title	Education	Experience	ASWB Exam
Licensed Clinical	DSW	2000 hrs POST	Clinical
Social Worker (LCSW)	or MSW	3000 hrs POST	Clinical
Licensed Social	MSW	None	Masters
Worker (LSW)	or BSW	3 yrs POST	Masters

INDIANA

Social Worker, Marriage & Family Therapist, and Mental Health Counselor Credentialing Board
402 West Washington Street, Room W
Indianapolis, IN 46204
317-234-2064
http://www.in.gov/hpb/boards/mhcb

Title	Education	Experience	ASWB Exam
Licensed Clinical Social Worker (LCSW)	MSW	3 yrs/2 yrs POST	Clinical
Licensed Social Worker (LSW)	MSW or BSW	None 2 yrs POST	Masters Masters

IOWA

Board of Social Work Examiners
Bureau of Professional Licensure
Lucas State Office Building
321 E. 12th Street
Des Moines, IA 50319-0075
515-281-4422
http://www.idph.state.ia.us/idph_pl/

Title	Education	Experience	ASWB Exam
Licensed Independent Social Worker (LISW)	DSW/MSW	2 yrs POST	Clinical
Licensed Master Social Worker (LMSW)	DSW/MSW	None	Masters
Licensed Bachelor Social Worker (LBSW)	BSW	None	Bachelors

KANSAS

Behavioral Sciences Regulatory Board
712 S. Kansas Avenue
Topeka, KS 66603-3817
785-296-3240
http://www.ksbsrb.org

Title	Education	Experience	ASWB Exam
Specialist Clinical Social Worker (LSCSW)	DSW/MSW	2 yrs POST	Clinical
Master Social Worker (LMSW)	MSW	None	Masters
Baccalaureate Social Worker (LBSW)	BSW	None	Bachelors

KENTUCKY

Board of Examiners of Social Work
911 Lenwood Drive, 2nd Floor
P.O. Box 1360
Frankfort, KY 40602
502-564-3296
http://www.state.ky.us/agencies/finance/

Title	Education	Experience	ASWB Exam
Licensed Independent Practice (LCSW)	DSW/MSW	2 yrs POST	Clinical
Certified Social Worker (CSW)	MSW	None	Masters
Licensed Social Worker (LSW)	BSW or BA	None 2 yrs	Bachelors Bachelors

LOUISIANA

State Board of Social Work Examiners
18550 Highland Road, Suite B
Baton Rouge, LA 70809
225-756-3470
http://www.labswe.org

Title	Education	Experience	ASWB Exam
Licensed Clinical Social Worker (LCSW)	MSW	3 yrs POST	Clinical/Adv. Gen.
Graduate Social Worker (GSW)	MSW	None	Masters
Registered Social Worker (RSW)	BSW	None	None required

MAINE   **State Board of Social Work Licensure**
35 State House Station
Augusta, ME 04333
207-624-8603
http://www.maineprofessionalreg.org

Title	Education	Experience	ASWB Exam
Licensed Clinical Social Worker (LCSW)	DSW/MSW	2 yrs POST	Clinical
Licensed Master Social Worker (LMSW)	DSW/MSW	None	Masters
Licensed Social Worker (LSW)	BSW or BA/BS	None 3200 hrs	Bachelors Bachelors

MARYLAND   **State Board of Social Work Examiners**
Department of Health and Mental Hygiene
4201 Patterson Avenue
Baltimore, MD 21215-2299
410-764-4788
http://www.dhmh.state.md.us/bswe/

Title	Education	Experience	ASWB Exam
Licensed Certified Social Worker—Clinical (LCSW-C)	DSW/MSW	2 yrs POST	Clinical
Licensed Certified Social Worker (LCSW)	DSW/MSW	2 yrs POST	Adv. Gen.
Licensed Graduate Social Worker (LGSW)	DSW/MSW	None	Masters
Licensed Social Work Associate (LSW)	BSW	None	Bachelors

MASSACHUSETTS Commonwealth of Massachusetts
Division of Registration
100 Cambridge Street
Boston, MA 02202
617-727-3073
http://www.state.ma.us/reg/boards/sw/default.htm

Title	Education	Experience	ASWB Exam
Licensed Independent Clinical Social Worker (LICSW)	DSW/MSW	2 yrs POST	Clinical
Licensed Certified Social Worker (LCSW)	DSW/MSW	None	Masters

Title	Education	Experience	ASWB Exam
Licensed Social Worker (LSW)	BSW	None	Bachelors
	or BA	2 yrs	Bachelors
	or college	5 yrs	Bachelors
	or HS	8 yrs	Bachelors
Licensed Social Work Associate (LSWA)	AA/BA	None	Associate

MICHIGAN

Board of Social Work
611 W. Ottowa Street
P. O. Box 30670
Lansing, MI 48909
517-335-0918
http://www.michigan.gov/healthlicense

Title	Education	Experience	ASWB Exam
Certified Social Worker (CSW)	MSW	2 yrs POST	Clinical
Social Worker (SW)	MSW	None	Bachelors
	or BA	2 yrs POST	Bachelors
Social Work Technician (SWT)	2 yrs college	None	Not Required
	or 1 yr exp	1 yr POST	Not Required

MINNESOTA

Board of Social Work
2829 University Avenue, SE, Suite 340
Minneapolis, MN 55414-3239
612-617-2100
http://www.socialwork.state.mn.us

Title	Education	Experience	ASWB Exam
Licensed Independent Clinical Social Worker (LICSW)	DSW/MSW	2 yrs POST	Clinical
Licensed Independent Social Worker (LISW)	DSW/MSW	2 yrs POST	Adv. Gen.
Licensed Graduate Social Worker (LGSW)	MSW	None	Masters
Licensed Social Worker (LSW)	BSW	None	Bachelors

MISSISSIPPI

**Board of Examiners for Social Workers
And Marriage & Family Therapists**
P.O. Box 4508
Jackson, MS 39296-4508

601-987-6806
http://www.msboeswmft.com

Title	Education	Experience	ASWB Exam
Licensed Certified Social Worker (LCSW)	DSW/MSW	2 yrs POST	Clinical/Adv. Gen.
Licensed Master Social Worker (LMSW)	DSW/MSW	None	Masters
Licensed Social Worker (LSW)	BSW	None	Bachelors

MISSOURI **State Committee for Licensed Social Workers**
Division of Professional Registration
P.O. Box 1335
Jefferson City, MO 65102
573-751-0885
http://www.ecodev.state.mo.us/pr/social

Title	Education	Experience	ASWB Exam
Licensed Clinical Social Worker (LCSW)	DSW/MSW	2 yrs POST	Clinical
Licensed Baccalaureate Social Worker (LBSW)	BSW	2 yrs POST	Bachelors/Masters/ Adv. Gen./Clinical

MONTANA **Board of Social Work Examiners &**
Professional Counselors
301 South Park, 4th Floor
PO Box 2309
Helena, MT 59620-0513
406-841-2369
http://www.discoveringmontana.com/dli/swp

Title	Education	Experience	ASWB Exam
Licensed Clinical Social Worker (LCSW)	DSW/MSW	2 yrs POST	Clinical/Adv. Gen.

NEBRASKA **Credentialing Division**
301 Centennial Mall South
P. O. Box 94986
Lincoln, NE 68509-4986
402-471-2117
http://www.hhs.state.ne.us/crl/mhcs/mental/
mentalhealth.htm

Title	Education	Experience	ASWB Exam
Licensed Mental Health Practitioner (LMHP)	DSW/MSW	3000 hrs POST	Clinical
Certified Master Social Worker (CMSW)	DSW/MSW	3000 hrs POST	Clinical/Adv. Gen.
Certified Social Worker (CSW)	MSW/BSW	None	Not Required

NEVADA

Board of Examiners for Social Workers
4600 Kietzke Lane, Suite C121
Reno, NV 89502
775-688-2555
http://www.socwork.nv.gov

Title	Education	Experience	ASWB Exam
Licensed Clinical Social Worker (LCSW)	MSW	3000 hrs POST	Clinical
Licensed Independent Social Worker (LISW)	MSW	3000 hrs POST	Adv. Gen.
Licensed Social Worker (LSW)	MSW/BSW	None	Bachelors or Masters

NEW HAMPSHIRE

Board of Mental Health Practice
49 Donovan Street
Concord, NH 03301
603-271-6762
http://www.state.nh.us/mhpb

Title	Education	Experience	ASWB Exam
Licensed Independent Clinical Social Worker (LICSW)	DSW/MSW	2 yrs POST	Clinical

NEW JERSEY

State Board of Social Work Examiners
P. O. Box 45033
Newark, NJ 07101
973-504-6495
http://www.state.nj.us/lps/ca/social/swlic.htm

Title	Education	Experience	ASWB Exam
Licensed Clinical Social Worker (LCSW)	DSW/MSW	2 yrs	Clinical
Licensed Social Worker (LSW)	DSW/MSW	None	Masters

Certified Social	BSW	None	Not Required
Worker (CSW)	or BA	1600 hrs. over 18	Not Required
		months (prior to 4/6/95)	

NEW MEXICO   **Board of Social Work Examiners**
2550 Cerillos Road
Santa Fe, NM 87505
505-476-7056
http://www.rld.state.nm.us/b&c/socialwk/index.htm

Title	Education	Experience	ASWB Exam
Licensed Independent Social Worker (LISW)	MSW	2 yrs POST	Clinical/Adv. Gen.*
Licensed Master Social Worker (LMSW)	MSW	None	Masters*
Licensed Baccalaureate Social Worker (LBSW)	BSW	None	Bachelors*

*Cultural awareness exam also required in New Mexico.

NEW YORK   **State Board for Social Work**
89 Washington Avenue
Albany, NY 12234-1000
518-474-3817
http://www.op.nysed.gov/csw.htm

Title	Education	Experience	ASWB Exam
Licensed Master Social Worker (LMSW)	MSW	None	Masters
Licensed Clinical Social Worker (LCSW)	MSW	3 yrs POST	Clinical

NORTH CAROLINA   **North Carolina Certification & Licensure Board**
357 S. Cox Street
PO Box 1043
Asheboro, NC 27204
335-625-1679
http://www.ncswboard.org

Title	Education	Experience	ASWB Exam
Licensed Clinical Social Worker (LCSW)	DSW/MSW	2 yrs POST	Clinical

Certified Social Work Manager (CSWM)	DSW/MSW/BSW	2 yrs POST	Adv. Gen.
Certified Master Social Worker (CMSW)	DSW/MSW	None	Masters
Certified Social Worker (CSW)	BSW	None	Bachelors

NORTH DAKOTA

Board of Social Work Examiners
P.O. Box 914
Bismarck, ND 58502-0914
701-222-0255
http://www.ndbswe.com

Title	Education	Experience	ASWB Exam
Licensed Independent Clinical Social Worker (LICSW)	DSW/MSW	4 yrs POST	Clinical
Licensed Certified Social Worker (LCSW)	DSW/MSW	None	Clinical/Adv. Gen./ Masters
Licensed Social Worker (LSW)	BSW	None	Bachelors

OHIO

Counselor, Social Worker, & Marriage & Family Therapist Board
77 South High Street, 16th Floor
Columbus, OH 43215-6108
614-466-0912
http://www.cswmft.ohio.gov

Title	Education	Experience	ASWB Exam
Licensed Independent Social Worker (LISW)	DSW/MSW	2 yrs POST	Clinical/Adv. Gen.
Licensed Social Worker (LSW)	DSW/MSW/ BSW	None	Bachelors
Registered Social Work Assistant (SWA)	AA	None	Not Required

OKLAHOMA

Board of Licensed Social Workers
5104 N. Francis, Suite E
PO Box 18817
Oklahoma City, OK 73154-0817
405-946-7230
http://www.state.ok.us/~osblsw

Title	Education	Experience	ASWB Exam
Licensed for Private Practice (LSW)	DSW/MSW	2 yrs POST	Clinical
Licensed Social Worker (LSW)	DSW/MSW	2 yrs POST	Adv. Gen.
Licensed Social Work Associate (LSWA)	BSW	2 yrs POST	Masters/Bachelors

OREGON **State Board of Clinical Social Workers**
3218 Pringle Road SE, Suite 240
Salem, OR 93702-6310
503-378-5735
http://bcsw.state.or.us/

Title	Education	Experience	ASWB Exam
Licensed Clinical Social Worker (LCSW)	DSW/MSW	2 yrs POST	Clinical
Clinical Social Work Associate (CSWA)	DSW/MSW	None	Not Required

PENNSYLVANIA **State Board for Social Workers, Marriage and Family Therapists, and Professional Counselors**
P. O. Box 2649
Harrisburg, PA 17105-2649
717-783-1389
http://www.dos.state.pa.us/bpoa/socwkbd/mainpage.htm

Title	Education	Experience	ASWB Exam
Licensed Clinical Social Worker (LCSW)	DSW/MSW	3 yrs POST	Clinical
Licensed Social Worker (LSW)	DSW/MSW	None	Masters

PUERTO RICO **State Board of Social Work Examiners**
PO Box 9023271
San Juan, PR 00902-3271
809-758-3588

Title	Education	Experience	ASWB Exam
Licensed Clinical Social Worker (LCSW)	DSW/MSW	3 yrs POST	Clinical
Licensed Social Worker (LSW)	DSW/MSW	None	Master's

RHODE ISLAND **Division of Professional Regulation**
Rhode Island Department of Health
3 Capitol Hill, Room 104
Providence, RI 02908-5097
401-222-2827
http://www.healthri.org/hsr/professions/s_work.htm

Title	Education	Experience	ASWB Exam
Licensed Independent Clinical Social Worker (LICSW)	DSW/MSW	2 yrs POST	Clinical
Licensed Clinical Social Worker (LCSW)	MSW/BSW	None	Masters

SOUTH CAROLINA **Board of Social Work Examiners**
P. O. Box 11329
Columbia, SC 29211-1329
803-896-4665
http://www.llr.state.sc.us/pol/socialworkers/

Title	Education	Experience	ASWB Exam
Licensed Independent Social Worker—Advanced Practice (LISW-AP)	DSW/MSW	2 yrs POST	Adv. Gen.
Licensed Independent Social Worker— Clinical Practice (LISW-CP)	DSW/MSW	2 yrs POST	Clinical
Licensed Master Social Worker (LMSW)	DSW/MSW	None	Masters
Licensed Baccalaureate Social Worker (LBSW)	BSW	None	Bachelors

SOUTH DAKOTA **Board of Social Work Examiners**
135 E. Illinois, Suite 214
Spearfish, SD 57783
605-642-1600
http://www.state.sd.us/dcr/socialwork/soc-hom.htm

Title	Education	Experience	ASWB Exam
Private Independent Practice (CSW-PIP)	DSW/MSW	2 yrs	Clinical/Adv. Gen.
Certified Social Worker (CSW)	DSW/MSW	None	Masters
Social Worker (SW)	BSW or BA	None 2 yrs	Bachelors Bachelors
Social Work Associate (SWA)	AA/BA	None	Associate

TENNESSEE

Board of Social Work Certification and Licensure
Cordell Hull Building
426 5th Ave. N
Nashville, TN 37247-1010
615-532-5132
http://www2.state.tn.us/health/boards/sw

Title	Education	Experience	ASWB Exam
Independent Practitioner (LCSW)	DSW/MSW	2 yrs POST	Clinical
Certified Master Social Worker (CMSW)	DSW/MSW	None	Not Required

TEXAS

State Board of Social Work Examiners
1100 West 49th Street
Austin, TX 78756-3183
512-719-3521
http://www.tdh.state.tx.us/hcqs/plc/lsw/lsw_default.htm

Title	Education	Experience	ASWB Exam
Licensed Clinical Social Worker (LCSW)	DSW/MSW	2 yrs POST	Clinical
Licensed Master Social Worker—Advanced Practice (LMSW-AP)	DSW/MSW	3 yrs POST	Adv. Gen.
Licensed Master Social Worker (LMSW)	DSW/MSW	None	Masters
Licensed Baccalaureate Social Worker (LBSW)	BSW	None	Bachelors
Social Work Associate (SWA)	BA—human sciences or related field	1 yr	Bachelors

UTAH

Social Work Licensing Board
Occupational and Professional Licensing
160 East 300 South
P.O. Box 146741
Salt Lake City, UT 84114
801-530-6396
http://www.dopl.utah.gov/licensing/
social_work.html

Title	Education	Experience	ASWB Exam
Licensed Clinical Social Worker (LCSW)	DSW/MSW	2 yrs POST	Clinical*
Certified Social Worker (CSW)	DSW/MSW	None	Masters*
Social Service Worker (SSW)	MSW/BSW or BA	None 1 yr POST	Bachelors* Bachelors*

*Law and rules exam also required in Utah.

VERMONT

Office of the Secretary of State
Licensing and Registration Division
109 State Street
Montpelier, VT 05609-1106
802-828-2191
http://www.sec.state.vt.us

Title	Education	Experience	ASWB Exam
Licensed Independent Clinical Social Worker (LICSW)	DSW/MSW	2 yrs POST	Clinical

VIRGIN ISLANDS

Division of Licensing & Consumer Affairs
Office of Boards & Commissions
Golden Rock Shopping Center
Christiansted, St. Croix, VI 00820
340-773-2226

Title	Education	Experience	ASWB Exam
Certified Independent Social Worker (CISW)	DSW/MSW	2 yrs POST	Clinical/Adv. Gen.
Certified Social Worker (CSW)	DSW/MSW	None	Masters
Social Worker (SW)	BSW or BA	None 2 yrs POST	Bachelors Bachelors

Social Work Associate (SWA)	AA/BA	None	Associate

VIRGINIA

Board of Social Work
6603 West Broad Street, 5th Floor
Richmond, VA 23230-1712
804-662-9914
http://www.dhp.state.va.us/social/default.htm

Title	Education	Experience	ASWB Exam
Licensed Clinical Social Worker (LCSW)	MSW	2 yrs POST	Clinical
Licensed Social Worker (LSW)	MSW or BSW	None 2 yrs POST	Bachelors Bachelors

WASHINGTON

Washington Department of Health Counselor Programs
1300 SE Quince
P. O. Box 47869
Olympia, WA 98504-7869
360-236-4900
http://www.doh.wa.gov/

Title	Education	Experience	ASWB Exam
Licensed Independent Clinical Social Worker (LICSW)	DSW/MSW	4000 hrs POST	Clinical
Licensed Advanced Social Worker (LASW)	DSW/MSW	3200 hours POST	Clinical/Adv. Gen.

WEST VIRGINIA

Board of Social Work Examiners
P. O. Box 5459
Charleston, WV 25361
304-558-8816
http://www.wvsocialworkboard.org

Title	Education	Experience	ASWB Exam
Licensed Independent Clinical Social Worker (LICSW)	DSW/MSW	2 yrs POST	Clinical
Licensed Certified Social Worker (LCSW)	DSW/MSW	2 yrs POST	Adv. Gen.
Licensed Graduate Social Worker (LGSW)	MSW	None	Masters

| Licensed Social Worker (LSW) | BSW | None | Bachelors |

WISCONSIN   **Examining Board of Marriage & Family Therapists, Professional Counselors, & Social Workers**
Department of Regulation and Licensing
P.O. Box 8935
Madison, WI 53708-8935
608-267-7223
http://www.drl.state.wi.us

Title	Education	Experience	ASWB Exam
Licensed Clinical Social Worker (LCSW)	DSW/MSW	2 yrs POST	Clinical*
Certified Independent Social Worker (CISW)	DSW/MSW	2 yrs POST	Adv. Gen.*
Certified Adv. Practice Social Worker (CAPSW)	DSW/MSW	None	Masters*
Certified Social Worker (CSW)	MSW/BSW	None	Bachelors*

*Laws and rules exam also required in Wisconsin.

WYOMING   **Mental Health Professions Licensing Board**
2020 Carey Avenue, Suite 201
Cheyenne, WY 82002
307-777-7788
http://plboards.state.wy.us/mentalhealth

Title	Education	Experience	ASWB Exam
Licensed Clinical Social Worker (LCSW)	DSW/MSW	2 yrs POST	Clinical/Adv. Gen.
Certified Social Worker (CSW)	BSW	None	Masters/Bachelors

Canadian Licensing Boards

ALBERTA   **Alberta College of Social Workers**
550-10707
100 Avenue, NW
Edmonton, Alberta T5J 3M1 Canada
(780) 421-1167
http://www.acsw.ab.ca

Title	Education	Experience	ASWB Exam
Clinical Social Worker (RSW)	MSW/DSW	2 yrs POST	Clinical
Registerd Social Worker (RSW)	Social work degree or diploma	None	Not required

BRITISH COLUMBIA

Board of Registration for Social Workers
302-1765 West 8th Avenue
Vancouver, BC V6J 5C6
604-737-4916
http://www.brsw.bc.ca

Title	Education	Experience	ASWB Exam
Registered Social Worker (RSW)	BSW/MSW	None	Not required
Registered Social Worker-Private	MSW/DSW/ PhD or	None	Not required
Practice	BSW	8 yrs POST	Not required

MANITOBA

Manitoba Institute of Registered Social Workers
103-2015 Portage Avenue
Winnipeg, MB R3J 0K3
204-888-9477
http://www.geocities.com/masw_mirsw

Title	Education	Experience	ASWB Exam
Registered Social Worker (RSW)	BSW/MSW	None	Not required

NEW BRUNSWICK

New Brunswick Association of Social Workers
P.O. Box 1533, Station A
Fredericton, NB E3B 5G2
506-459-5595
http://www.nbasw-atsnb.ca

Title	Education	Experience	ASWB Exam
Registered Social Worker (RSW)	BSW/MSW	None	Not required

NEWFOUNDLAND   Newfoundland & Labrador Association of
& LABRADOR   Social Work
P.O. Box 5244
St-John's, NF A1C 5W1
709-753-0200

Title	Education	Experience	ASWB Exam
Registered Social Worker (RSW)	BSW/MSW/ DSW	None	Not required

NOVA SCOTIA   Registrar's Office Board of Examiners
Plaza 1881
1891 Brunswick St., No. 106
Halifax, NS B3J 2G8
902-429-7298
http://www.nsasw.org

Title	Education	Experience	ASWB Exam
Registered Social Worker (RSW)	BSW/MSW/RW	3 yrs. POST	Nor required
Registered Social Worker-Private practice	MSW/DSW	None	Not required

ONTARIO   Ontario College of Social Workers & Social
Service Workers
80 Bloor St., West #700
Toronto, ON M5S 2V1
416-972-9882
http://www.ocswssw.org

Title	Education	Experience	ASWB Exam
Registered Social required Worker (RSW)	BSW/MSW/DSW	None	Not

PRINCE EDWARD   Prince Edward Island Social Work Registration
ISLAND   Board
81 Prince St.
Charlottetown, PE C1A 4R3
902-368-7337

Title	Education	Experience	ASWB Exam
Registered Social Worker (RSW)	BSW	None	Not required

QUEBEC   **Ordre Professionel des Travailleurs Sociaux du Que**
5757 av Decelles, bureau 335
Montreal, QC H3S 2C3
514-731-3925
http://www.optsq.org

Title	Education	Experience	ASWB Exam
Social Worker (SW)	BSW/MSW	None	Not required

SASKATCHEWAN   **Saskatchewan Association of Social Workers**
2110 Lorne St.
Regina, SK S4P 2M5
306-545-1922

Title	Education	Experience	ASWB Exam
Registered Social Worker (RSW)	Certificate in Social Work	None	Not required

Appendix D

MSW Application Tracking Sheet

This sheet is provided as a tool to help you organize your application process. Use one tracking sheet for each school to which you apply.

Name of School _____

Address _____

Telephone _____

Fax _____

E-Mail _____

Contact Person _____

Application Deadline _____

Program begins: ❑Fall   ❑Winter ❑Spring   ❑Summer

Admissions Information Checklist:

Item	Date Submitted	Date of Notice of Receipt by School
Completed Application	_____	_____
Letters of reference		
Source	_____ _____	_____
Source	_____ _____	_____
Source	_____ _____	_____
Source	_____ _____	_____
Source	_____ _____	_____
Transcripts		
School	_____ _____	_____
School	_____ _____	_____
School	_____ _____	_____
School	_____ _____	_____

Item	Date Submitted	Date of Notice of Receipt by School
Standardized Test Results		
Type of Exam _____	_____	_____
Biographical Statement	_____	_____
Financial Aid Information		
Free Application for Federal Student Aid (FAFSA)	_____	_____
State Aid Form (if applicable)	_____	_____
School Financial Aid Form	_____	_____
University Financial Aid Form (if applicable)	_____	_____
Copy of Previous Year's Personal Tax Return	_____	_____
Copy of Previous Year's Parents' Tax Return (if requested)	_____	_____

Response from School:

Item	Date Received	Date Returned
Offer of Admission or Rejection	_____	_____
Deadline for Acceptance or Rejection of Offer of Admission _____		_____
Offer of Financial Aid Award	_____	_____
Deadline for Acceptance of Offer of Financial Aid Award _____		_____
Deposit to Hold Place in Class (Amount: _____)	_____	
Deadline to Receive a Refund of Deposit (if any) _____		

Appendix E

Making Your Visit Count: Questions to Ask and Things to Look For

I strongly advise that you visit the schools you are seriously considering before you make a final selection of school. The visit can take place either before or after you are offered admission. The advantage to making the visit while your application is still being considered is that you may be able to interview with an admissions person and, in essence, make a case for yourself by the impression you make. As mentioned in Chapter 8, not all schools grant applicants a formal admissions interview. Nevertheless, even in the schools that formally do not make interviews a part of the evaluation process, making a favorable impression during a visit may yield positive results. (Be on your best behavior during the visit, because a negative impression can just as easily have the opposite result!) On the other hand, visiting the school after you are offered admission can also have some advantages. Given that the school has already opened its doors to you, admissions staff may have more of an investment in taking the time to answer many questions. In either event, a visit to a school is an excellent idea, because it will allow you to get a sense of the intangibles that no catalog or video about a school and its community can fully convey.

Some readers may think the checklist that follows is too long, while others may think of items that are not included. It is, of course, not mandatory that you cover all the items posed here. Neither should you limit yourself only to these issues. Rather, they are offered as a starting point in making your own checklist.

1. Make prior arrangements with the admissions office to sit in on classes.

    Class Visits:

    Class _____ Professor _____ Date and Time _____

    Class _____ Professor _____ Date and Time _____

    Class _____ Professor _____ Date and Time _____

2. Make prior arrangements to meet with faculty who are doing work that interests you.

    Professor _____ Date and Time _____ Bldg. and Room _____

    Professor _____ Date and Time _____ Bldg. and Room _____

    Professor _____ Date and Time _____ Bldg. and Room _____

3. Is there knowledgeable and accessible academic advice?

    [   ] Advisors within the school

    [   ] Advisors at the university level (How well do they know social work?)

4. Ask to meet with students from similar backgrounds and circumstances as you.

    Student _____ Date and Time _____ Bldg. & Room _____

    Student _____ Date and Time _____ Bldg. & Room _____

    Student _____ Date and Time _____ Bldg. & Room _____

5. Physical facilities:

    Are the classrooms and seating comfortable?   [   ] Yes   [   ] No
    Are they adequately heated or cooled?   [   ] Yes   [   ] No
    How large are typical classes? _____

6. Is the school accessible to the physically disabled? [   ] Yes   [   ] No

What services has the school provided for students with disabilities?

_____

_____

7. What provisions does the school (and the university) provide for the safety of students?

    Have any students been victims of crimes on campus in the last year?
    [   ] Yes   [   ] No

    If yes, does the university police department provide information about the locations and nature of recent incidents on campus?

    _____

    _____

    Does the university have van or bus service for students to and from their dormitories and apartments during certain hours of the night?

    [   ] Yes   If yes, is it free? [   ]   Or at what cost? _____

    If you will be living off campus without a car, is there safe and reliable public transportation?

    [   ] Yes   Cost? _____

8. Library services:

    Does the school have its own library?   [   ] Yes[   ] No

    If it does...

    How well-stocked is it? _____

    Is there a full-time librarian and other qualified staff available during all operating hours?   [   ] Yes   [   ] No

    Is there electronic access to library materials?   [   ] Yes   [   ] No

    If the school does not have its own library...

    How well-stocked is the university's main library with social work matter?

    _____

    Are other campus libraries available to you?
    [   ] Yes   Which? _____   [   ] No

Does the library have cooperative arrangements with other universities for sharing materials?   [   ] Yes   [   ] No

If yes, how long does it take to actually receive materials from sister libraries?   _____

Do the libraries have state-of-the-art computers that allow you to access materials from other libraries online?   [   ] Yes   [   ] No

9. Does the school have its own computer center?   [   ] Yes   [   ] No

   If it does not, is there one at the university?   [   ] Yes   [   ] No

   Are its hours adequate and accessible to students?[   ] Yes   [   ] No

   Is it staffed all of the time or only part of the time by qualified personnel who can answer your questions?   [   ] Yes   [   ] No

   How current are the computers and related equipment?

   _____

   Are the computers compatible with your personal computer?
   [   ] Yes   [   ] No

   Does the university have a computer store with reduced prices to students?
   [   ] Yes   [   ] No

   Does the school provide low-interest student loans for the purchase of a computer?   [   ] Yes   [   ] No

10. Living arrangements:

    Appointments to view dorms and apartments:

    Contact Person _____ Date/Time _____ Bldg. & Room _____

    Contact Person _____ Date/Time _____ Bldg. & Room _____

    What is the range of rental costs?   _____

    Are utilities included? [   ] Yes   [   ] No
    If not, what is the estimated cost? _____

    Are pets permitted?   [   ] Yes   [   ] No

Are the buildings smoke-free? [   ] Yes   [   ] No

Do the buildings and neighborhoods appear safe? _____

If you have children, what schools are available? _____

11. Bookstores:

How are the prices at the university bookstore? _____
Are there independent cooperative bookstores in the area and how do prices compare?   _____

12. Health Insurance:

Is health insurance available through the university? [   ] Yes   [   ] No

Is it required of students to carry health insurance, and is the requirement waived for students who show proof of alternative coverage?
[   ] Yes   [   ] No

13. Eating Facilities:

Are campus dining facilities reasonable in cost and do you like the food?
_____

14. Recreational facilities:

Athletic fields for sports of your choice: _____

Swimming pool: _____

Other activities that interest you: _____

15. Community offerings:

Museums: _____

Concert facilities: _____

Theaters: _____

Other entertainment: _____

Appendix F

Biographical Statement Worksheet

The following is one approach that may prove useful in writing your essay. It is important to emphasize that it is not intended as a "recipe" for composing a biographical statement. The task is much too important to think of it as a series of steps that will always lead to a common outcome. Instead, the approach suggested is intended as a tool to help you organize your thoughts.

1. Make a thorough self-assessment of your experiences before writing your statement by making a list of all jobs, including those not directly related to social work:

    Employer   *Position*

    _____   _____

    _____   _____

    _____   _____

    _____   _____

    _____   _____

2. List all internships you have ever held:

    Agency/Location   *Position*

    _____   _____

    _____   _____

    _____   _____

    _____   _____

    _____   _____

3. Once you have a list of all the experiences, look at what you did in each of your positions. Make sure to list every task you had to perform on a daily basis:

   Position   *Tasks Performed*

   _____   _____

   _____   _____

   _____   _____

   _____   _____

   _____   _____

4. Once you've identified each task, list the skills that you needed in order to perform each task.

   Task   *Skills Required*

   _____   _____

   _____   _____

   _____   _____

   _____   _____

   _____   _____

5. Once you've identified the skills, establish a connection to your future goals by identifying how those skills are applicable to social work. The section on social work settings in Chapter 9 of this book discusses social work skills and may help you in this process.

   Skill   *Applicability to Social Work*

   _____   _____

   _____   _____

   _____   _____

   _____   _____

   _____   _____

6. List classes that you've taken that contributed to your understanding of social work skills:

   Class   *Skills Identified*

   _____   _____
   _____   _____
   _____   _____
   _____   _____
   _____   _____

7. Use the list of skills from jobs, internships, and classes to identify the areas of social work where you may want to go in the future. Once again, Chapter 9 of this book can help you in identifying areas of social work practice.

   Social Work Skills   *Specific Social Work Area of Practice*

   _____   _____
   _____   _____
   _____   _____
   _____   _____
   _____   _____

8. Make the connection between your goals (i.e., areas of social work practice that interest you) and the particular school's program.

   Settings   *Programs That Train For That Setting*

   _____   _____
   _____   _____
   _____   _____
   _____   _____
   _____   _____

Completing this worksheet should help you see more clearly how your past experiences have helped you develop skills that are applicable to specific social work areas of practice. That knowledge, in turn, will help you better identify the schools that have programs best suited to prepare you for your goals.

Armed with this knowledge, carefully read Chapters 10 and 11 of this book to help you address the specific points requested by the schools to which you are making application.

Appendix F: Biographical Statement Worksheet. From *THE SOCIAL WORK GRADU-ATE SCHOOL APPLICANT'S HANDBOOK.* © 2005 Jesús Reyes. Permission is granted to photocopy this appendix for your personal use.

Appendix G

For More Information

Books

Association of Social Work Boards. (2001). *Social Work Laws and Board Regulations.* Culpeper, VA: Author.

Council on Social Work Education. (2004). *Summary Information on Master of Social Work Programs, 2003-2004.* Alexandria, VA: Author.

Doelling, Carol Nesslein. (2004). *Social Work Career Development.* (2nd Ed.). Washington, DC: NASW Press.

Ginsberg, Leon. (2000). *Careers in Social Work, 2nd Edition.* Needham Heights, MA: Allyn and Bacon.

Grobman, Linda M. (Ed.). (2005). *Days in the Lives of Social Workers. (3rd Ed.).* Harrisburg, PA: White Hat Communications.

Grobman, Linda M. (Ed.). (2005). *More Days in the Lives of Social Workers.* Harrisburg, PA: White Hat Communications.

Lennon, T. M. (2004). *Statistics on Social Work Education in the United States: 2002.* Alexandria, VA: Council on Social Work Education.

Melcher, Manfred J. (2002). *Becoming a Social Worker.* Harrisburg, PA: White Hat Communications.

Organizations

Association of Social Work Boards (ASWB)
400 South Ridge Parkway, Suite B
Culpeper, Virginia 22701
800-225-6880 or 540-829-6880
Fax: 540-829-0142
http://www.aswb.org

Canadian Association of Schools of Social Work
1398 ch. Star Top Road
Ottawa, ON K1B 4V7

Canada
613-792-1953
Fax: 613-792-1956
http://www.cassw-acess.ca

Canadian Association of Social Workers
383 Avenue Parkdale Avenue, Suite/Bureau 402
Ottawa, Ontario K1Y 4R4
Canada
613-729-6668
Fax: 613-729-9608
http://www.casw-acts.ca

Council on Social Work Education (CSWE)
1725 Duke Street, Suite 500
Alexandria, VA 22314-3457
703-683-8080
Fax: 703-683-8099
http://www.cswe.org

National Association of Social Workers (NASW)
750 First Street, NE, Suite 700
Washington, DC 20002-4241
800-638-8799
http://www.socialworkers.org

Web Sites

Canada Online—Student Financial Assistance
http://canadaonline.about.com/od/studentaid/

Free Application for Federal Student Aid (FAFSA)
http://www.fafsa.ed.gov/

GradSchools.com
http://www.gradschools.com

The New Social Worker Online
http://www.socialworker.com

Peterson's Education Center
http://www.petersons.com

Social Work Graduate School
http://www.socialworkgradschool.com

Student Aid on the Web
http://studentaid.ed.gov/PORTALSWebApp/students/english/index.jsp

Index

ABOUT THE AUTHOR

Jesús Reyes, AM, ACSW, is a graduate of the School of Social Service Administration (SSA) of the University of Chicago and former Assistant Dean for Enrollment and Placement at SSA. Prior to his administrative work in recruitment, admissions, and job placement at SSA, he practiced social work in a wide variety of settings, including schools, mental health and community settings, health care, and private practice. He is currently Director of Social Service of the Circuit Court of Cook County, Illinois, the largest unified court system in the nation. His Department receives approximately 24,000 court referrals yearly consisting of felony, misdemeanor, ordinance, and traffic violation offenders. With a staff of 260 encompassing 13 court locations, the Department develops and implements an individualized supervision plan for each offender and guides and monitors the offender while he or she remains under the court's supervision. Reyes' broad social work experience, coupled with his experience in admissions at one of the most selective social work programs in the nation, provides a rich source of information for anyone considering entering the profession of social work and applying to graduate social work programs.

DAYS IN THE LIVES OF SOCIAL WORKERS
54 Professionals Tell "Real-Life" Stories from Social Work Practice (3rd Edition)
Edited by Linda May Grobman

"When I read the first story, 'Social Work in the ER,' I found myself saying, 'What an exciting day.' Thank you for your work in bringing not just good stories to print, but a resource for me and others." Delores W. Shirley, MSW, Faculty Liaison/Advisor and Director of Recruitment, University of North Carolina-Chapel Hill School of Social Work

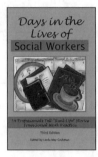

Each chapter is a first-person account written by a professional social worker in a different setting. Readers can take a look at the ups and downs and ins and outs of the writers' real-life days in the "trenches" of social work practice. This book has helped many students decide whether social work is the profession for them, and beyond that, which areas of social work to focus on in their studies and their careers.

Read this book to observe social work practice in the following settings and roles:

- Community and inpatient mental health
- Inner-city and rural schools
- International social work with "raskal" gangs in Papua New Guinea
- Prisons
- Hospitals
- The military
- Managed care
- Residential treatment centers for adolescents
- Homeless outreach
- College counseling centers
- Public child welfare
- Nursing homes
- Hospice
- Adventure-based therapy
- Private practice
- HIV/AIDS research
- Public health
- Administration
  ....and many more!

This book is an **essential guide** for anyone who wants an inside look at the social work profession. You will learn valuable lessons from the experiences of social workers described in *DAYS IN THE LIVES OF SOCIAL WORKERS, 3rd Edition.*

ISBN: 1-929109-15-6   2005   Price: $19.95 (U.S.) + shipping

410 pages, 5 ½ x 8 ½   Softcover

Order from White Hat Communications, P.O. Box 5390, Harrisburg, PA 17110-0390 with order form in the back of this book.

MORE DAYS IN THE LIVES
OF SOCIAL WORKERS

35 "Real-Life" Stories of Advocacy, Outreach, and Other Intriguing Roles in Social Work Practice

Edited by Linda May Grobman

Like its popular predecessor, *Days in the Lives of Social Workers*, this book illustrates through first-person narratives that there are no "typical" days in social work, but that professionally trained social workers take on a variety of different roles. In this volume, there is more of a focus on macro roles than in the first, although this book also includes micro-level stories and illustrates ways in which social workers combine macro, mezzo, and micro level work in their everyday practice.

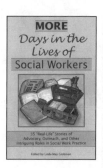

Read this book to observe social work practice in the following settings and roles:

- Working on a national level
- Program development and management
- Advocacy and organizing
- Policy from the inside
- Training and consultation
- Research and funding
- Higher education
- Specialized roles in the court system
- Faith and spirituality
- Domestic violence
- Therapy and case management
- Employment and hunger

This easy-to-read, hard-to-put-down book will make a welcome supplement to the theory found in traditional textbooks. Find out how social work managers and practitioners put theory into practice on a day-to-day basis.

Organizations, Web sites, and additional readings are listed to assist you in further exploring areas of social work practice that are of interest to you.

ISBN: 1-929109-16-4   2005   Price: $16.95 (U.S.) + shipping

252 pages, 5 ½ x 8 ½   Softcover

Order from White Hat Communications, P.O. Box 5390, Harrisburg, PA 17110-0390 with order form in the back of this book.

ORDER FORM

I would like to order the following publications from White Hat Communications:

Qty.	Item	Price
_____	Days in the Lives of Social Workers @ $19.95	_____
_____	More Days in the Lives of Social Wkrs @ $16.95	_____
_____	Field Placement Survival Guide @ $21.95	_____
_____	Social Work Grad. School App. Hdbk @ $19.95	_____
_____	New Social Worker Subscription $15.00	_____
_____	Other _____	_____

Please send my order to:
Name _____
Organization _____
Address _____
City_____ State____ Zip _____
Telephone _____

Please send me more information about ❑social work and ❑non-profit management publications available from White Hat Communications.

Sales tax: Please add 6% sales tax for books shipped to Pennsylvania addresses.

Shipping/handling:
❑Books sent to U.S. addresses: $6.00 first book/$1 each add'l book.
❑Books sent to Canada: $9.00 per book.
❑Books sent to addresses outside the U.S. and Canada: $12.00 per book.

Payment:
Check or money order enclosed for $_____
U.S. funds only.

Please charge my: ❑Mastercard ❑Visa ❑AmEx ❑Discover
Card #: _____
Expiration Date: _____
Name on card: _____
Billing address (if different from above): _____
_____
Signature: _____

Mail this form with payment to:
WHITE HAT COMMUNICATIONS, P.O. Box 5390, Dept. SWG
Harrisburg, PA 17110-0390
Phone orders: 717-238-3787/Fax orders: 717-238-2090
or order online at http://www.socialworker.com